Praise for Bang Boom Burn

Wayne Miller has done it all in his distinguished 25-year career with ATF. I've had the distinct pleasure of working with Wayne on numerous fire investigations, including the God and Country Arsonist, during my career with the Mass State Police. A great investigator, a true gentleman and the distinguished author of *BURN BOSTON BURN*, he has done it again with this latest book, *BANG BOOM BURN*. A great read from someone who has personally experienced the thrill, fear and adrenaline rush of undercover work, the sadness, gruesomeness and despair investigating violent deaths and the highs of making the big case!

—**Michael J. Crisp**, Major,
Deputy Commander of Investigations,
Massachusetts State Police (Ret)

"Miller's first book, "Burn Boston Burn," was a deep dive into the biggest arson case in history, a meticulous study of a massive arson ring and the amoral oddballs behind it. His new book, "Bang Boom Burn," is no less meticulous but provides a sweeping, more comprehensive view of the career of a federal ATF agent charged with investigating and taking off the streets those who would use guns, explosives and fire to harm others – hence, the bang boom and burn. It's more true life than true crime, revealing the painstaking, and even sometimes mundane, world of a professional investigator. These aren't TV police procedurals that are neatly resolved in an hour. This is real life, where the depraved conceal their devices in Christmas wrapping, and where dedicated agents like Miller do more than punch a clock, investing their own lives, at some loss to their families, to track down criminal minds. The personalities that emerge, the cops and the criminals, are not stereotypes. Reading this book, the layman will likely conclude that interpersonal relationships, particularly among investigators, are as important as forensics that human instincts are just as important as anything taught at the various law enforcement academies. That Miller and his colleagues weren't always successful, that they approached each investigation with humility more than hubris, makes this book far more realistic, revealing and entertaining than the usual run-of-the-mill cop empties his notebook genre. It should be required reading for anyone in law enforcement, a primer in real life."

—**Kevin Cullen,** Columnist for The Boston Globe,
Pulitzer Prize Winner team member,
Co-author of The New York Times bestseller *Whitey Bulger*

"BANG BOOM BURN is an interesting and captivating great read as Wayne walks you through the intricacies and difficulties of the investigative processes with precision and emotion!"

—**Joe Finn,** Commissioner/Chief of the Department (Ret),
Boston Fire Department member 35+ years

BANG
BOOM
BURN

Explosive True Crime Gun, Bombing
and Arson Cases from a Federal Agent's Career

WAYNE M. MILLER

BANG BOOM BURN

Cover design by Mike Clark, MikeClarkDesign.com
Cover Worcester Warehouse Photo courtesy of Roger B. Conant
Cover Explosion Image: Slow-motion image provided by The Slow Mo Guys
Editor: C. Susan Nunn, csusannunn.com
Book Interior and E-book Design by Amit Dey | amitdey2528@gmail.com

Publishing Consultant: Geoff Affleck, AuthorPreneurPublishing, Inc.

ISBN: 978-1-7333403-4-2 Hardcover
ISBN: 978-1-7333403-5-9 Paperback
ISBN: 978-1-7333403-6-6 E-book

Dedication

To all first responders, past, present and future
Thank you for putting your lives on the line every day
And for those lost to fire or crime
You will not be forgotten

Contents

**Get your bonus chapter to _Bang Boom Burn_
by scanning this QR Code with your phone.
It will bring you to a link on my burnbostonburn.com
website! Enjoy!**

Foreword

What started as a simple social media search to find an interesting guest for my Badge Boys podcast, became something quite unexpected. What came to pass upon connecting, meeting and befriending author Wayne M. Miller was nothing short of a life-altering encounter with a kindred spirit–a fellow detective.

The author of *Burn Boston Burn*, Wayne M. Miller is more than just a master craftsman who penned a riveting true-crime saga about a criminal conspiracy of Boston area police and firefighters turned arsonists. More importantly, for a quarter-century, this dedicated ATF Special Agent tirelessly participated in investigations of one high-profile crime after the next, all of which involved a "Bang! Boom! (or) Burn!"

Retired Special Agent Miller's professional path is a journey few have taken. If not for his tenacious efforts, along with a team of like-minded investigators, incarcerating sadistic shooters, bomb builders, and psychotic pyromaniacs, untold lives would have perished. As a community, we are truly safer due to Special Agent Miller's deep dive into an abyss filled with dangerous and depraved derelicts, all of whom share a common trait: their acts destroy lives.

Just one example of the cruel carnage caused by such homicidal monsters is chronicled in the disturbing Michael Stevens-Earl Figley Bombing Case. This chapter wastes no time, delving into the glass-eyed, scar-faced murderer's explosive crime in which four family members and a bystander were obliterated by separate bombs mailed to their individual homes. The bombers packaged the devices to look like gifts, insidiously meant to deceive the victims, killing them over the Christmas holiday.

Upon working these horrific scenes, Miller mentions, "Training, along with having the proper equipment, helps prepare you to do the job. But nothing prepares you mentally for the savagery one human being can inflict on another. Those appalling images are still vivid in my mind's eye today."

He not only helped to solve crime after crime, stopping these monsters who lurked in the abyss, but he came out the other side a better person. As Nietzsche cautioned, "those who fight monsters risk becoming one." Special Agent Miller took heed. Instead, he channeled a career filled with pain and sorrow into compiling a book containing story after story of the most manic encounters to both entertain and forewarn–there are real monsters among us. Despite all the bad he faced in the criminal world, Agent Miller still managed to add humor to some of his stories.

Thankfully, there are special women and men like Special Agent Miller who risk their lives and sanity to keep these monsters at bay, so we can not only sleep safely at night, but thanks to this cop-turned-author, we also have something to read while lying in bed.

Ret. Phoenix Police Sergeant Darren Burch,
Badge Boys Podcast Host, Author of *Twisted But True*
& *Twisted But True Book II–Filling in the Cracks*,
and Featured Detective in ID Channel's
"American Detective with Lt. Joe Kenda" episode

Introduction

After completing my first book, *Burn Boston Burn*, which was totally enjoyable to write and was fairly successful, I got the bug to write another. That book, over 470 pages long, told the story of one major serial arson case involving nine men. In contrast, this book contains several short stories of Bureau of Alcohol, Tobacco and Firearms (ATF) cases I worked on. I chose from many interesting investigations during my 25-year career. These are only a small sampling of the type of work conducted by ATF Special Agents throughout the country. Most agents could add their own stories to this sampling.

As I looked back at those years which flew by, sometimes I felt I didn't make many cases. However, when I examined my career more closely, I realized I had worked on many significant investigations. Some did not result in successful prosecutions. Those cases that didn't culminate in convictions were because the evidence was lacking or we failed to present a convincing case to jurors.

I have asked myself when I only averaged two convictions per year, were my efforts, my job, and a career as a Federal Agent worth it to you as a taxpayer, or to me as a person? But when you look at some of those convictions—a man with 46 stolen machine guns, nine men who burned 264 buildings, bombers who killed one police officer while maiming another and killed other innocent people, arsonists who burned people's properties and more—we should all be happy there are public servants willing to put in the effort to stop these criminals. To use baseball analogies, nobody batted a thousand on the job, but I had a decent average, a lot of good swings, and my share of whiffs.

During my first four years on the job, I primarily worked gun cases, but there were only a couple cases I thought the readers would find attention-grabbing. I don't want to get into the politics behind the discussion between gun rights and some people's thoughts about ATF. But, after being an agent for 25 years and knowing hundreds of other agents, I can clearly state most agents believe in the rights established in the Second Amendment and have no desire to take citizen's guns or restrict law-abiding people from using, carrying or buying guns. We just wanted to stop real criminals from using guns to rob and kill people.

Undoubtedly, ATF has been involved in some high-profile cases gone wrong. But the street agents, by and large, have acted with the utmost integrity and diligence to get the job done, and done well. The stories herein will give people a sense of what we, as agents, go through during our careers.

During the 25 years, I worked several bombing cases including one which killed a Boston Police Officer and maimed another. The facts, in that case, were intriguing. I also worked on the Atlanta Olympics bombing in 1996. Because it has been thoroughly covered, I did not write a chapter on it. I only mention it as part of another bombing story.

Finally, since I spent 20 years working fire investigations, I include several fire cases here. Two serial arson cases involving a single arsonist in each case will captivate the reader. I cover several arson-for-profit investigations in great detail. These cases show how difficult it is to prove and prosecute intentionally set fires involving business owners. Each story serves as training for this type of case, but they are also entertaining.

You will find some stories funny, others serious and fascinating. Some will pull at your heartstrings and make you cry. Others will make you shake your head in disbelief. You'll feel my personal frustrations and satisfactions, sometimes even elation at the outcomes.

This is the life of many first responders and follow-up investigators. Part of the reason for writing this book is I wanted the general public to understand the life your first responders and Federal investigators live, what we see and what we feel.

One difference between local authorities and Federal Agents is that the Feds work anywhere and everywhere in and around the United States, not bound by local or state lines. During my last three years on the job, I was away from home for 12 weeks, then 14, and finally, 16 weeks. That was time away from my family which I'll never get back. Don't get me wrong. I loved the job, but I was always uncomfortable being away so much.

During all those years and cases, I worked with many excellent ATF Agents, other Federal Agents plus State and local investigators. We worked our butts off on these investigations with lots of frustrations and varying degrees of success. Working with these professionals provided me with opportunities to develop long-lasting friendships. As I think back on these investigations, I wonder what else we could have done to bring more of them to successful conclusions. All these cases date back from 20 to over 40 years ago.

This country is fortunate to have so many good people taking up the cause. Today's active investigators have the benefit of advanced technology and limitless data available at their fingertips. The advances in DNA, security cameras at nearly every turn, cell phone and GPS tracking, plus social media all greatly assist in investigations.

To those on the job today, when out on the streets working your cases, imagine not having these developments and look at your investigations from a different viewpoint. The ability to do this will help make your cases even stronger.

Interviews are still key to making cases. This hasn't changed. Talk to as many people as possible. You never know who will help make your case. Also, putting in the hard work will often reward your dedication. Leave no stone unturned; look under the stone that's under the stone.

The years on the job go by quickly. To reflect on your years of service, knowing you gave your best will give you great satisfaction during your second career or retirement years. Keep up the outstanding work. Remain passionate, compassionate, flexible and honest. Never let complacency get the best of you. And always, always keep your head on a swivel. Stay safe.

CHAPTER 1

Machine Guns in the Suburbs

On any one day, a well-dressed man in smart casual clothing comprising of patterned double knit pants, topped by a cardigan sweater over a button-down dress shirt walked into a house not his own. The man's hair, perfectly coiffed, a light brown, swept to the side slightly over both his forehead and the tops of his ears. Charlie carried a large suitcase with him. He used something other than a key to enter either a rear or side door. Nobody was home. Just Charlie, all by himself. Anybody who saw this man never suspected his nefarious intent.

Charles Gallant was an old-time thief, a b & e guy who spent his adult life breaking and entering into your neighbor's house or maybe yours. This was his career choice, his job. He was not a violent man. Charlie did not commit violent crimes like armed robberies.

Once in your house, he nonchalantly looked through your belongings. Charlie knew what he wanted. He also had a good idea what you had. He cased your house and your habits before he chose you as his target. This was during the 1970s, on the cusp of the 80s. There was no internet or social media for him to check you out. Much like the gumshoe detective pounding the streets for the evidence needed to solve a crime, Charlie put in similar work preparing for his day's work.

He would fill his suitcase with your cash, jewelry, and handguns if he could get them into the suitcase. He rarely took any electronics, but he always took Hummel and Lladró figurines, both heavily collected in the 1970s. The Hummels, created in Germany in 1935 when porcelain company owner, Franz Goebel turned the artwork of Berta Hummel into figurines. Three Lladró brothers from Spain created their Lladró decorative sculptures and figurines in the 1950s. Charlie took whatever wasn't nailed down if he thought it had any value.

✳   ✳   ✳

The day after Easter, Monday, April 7, 1980, I was at the Boston Arson Squad relative to a major arson-for-profit scheme that was just unfolding. This investigation was interrupted when I received word to head immediately to Walpole, Massachusetts because the locals had just discovered a large cache of guns. A phone call had come directly for me from my good friend, Walpole Police Detective James "Dunny" Donahue.

Earlier that morning, the Walpole Fire Department received a report of smoke coming from a raised ranch garage on Lee Street, a packed middle-income residential area. According to Walpole Firefighter (later Chief) Ed Hartmann, he was with the first due firefighters who saw dark smoke pushing out from the closed garage overhead door. He said they had to force their way into the garage located under the house where they encountered a heavy smoke condition, but minimal flames.

In the garage, once they saw through the smoke, firefighters flipped over a discarded carpet. It covered a smoldering trash can. After hitting the container with water, the firefighters made the discovery of a lifetime.

There were 17 rifles in the trash barrel. A quick check of the residence for any people or other fire revealed dozens of other guns throughout the house, but no bodies, either dead or alive. The Officer in Charge reported their find to the police, who automatically responded to the scene. The responding police officer radioed back to the PD to notify Chief Armando Betro of what was unfolding and to request detectives and superior officers.

That's when my friend, Detective Donahue, arrived on the scene. Normally, protocol would have the Walpole Police first notify the Norfolk County District Attorney's Office about a major case such as this. The DA was the chief law enforcement officer of the county. All the State's District Attorneys had a cadre of Massachusetts State Police Detectives assigned to their office. They were often the elite state investigators.

Instead of making that first call to the DA's Office, Detective Donahue called me. We had quite a history together in the three years since we met. We had worked on the Klosieski drugs and gun case where we spent hundreds of hours together. He had been part of my wedding party after having introduced me to my first wife. We knew and trusted each other as friends and colleagues. Jimmy's thinking was this case should involve the premier firearms investigative outfit, the Bureau of Alcohol, Tobacco and Firearms with me as his primary contact.

I immediately raced out of Boston. The normal 45-minute drive to Walpole took about 20 minutes with my blue light flashing and siren blaring. I wanted to beat the Troopers to the scene. I did. Once on-site, I learned more about the unfolding mystery.

The house belonged to Charles A. Gallant, Jr. Around 7:30 a.m., a neighborhood woman walking her dog noticed smoke coming from the garage as she passed the house. She knocked on the front door of the house. A man, later identified as Gallant, came to the door. The woman advised him there may be a fire in his garage. Charlie responded, "Oh, yeah, I've taken care of it." The woman thought his response meant he had called the fire department. She continued on her way.

So did Charlie. He hightailed it out of his house to parts unknown. Knowing firefighters followed by police would soon come down his street, and with a house full of weapons and other evidence of crimes, Gallant moved quickly to protect himself from arrest on this sunny Monday morning.

Detective Donahue informed me there were dozens of military M16s in the house, along with other weapons and tons of other potentially stolen goods. He had already checked one of the M16 serial numbers through the National Crime Information Center (NCIC) database and found it was actually an M16A1 stolen from an armory years before. The military rifle Model M16A1 was an updated version of the original M16s. These had a selector switch to change between firing modes, including fully automatic.

✳ ✳ ✳

According to a March 2019 article by Daniel A. Gagnon in the Danvers (MA) Herald, a few men over a weekend in August 1976 cut through a seven-foot-tall chain-link fence surrounding the Danvers National Guard Armory, about 17 miles northeast of Boston. These men also disabled the security system and burglar alarm before locating the gun vault inside the building.

The vault was built with reinforced concrete, a steel door and a combination lock. The burglars used pickaxes to bang away at the steel door. Gagnon reported they also used the tools to break into a Coca-Cola cooler to quench their thirst as they worked hard to bust through the door.

The thieves loaded armfuls of weapons from the vault into a van and vanished into the night. The weapons took an unusual trip from there. No arrests were ever made for the theft.

Authorities discovered the break-in on the following Monday. A check of the inventory revealed 92 M16A1 assault rifles, 7 M60 machine guns, a .45 caliber automatic pistol, two grenade launchers, flak jackets, infrared binoculars and a missile launcher were missing. Somebody had enough equipment to start a war.

That night, the headlines in the Boston Globe read 100 'useless' guns stolen in Danvers. The article cited law enforcement personnel who believed a group of professional thieves committed the theft. But, according to the article, the automatic weapons were useless because the firing mechanisms or pins had been removed and stored separately at the Danvers Police Department. Another interesting part of the article mentioned the FBI and Massachusetts State Police immediately started investigating 1970s terrorist groups for the theft, even stating their names in the article.

Apparently, somebody found how to make these weapons work. It is amazing how those 'useless' M60s and half (46) of the M16s ended up being used by the Irish Republican Army (IRA), a guerilla group from Northern Ireland fighting to reunite Ireland. The Irish enclaves of Boston regularly transported shipments of weapons via fishing boats to their ancestral country.

Boston ATF Agents had a different theory of suspects who committed the Danvers larceny. One theory included hijackers, alarm system specialists and expert safecracker Arthur "Bucky" Barrett, later murdered by infamous South Boston gangster Whitey Bulger. Nobody was ever implicated in the armory theft, but now, with the discovery

Boston Globe headlines re: Danvers Armory theft.

of half of the M16 stockpile in Charlie Gallant's house, there was a new avenue of information.

*   *   *

Before heading into the house, I telephoned my ATF Group Supervisor Ed Hoban to see what we could do about obtaining a search warrant as fast as possible. After all, the State Troopers assigned to the DA's Office were only miles away from the crime scene with ready access to numerous attorneys and judges in the Norfolk Superior Courthouse.

Eddie was a heavyset smoker, approaching 50 years old. He was sharp-witted, funny, yet a serious, very smart investigator and an attorney. He was a wealth of information on Boston area criminals. Hoban made ATF Boston history that day.

Taking information from me via a lengthy series of landline phone calls, Ed wrote up the affidavit to support a search warrant. He faxed it over to the US Attorney's Office, where the draft was reworked before being brought to a United States Magistrate. The judge granted the warrant. We now had the legal right to search the entire house and property.

Reinforcements from the Walpole Police and our ATF gun group arrived on the scene. Every pair of hands, set of eyes and brains were put to good use.

The State Troopers also arrived at the house. They were shocked, dismayed, and generally pissed we had custody and control of the property based upon the search warrant. But we let them play in our sandbox. You never know how a professional gesture might play out on another day.

Walking through the house, we were all amazed by what we were seeing. Besides the 17 rifles of various makes and models in the trash container firefighters first discovered, there were piles of other weapons throughout the lower level of the house. Everyplace we turned, there were more and more rifles.

After photographing everything in place, we took the guns outside where we aligned them on the grass to catalog them by make and serial number. Forty-six M16s in total were lined up neatly on the lawn. Upstairs, besides the usual contents in the house, there were Hummel and Lladró figurines everywhere.

I tried to open the door to one bedroom, but when I met resistance, I pushed the door with my shoulder. I couldn't quite understand how the door could have been closed with debris behind it preventing its free movement. Once inside the room, I understood the situation better. The room was chock full of stuff later identified as stolen property. There were more figurines, pictures, boxes of jewelry and lots of other items that filled every inch of the room piled several feet deep. Not counting the weapons, once itemized, we valued the stolen property at one million dollars.

At one point, early in the afternoon, while several of us were outside, a shiny, mid-70s big old boat of a black Cadillac slowly drove past our location. Two White guys, between 35 and 45 years old, craned their necks in our direction.

With what was going on at this property, it was understandable someone driving by would gawk at the happenings, but ATF Special Agent Terry Barry felt these guys were wrong. This was a middle-income, working-class neighborhood on a back road. The car and its occupants didn't fit in this area. Profiling at its best. The Cadillac made the left turn at the end of the street.

Terry always was a talented investigator with excellent instincts. He immediately jumped into his car with another agent and chased after the Caddy. A short time later, the agents returned. Terry told us the two men were brothers, the McLaughlins, who came from West Roxbury and Charlestown. They told Terry they were just out for a ride when they drove past us. They said they knew nobody on the street, including Charlie Gallant.

Two hours later, during our search of the house, we found a photo with three men at an amusement park, their arms interlinked around shoulders as if best buddies. We knew the middle guy was Charlie. When Terry saw the photo, he immediately recognized the other two men as the lying McLaughlin brothers.

Now, we were itching to know what this entire day was about. There were far more questions than answers. Why was there a fire at Gallant's house? Where is Charlie? What is the relationship between Gallant and the McLaughlins? Why did they drive by the house that day?

And why did Charles Gallant have 46 M16s in his Walpole house which someone stole four years earlier with half of the stolen guns found in Northern Ireland?

For the moment, we dealt with what was in front of us. There were many aspects of this breaking investigation needing to be addressed simultaneously.

The nearly two dozen law enforcement officers on the scene worked until well after dark, looking in every nook and cranny for more evidence. Then they tagged and cataloged every piece. Back at the office, an all-points bulletin (APB) went out for the missing Charles A. Gallant, Jr. We identified vehicles registered to him and the search for them began.

We determined Charlie had a common-law wife, but where was she? His criminal record was scrutinized for any hints as to his whereabouts, including checking his family and friends.

As I was the case agent, it was my job to follow up on everything and anything that presented itself as a lead in this investigation. The first night, Supervisor Hoban, Agent Barry and I traveled back to Boston with all the evidence where we stored it in the ATF evidence vault. Tired, but excited by the possibilities and complexities presented by this new case, I headed home for a brief night's sleep, hitting my bed after midnight.

The Walpole Police secured the Gallant property overnight. During the next couple days, we excavated the yard around the house with heavy equipment seeking additional evidence, but we found nothing but dirt.

The following morning, I was back in Boston by 8:30 a.m., taking care of lots of paperwork. The evidence still needed more processing. I completed an opening report and an additional status report. A formal message was electronically sent to ATF HQ to update them.

Then we drafted an affidavit with the US Attorney's Office to obtain an arrest warrant for Charles Ambrose Gallant, Jr. We conferred with the FBI, the Army Criminal Investigation Division (CID) and US Customs. They all had something to offer about the original theft of the weapons and about the weapons that traveled to Northern Ireland.

That same night I was back in Walpole for a conference with Norfolk County Assistant District Attorney Jerry Kirby and several Walpole Police Detectives, including Jimmy Donahue. We went to the nearby towns of Norwood and Canton, where we attempted to interview the woman who first saw the smoke coming from Gallant's garage notifying Charlie about the fire. She was not at either location where she allegedly was staying. So much for another day's work, ending at 11:30 p.m.

Two days after discovery of the weapons cache, I served a subpoena on Denise Carpenter, the common-law wife of Charlie. She was staying in Hyde Park, the most southwest neighborhood of Boston. We tried to interview her, but she referred us to her attorney. Word was Charlie had won his wife in a card game.

Late in the afternoon, based on information received, eight of us agents traveled to an apartment building in Seabrook, New Hampshire, a coastal town just over the northern Massachusetts border. We heard Gallant may stay there. Also, one of the two McLaughlin brothers who had driven by Gallant's house, Dennis, was living there temporarily.

He wasn't, but two Boston ex-cons were living there. Both had ties to Gallant, but, of course, neither knew anything about Gallant's recent activities or about the firearms in his house. After obtaining consent to look around the apartment, we found a couple guns stashed in a closet.

Since both men were prohibited from possessing guns because of their felony convictions, this violated Federal firearms laws.

We noted the gun information but didn't mention the violation directly to the men. One man told us the one gun found in the closet of McLaughlin's bedroom belonged to Dennis. At the time McLaughlin was out of the country, but due back on Monday, April 14.

Because of the newest discovery of firearms violations, the next day was another straight-out day. First, I testified before a Federal Grand Jury seeking indictments against Gallant, Dennis McLaughlin, and the other convicted felon who lived in the Seabrook apartment. Next, I traveled to Concord, New Hampshire to obtain a search warrant from the proper jurisdiction, so we could seize the firearms from the Seabrook apartment. We did this without incident that evening. Again, I arrived home just before midnight.

On Friday, the firearms were traced and secured. We returned the search warrants to the court. Subpoenas were obtained. The indictments were returned, so we planned the arrest of Dennis McLaughlin and his roommate.

All this activity and peripheral work was being done in an effort to find Charlie Gallant and solve the riddle of the path taken by the M16s. These types of cases, with seasoned criminals, often required a lot of extra work to put pressure on associates of the primary target to cooperate. The work we were doing at least provided us with a potential route to get information from these guys.

On Monday afternoon, we grouped at Boston's Logan Airport, preparing to arrest Dennis McLaughlin. His flight arrived at the International Terminal at about 4:45 p.m. As he cleared US Customs, we placed him under arrest for firearms violations. McLaughlin was more than a bit surprised to be met by a welcoming party.

We transported him to the JFK Federal Building to process him and lodged him at Boston PD for the night.

Over the next few days, we conducted various interviews in our quest for more information on Gallant. Dennis McLaughlin and his felon roommate were released on low surety bail. Neither one provided any information about Charlie or any other crimes. This was a tight-lipped, experienced crew of criminals. With the seriousness of the loss of the weapons and their situation, these guys had much to lose by cooperating with us.

The case reports required by ATF to be presented to the prosecutors were also completed during this period. There was no recent news on the whereabouts of Charlie, but that was about to change, somewhat.

One day, I played a hunch. I guess it was the gut feeling investigators have talked about and acted upon for many years, those types of feelings that end up breaking a case wide open. With all the recent flurry of activity but lack of information on Charlie, I was getting fidgety. I wanted something to happen, so I took some initiative to make it happen.

On Thursday or Friday, the last week of April, I headed to the Hyde Park section of Boston, the hometown of Gallant. I learned Charlie was a big drinker, so I went to the biggest and busiest liquor store in the area, Kelly's Liquor Mart on the main thoroughfare, Hyde Park Avenue. The owner of the store owed me a favor. He was about to pay off.

Back in the summer of 1977, I had been working undercover in Hyde Park, trying to buy illegal guns off the street. I remember the day Elvis Presley died on August 16, 1977. I was buying some guns from guys I had met in D'Amateos Bar on River Street on the bridge outside Cleary Square. Two of the handguns had been stolen from Kelly's Liquors.

In those days, once the courts adjudicated a case, the guns were no longer needed as evidence. We returned the firearms to their rightful owners, in this case, the owner of Kelly's. The day I dropped the guns off to him, he said to me, "Anytime you need or want something, come see me. I'll take care of you."

I never saw him again until this 1980 April day. When I popped in on the owner, I showed him a picture of Charlie, asking him if he had ever seen him. He gave the photo a good look but shook his head and said he didn't look familiar. Slightly disappointed, I handed him my business card and said if he thinks of anything, hears anything or sees anything, to call me. Although he seemed honest and helpful, I wasn't holding my breath.

Lo-and-behold, about 9 p.m. on Saturday night, a man fitting Charlie Gallant's description came into the store and purchased a couple bottles of booze. Mr. Store Owner spotted him right away and took note. When Charlie left, the owner waited a few moments, then followed him out the door. This guy got the description of the car and noted the license number on the vehicle. It was a Maryland tag. Not only that, when he closed the store, as he headed home, he spotted the same car parked on Hyde Park Avenue a couple blocks from his store.

This upstanding citizen called the number on my card, but, in those days, the call was directed to a 24-hour ATF Headquarters phone. Someone took the message, but for some reason, I didn't get the message until Monday morning. Ahh, those were the days!

With that information, we learned a couple things. Charlie may still hang around his old haunts, and he had a stolen car with Maryland plates. The car had been stolen the week before from Charlestown, Massachusetts. That area of Boston was a notorious hotbed of crime committed by White boys and men often associated with the housing projects.

The owner of the stolen car was located and interviewed. Surveillances were arranged and conducted all over Hyde Park and Charlestown trying to locate Charlie. We set up on his woman, Denise Carpenter. She lived in Hyde Park and worked downtown.

Agents sat on the other McLaughlin brother, John, who lived in West Roxbury. We knew the brothers had lied on the first day of this investigation. We could have charged them with lying to a Federal Agent violating 18 United States Code, Section 1001. Rarely used, this section could have helped to further this investigation, but it was not charged here.

Over the seven weeks, from the discovery of the weapons to the first week of June, I worked 12 to 14-hour days chasing every single lead, interviewing people and double-checking every piece of evidence to no avail. The activity just started waning when everything suddenly came to a head.

*   *   *

On Monday, June 2nd, I received word the local police had arrested Charlie Saturday in the Town of Groton, Connecticut, a seaside town at the eastern end of the state, for operating a motor vehicle under the influence of alcohol. The race was on again. We Feds wanted to grab Gallant before the Massachusetts Staties got to him. Blue lights all the way with a little siren as needed to push slower-moving vehicles out of the high-speed lane. This 115-mile trip took a little over an hour. A couple Hartford-based ATF Agents met me to assist with transporting Charlie.

Upon arrival at the Town of Groton PD, I learned further details of Gallant's arrest from young Police Officer Michael Lewin, who stopped Gallant. Charlie was completely loaded when spotted driving haphazardly.

When Officer Lewin put him in the cruiser, Charlie blurted out, "You would call the FBI if you knew who you had." But Charlie wasn't telling anybody who he was and he only had a fake license with him. Plus, he was driving the same stolen car with the Maryland license plates as seen weeks before outside the Hyde Park liquor store.

Officer Lewin told me later on Sunday, a sober Gallant finally revealed his identity but nothing else. At 3 p.m., I placed Charles Ambrose Gallant under arrest for several federal charges. The Groton Police turned Charlie and some evidence over to me. We had to get him to Hartford to house him there until his appearance before a Federal Magistrate.

The evidence had all come from Charlie's person and from the vehicle which they had impounded. There were no weapons of any kind, which was quite a surprise. Maybe it shouldn't have been. When

I got to know Charlie better, he was a thief. He had no need to carry a gun as he was not a violent man and he didn't need any protection. The most important items he had were a single key and map books.

The key had an orange plastic square stuck to it, one of those cut out with those simple handheld label makers. Imprinted on the square was the numeral "5" with no other identifying information. The map books were of Connecticut and Maryland with large circles on each, covering the Groton/New London area and Baltimore.

As we transported Gallant to Hartford, I conferred with him. He repeatedly begged me to stay with him in the Hartford City Jail overnight. Charlie said he was fearful some associates put a "hit" out on him for losing all those weapons at his house. I appealed to him, "Charlie, I'll stay with you or we'll figure out something to protect you, but you have to tell me who might be after you. Who are you afraid of? Who were you holding the weapons for?"

His only reply came with a defeated, soft sigh, "I can't tell you." He shrunk into his seat and sat silent except to tell me he was going to send Denise out to see if there was a hit on him.

Before we lodged Charlie for the night, I again implored him to give up the information so we could protect him. He said, "Thanks, but no thanks." We spoke for a few more minutes. This old-style criminal respectfully told me, "You have your job to do. I have my job. That's all I know how to do. I can't change. I'll be at it again when I get out."

With that, he disappeared behind the first set of bars into the bowels of the jail. It was a long 100-mile journey back home. I replayed in my head over and over how maybe I could have said something more or different to get Gallant to tell me the story of the guns. But it made no difference what I thought. Maybe, if he lived through the night, he would tell me sometime soon when he felt the pressure of years in prison looming over him.

Charlie didn't die that night, or many more nights to come. Denise found out there was no hit out on him. Gallant stayed mum, a stand-up guy according to the criminal code.

Three months later he pled guilty to possession of all those weapons and to a few other charges. The Federal judge sentenced Charlie to eight years. He served the full sentence.

The McLaughlin brothers and their two buddies all pled guilty to Federal Firearms violations and spent some time in federal prisons. Questions on the theft of the guns, why they were in Gallant's house four years later, and who they were being held for went unanswered. With half of the M16s found in Northern Ireland, there was unsubstantiated information that the 46 M16s at Charlie's house were being held for Boston Mafia boss Frank Salemme. He was due to be released soon from prison, where he was serving time relating to blowing up a car with an informant inside. The theft at the Danvers Armory remains unsolved as of this writing.

Ten years after I last saw Charlie when Marshals escorted him away after his sentencing, I was coming out of the beautiful Norfolk County Superior Courthouse in Dedham, southwest of Boston. The white-gray expansive 1820s Greek Revival structure sits atop a double tier of a dozen stairs. The front facade is adorned with four magnificent granite 20-foot-tall round columns whose diameter each stretches some three feet. Looking to my left, between two of those pillars, stood a familiar-looking man, a 10-year older Charlie Gallant. When our eyes met, I pointed toward him, and with a friendly tone, I said, "I know you!" He replied the same.

While we spoke for a few minutes, Charlie told me as he laughed, "I told you I wouldn't change!" He had been arrested and convicted of another burglary. I miss the old-time bad guys like Charlie. They were so honorable in their dishonorable way!

Charles Gallant died in 2016.

Walpole police officers and federal agents sort guns found after firefighters responded to alarm of fire at Walpole house yesterday. At right, agent of Bureau of Alcohol, Tobacco and Firearms examines one of the weapons. (Globe photos by Joe Dennehy)

Stolen weaponry found

Large cache of weapons found in burning garage: WALPOLE, Mass. AP State and local police, using mine detectors and other instruments, hunted inch-by-inch through a Walpole man's home and yard Tuesday, after finding a cache of automatic weapons in his burning garage. (Boston Globe headline and picture, April 8, 1980)

Boston Globe picture and headline on the front page, Robert Anglin, Globe Staff, August 17, 1976)

Picture from January 1978, when the IRA first revealed the M60s from Danvers. Source: https://www.newsletter.co.uk/news/crime/bogside-held-in-fear-by-ira-for-years-it-was-dictatorship-1-6797214

IRA Probe Yields Arms Cache, Washington Post, James Naughtie, July 30, 1981

https://www.washingtonpost.com/archive/politics/1981/07/30/iraprobe-yeilds-arms-cache/289ce86d-b6b8-4d4f-9200-f7d7e28b6062/

Danvers Armory Robbery, 1976, Danvers Herald, Dan Gagnon, March 17, 2019

CHAPTER 2

Boston Mounties to the Rescue

Here's a funny one for you.

I was on the job for about two years, working out of the gun group under my second supervisor in three years, Ed Hoban. All of us junior agents were under some pressure, often self-imposed, to produce cases under the 1976 project named Concentrated Urban Enforcement (CUE).

ATF designated several cities as CUE cities. CUE's aim was to assist state and local authorities to make a significant impact by reducing serious crimes involving firearms and illegal gun trafficking. Therefore, in 1976, ATF hired 40 new agents to double the number of investigators in the greater Boston area. Boston was, and is, the headquarters for the New England division. Over the next 20 years, ATF only added another 40 agents.

All being young bucks trying to prove our worth, we agents in Boston clawed to make cases on illegal firearms violations. We often stumbled over each other trying to do so. It was a very competitive atmosphere. Often, we operated on the streets somewhat recklessly by putting ourselves in unnecessary danger, all in the name of making cases. We all took too many chances.

A lot of us worked undercover trying to make cases. Sometimes we worked alongside the informants.

Other times we tried cold approaches in targets such as bars or other locations where drugs, illegal guns and other crimes were suspected of being committed.

Many times in those days, we worked alone or with one other agent, but we often had no cover team, backup or surveillance, whether mobile or electronic.

Enough about the danger and all the serious stuff. Let's get back to the funny part of the story.

It was a Monday morning. I had been in the office for a short while when a new confidential informant (CI) of mine called the office. I hadn't made any cases with this source yet, but I was trying to build a relationship with the guy. He related a story to me concerning an associate of his who had two handguns for sale. It gets a little juicier, though.

Over the weekend, thieves broke into Gartman Arms, a gun store and gunsmith for some 20 years on Route 1 in Wrentham, Massachusetts (just south of the home of the New England Patriots). They got away clean with several handguns. This was the first I had heard about this theft, as I hadn't listened to any local news that morning.

A quick phone call to Wrentham PD verified a theft did, in fact, occur. I then called the CI back, setting up a meet with him and the "bad guy" for noon in West Roxbury at a convenience store parking lot.

My boss, Ed, and I got a plan together. I was the plan, just me, myself and I. We had nobody available to cover me, and Ed suspected this newly minted investigation could be a wild goose chase.

Armed with my little 2-inch barrel, .38 caliber Smith & Wesson Model 36 Chiefs Special, I headed out in my assigned government-issued 1975 Ford Mustang.

*   *   *

Agents referred to their vehicles as G-rides. This 2-year-old undercover car, powder blue with a partial white vinyl roof, already had quite a history in its brief existence.

First, ATF had seized it from a gun-carrying drug dealer about a year before it was being assigned to me. Privately owned vehicles used during violations of certain Federal firearms laws can be subject to seizure and forfeiture by the US Government. But this car nearly ended my brief career.

During the fall of 1976, after I completed my training at FLETC (the Federal Law Enforcement Training Center) in Brunswick, Georgia, I was temporarily living in an agent pad, an apartment on Pond Street in Quincy, south of Boston. The one mainstay at the apartment was Special Agent Billy Murphy, a local Irish kid, Vietnam vet who would become a lifelong adult friend and occasional partner on the job. Other agents, including myself, and Tom Perret, bounced in and out as necessary. None of us had long-term individual living arrangements yet.

One Friday night, late in the fall of 1976, only five months on the job, I had a date with a girl I had known from Bryant College (now University), from which I had graduated 18 months prior. We scheduled our rendezvous for 9 p.m.

The only problem was I was part of a surveillance team covering a gun deal in Boston. The deal was to go down about 7 p.m., but as these things often happened, it ran late.

Once we finished, I scurried back to the Quincy apartment where I dropped the G-ride in the small parking lot behind the building. After hastily changing, I called my date and headed out in my personal vehicle, a '72 Chevy Malibu, knowing I was already 20 to 30 minutes late.

After apologizing profusely to my date, we went out for the evening. We had a good night, and after dropping her back at her parents' house, I arrived at my place at about 2 a.m. I was dead tired. As my head hit the pillow, the last thing that flashed through my head before falling asleep was, "I don't remember seeing my Mustang in the parking lot."

When I awoke about 10 a.m., I never gave the G-ride a thought. But when I went out an hour later, the car was nowhere to be seen.

My instant panic was palpable. Someone had freaking stolen my car right out of the parking lot. As I headed inside the apartment to report the missing vehicle, I remembered I had put my two-way radio, which I used the night before to communicate with the other surveillance units, under my driver's seat. My dread now grew exponentially to "I'm screwed!"

As a rookie agent, I knew they could fire me, without cause, during this first year of employment with ATF. That's the rule. I should have secured the radio in my residence. It didn't matter I had simply forgotten it in the car.

My first phone call was to my first Supervisor, Jack Dowd, who had only recently been promoted to that position. Jack advised he would handle everything with the front office (that is, the Special Agent in Charge, SAC) while telling me to notify the Quincy Police about the theft.

A few hours later, Boston Police recovered my car on Magazine Street in the Roxbury section of Boston. No perpetrators were found. Besides a nice dent in the passenger side front quarter panel, the car was otherwise fine. The portable radio, valued at $1200, was missing. The only good part about the stolen radio was that, without the special battery charger, the radio would quickly be useless.

Supervisor Dowd worked some magic, saving my ass from being fired. This fiasco resulted in my first encounter of several over my career, with Internal Affairs.

✳   ✳   ✳

Back to the funny part of the story. With the dent still in my G-ride, since it added to the credence the guy driving the car couldn't be a cop, I drove the few miles to the West Roxbury rendezvous site.

My informant was standing in the store parking lot with a guy who I assumed had the guns. It took one glance at the guy to see he was merely a kid, probably 16 years old, a White male, very slight, probably all of 140 pounds. With his black hair and dark complexion, he had a Mediterranean look. Turns out, he was a first-generation Greco-American. Immediately after the CI made introductions, the first thing I said to the subject was, "Man, you're just a kid, how old are you anyway?" When he confirmed he was 16, I knew there was a minor problem.

The Feds, or at least ATF, had logistical issues with arresting juveniles, which was anyone under the age of 18. Part of the problem was housing a juvenile prisoner. So, I had some decisions to make.

The three of us sat in my vehicle. The kid showed me the guns, a revolver and a small semi-auto pistol. I checked them out, making sure they were empty of any ammo and asked the kid if he had any rounds with him. He responded he didn't have any. There was a good chance I would not be shot that day.

I then inquired about the theft, but the kid only had partial information. Speaking freely, he told me he had not taken part in the burglary, but he was friendly with the thieves who sold him the two guns. He suggested more guns might be available if I was interested. I told him I could use some more pieces for some robberies, and I also had a few friends who could use them. We rode around for several minutes, so we didn't attract attention in the store parking lot. This also gave me time to make a plan.

"I think I can get rid of these guns this afternoon," I told the two guys in my car. "I'm going to find a phone and give my guy a call." This was still during the pre-cell phone era.

Within a minute, I spied a roadside payphone on Washington Street in West Roxbury. I dialed Area E of the Boston Police Department, located only minutes away. After identifying myself and explaining the situation, I asked if a couple of officers could meet me at the Dunkin Donuts just outside Roslindale Square, another Boston neighborhood. They agreed to meet me there within 10 to 15 minutes.

Once I hopped back into the car, I told the two guys who were sitting in my backseat my guy would meet us in a few minutes. We headed over to the Dunkin' Donuts.

The small parking lot in front of the donut shop had several cars parked in it. I pulled into a parking spot facing the street. Then, I got out of the car, telling them I could wave my friend over to our car. I left them to chat.

Standing next to the car, I leaned with my arms on the roof, tapping a little tune on the roof as I waited for BPD to arrive. Within minutes, I heard a clipity-clop, clipity-clop, clipity-clop sound, and then saw two mounted Boston Police officers astride beautiful chestnut-colored horses bounding toward the Square on Washington Street. I couldn't believe what I heard and saw. I shook my head, laughing to myself.

Pulling out my credentials and badge, I waved my creds in the air above the roof of the car so those in my car couldn't see my actions.

As the mounted cops arrived next to my car, I motioned that a guy in the vehicle had two handguns. The officers dismounted. I opened the car passenger door with my sidearm in hand, identified myself and commanded the perp to get out of the car as he was under arrest for gun charges.

The kid was not only flabbergasted, he started crying! Doesn't he know there's no crying when being arrested?

I could only roll my eyes toward the police officers as they cuffed him and patted him down. No, they didn't throw him on a horse for transport to the station for booking. They radioed for a cruiser, which arrived within minutes. While we waited, all the kid could do was sniffle.

Once back at the Area E station, after dropping my CI off, I interviewed the young prisoner. He readily gave up what he knew about the guns, the theft, and the perpetrators.

The next day, I showed up at West Roxbury District Court for the kid's arraignment. I met with the Assistant District Attorney and explained how the case unfolded.

In the courtroom, I saw the kid's parents. They were about the same size as their son, very slight and short, but what first attracted my eyes in their direction was they dressed head-to-toe completely in black. Mom was in a black dress, black pumps, and a black shawl reminiscent of what my Italian grandmother wore when attending a funeral. Dad had on a black suit with shoes that looked like he brought them with him from the old country. And they had their Greek Orthodox priest with them, all decked out in his floor-length black robe, the traditional kalimavkion (high hat) and a full beard. The trio looked solemn and shell-shocked.

I spoke to them through their priest telling them what I was about to do. A short time later, a court officer escorted me into the Judge's chambers where I again explained the details of the case.

In Massachusetts, state law mandates a one-year prison sentence for possession of a firearm without a license to carry. I also told the Judge the kid had no previous arrests, and he cooperated fully with us. And I explained the kid's arrest devastated him, most likely scared straight. I asked if he could see his way to not incarcerate the juvenile.

Some of you may think I am a bleeding-heart liberal for not wanting the kid to go to jail. You may be in the same group that thinks all of us ATF Agents are jack-booted thugs. Well, I included this narrative to present an example of compassion, of not sending someone away for his crime but giving him a second chance. We wanted to work gun cases involving true criminals, to enforce the existing gun laws.

The Judge gave the kid a year's probation, plus he would expunge his record if he kept his nose clean. And we solved the rest of the theft with the recovery of the guns, arrests and jail sentences for those responsible for the thefts. To my knowledge, the kid was never arrested again.

*   *   *

In the late 1970s, agents in my gun group worked an investigation into the activities of Myles J. Connor, Jr., a notorious Boston-area criminal, now turned celebrity with a docu-series and a book. It seemed everybody worked cases on Myles (he was referred to by his first name often) in those days. If you made a case against him, it would be a feather in your cap.

Myles was into everything, a legendary art thief, drugs, guns, robberies, and possibly, murder. He had quite the criminal career, considering his father was a career police officer.

I developed a female source who became an informant. I'll refer to her as Diane. She told us about a shocking scene at her apartment. When she arrived home one day, she found blood all over the place, including on the telephone receiver. Allegedly two women who witnessed a murder were themselves murdered so they wouldn't testify about what they saw. It was these women who were murdered in Diane's apartment.

The story implicates Myles after the fact. He allegedly helped his buddies dispose of the women's bodies in the woods of a northwestern Massachusetts town. This story had some credence because Myles had a Massachusetts State Police Major and a District Attorney as his allies. Myles had a knack for giving up some significant evidence on an unsolved investigation whenever he got in trouble. This was his "Get out of jail card."

He showed his "handlers" where the bodies of the women were buried. How would anybody know where they were unless you had been there originally?

Loaded with information connecting Myles to two of the highest law enforcement officers in the area, caught their attention. One day, my supervisor, Jack Dowd, accompanied me to the office of the State Police Major, after he beckoned us to meet with him.

He tried to feel us out about what we knew and what our informant was telling us. Without giving everything up, we alluded to her implicating his involvement with Myles. His activities bordered on criminal behavior or at least protecting a criminal when it suited their needs.

The Major went bullshit. Red-faced and screaming, he pounded his desk while screaming at us that this was unprofessional and liable to get us in trouble. For the next year, I made sure I drove extra carefully and always kept a watch in my rearview mirror waiting for his henchmen to take a bite out of me.

The first time I interviewed Diane with a local police officer, we recorded the interview for four hours. She provided details of all sorts of crimes she alleged Myles to be involved with. One of the crimes was a bank robbery where she described the getaway car as a brown Lincoln rather than the blue Cadillac that was actually used. Letting her ramble on for a while, I called her on this one piece of information where I already had the facts.

I asked, "Diane, why did you lie to me about the car?"

She explained she still didn't know us or trust us so she wasn't truthful about every fact she told us. Diane then filled in the blanks with more of the truth.

Here's the kicker. Several months later, as a case was being built against Myles, the tape-recorded interview was turned over to the US Attorney's Office and eventually to Myles' defense attorney. On an episode of either *60 Minutes* or some similar show where they were pushing an agenda that paid informants were often liars, they played a snippet of the four-hour interview.

There was my voice asking Diane the one question about her lying to me not accompanied by her response. They took it completely out of context, using 15 seconds of the recording, to make her appear to be a lying informant willing to say anything for money.

When I mentioned earlier that Internal Affairs (IA) and I had a close relationship, this was one of those occasions they wanted to talk to me. In Supervisor Dowd's office, the IA investigator asked me how the tape got on TV. Did I give it to the newsies?

No way had I done that. There was no reason I would have sabotaged my own informant and cases that way. I had no idea how the tape got on TV, except for the most obvious answer. The defense attorney gave it to the show to help discredit my informant along with all others. Give me a break, will you? I was told as a young agent if you are out on the streets truly working investigations, it was not uncommon to be investigated by IA for some perceived infraction over the years. Well, it was always unsettling to be questioned by IA when I never did anything outside the lines.

CHAPTER 3

More Undercover Stints

Working gun cases in Boston, and most likely other locations across America, could definitely be hazardous to one's health. I never was shot at, but I knew a couple guys from our Boston ATF Office who were. Luckily, those agents received no injuries from those encounters. But I also knew a couple other ATF Agents who were shot and killed during my 25 years on the job. May these heroes rest in peace.

There were many instances where agents performed undercover work without the safety benefits of being wired or having a backup surveillance team. Since working an investigation while in an undercover capacity involved much danger and the agent had to assume the character of a criminal, not everyone could be good at it.

We considered it a badge of honor, in a macho sort of way, to be a success in that role. An undercover agent was admired by his or her peers. Every one of us wanted to be a "Serpico." Once you made a successful undercover buy of evidence, other agents considered you to have "made your bones" that phrase meaning to take actions to establish achievement, status, or respect.

Within a few years, when the Bureau recognized the dangers inherent with the way we worked undercover cases, everything changed. Today, with the precautionary measures in place, nothing like the way we worked in 1976 is allowed to occur.

*   *   *

Now, for those of you who know me, can you imagine I was a colors-wearing member of the Latin Kings? In 1978, the Bureau sent 10 Boston agents, including local Polish boy, my friend and sometimes partner, Tom Wlodyka (pronounced "Wa-dick-a") to the local branch of the Berlitz School of Languages. I remember it clearly, but not for the deep immersive dive into Spanish. This instruction lasted eight weeks, 40 hours per week.

On one of those days, it started snowing by mid-day. The weather reports issued dire warnings of impending snow amounts. The instructor only lived blocks from the school. He couldn't care less about the snow. The Boston ATF Office closed down operations at noon. We stayed in class until 3 p.m.

I still drove the same undercover Mustang, which didn't do well on snowy roads. By now, the snow fell at the rate of one to two inches per hour. I had to drop off a fellow agent who I had picked up that morning. He lived on the coast, just south of Boston, in Quincy. My condo was another 15 miles from his place.

As we drove along the shore drive with the ocean to our left, the wind howled, blowing the blinding snow sideways. There was only the sea wall on one side and buildings on the other to keep us on the road. Nothing had been plowed. No street lines were visible.

After dropping him off, I got onto the Route 128 loop south of Boston going westbound. It was only a four-mile stretch before my exit. But it was a white-knuckle drive as I gripped the steering wheel to keep my steed in its lane. On the slight incline, cars to my left and right fishtailed as the underside of my Mustang brushed against the deepening snow. I kept slow and steady pressure on the gas pedal, not willing to lose traction.

Winding around the long curve of the exit, I passed several stuck drivers. Plowing forward, I made it to my parking spot where I forcefully slid my vehicle sideways into its resting place. It wouldn't move again for seven days. Between 30 and 40 inches of wind-blown snow covered the state, shutting everything down. Drifts were over five feet deep in places from the Blizzard of 1978.

* * *

Shortly after completing the Spanish course, I worked undercover as a member of a new chapter of the Latin Kings in Brockton, Massachusetts. My Spanish was immediately put to use, but all the members also spoke English.

Now don't be mistaken. I quickly learned the few members of this group weren't the same as the dangerous thugs associated with the established Kings in other parts of the country. You could grab most of these guys by the scruff of their neck with no concern about deadly retaliation.

I don't know why they accepted me because even when I have my darkest tan, I hardly look like I have Hispanic heritage. And my Spanish was así así.

Within a couple weeks, the Chapter President took a liking to me. He said he thought I was pretty smart, so he asked if I would be his vice-president. He awarded me with the Latin Kings vest, with their colors on the back of the Puerto Rican flag. The colors are the club's logo worn by all club members. I accepted, but I ghosted the group shortly thereafter since I detected no criminal activity. My proficiency in Spanish rapidly declined with lack of use. Hoy solo hablo un poco de Español. I still have my colors.

* * *

Another strange undercover stint occurred in Boston. I partnered with Special Agent Dave Sherman, another agent from the class of 1976. We knew each other well as we spent a lot of time together, both on the job and during our personal time. But you never really get to know another person, do you?

Dave opened an investigation on the Red Emeralds Motorcycle Club (MC), which originated in Boston in 1964. One Monday evening, while acting in an undercover capacity, Dave and I visited a bar in the Mattapan neighborhood of Boston. This was one of the main hangouts for the Red Emeralds.

We ordered beers at the bar, nodded to a couple bikers, but otherwise kept to ourselves. Being a Monday, the place was quiet with only a handful of patrons. Our plan was to watch and listen and be seen.

This was a cold introduction to the MC. We had no informant to pave the way for us. If this was to succeed, it would be through our own wits.

About 10 p.m., the bartender announced he was closing because it was so slow. We overheard two bikers say they were heading to the infamous Combat Zone downtown, the now-defunct sleazy adult entertainment district. We knew the Emeralds ran a bar in the Zone, so we went there too.

The dive bar was very narrow inside. It was only about 20 feet wide, sandwiched between two other joints. There was a single front door. The rear door, not visible from the bar, opened into an alley. We sat at the bar, which took up most of the 60-foot-long room. Again, there were only a few patrons. The bartender here was also a Red Emeralds member.

While sipping on a beer, the two guys who were at the first bar eyed us, then one of them sidled over to our seats. This looked like trouble brewing, my senses prickling. Dave and I slowly spun our stools to face the interloper.

We both carried handguns concealed inside our belted hips. I also carried a rough walking stick that I fitted with a brass T-pipe handle. I wrapped the pipe with leather. The cane served as a prop to accompany my fake limp. Plus, it was another weapon readily available in my hand. I could just swing the sturdy stick between a guy's legs, employing a blow to the groin, quickly disabling an attacker. The handle could also be used if an all-out fight erupted. I readied myself.

The biker invaded my space. "What are you doing here? You were at the other bar a little while ago." He stood between my knees as I was still seated on the barstool. I explained we weren't ready to go home. When the other place closed, we came here to continue drinking. No harm, no foul.

He wasn't satisfied. He continued jawing at me, while he put his hands on me, feeling my chest, stomach and waist checking for a weapon or something else. I returned the favor. Aggressively, I felt him up, too, saying, "If you're looking for a fight, I like a good fight." My partner's eyes widened.

"We're out of here. Let's go," I motioned to Dave. Standing face to face with the biker, we slowly backed out, never taking our eyes off the group. Once outside, I started breathing again.

Dave let me have an earful, screaming, "What do you mean, you like a good fight?"

Sometimes a good defense is a good offense. That was my last day working on the Red Emeralds.

CHAPTER 4

Lost and Found in Maine

I know the first stories in this chapter had their comical side, but it also was dangerous to meet an unknown perpetrator who had stolen firearms without a backup team. Let me give you an example that could have brought about my demise.

I was working in my first gun group under Supervisor John "Jack" Dowd, about 16 to 17 months on the job, so mid-fall 1977. I had another confidential informant (CI) with information on a stash of guns. His story centered on stolen military assault rifles, M16s, which can fire automatically up to 800 rounds per minute.

The M16 came into prominence in 1964 when the military adopted it for use in the Vietnam jungles. The rifle initially had mixed reviews because of corrosion and cleaning issues. In the years following the war, armories around the United States stored various models of the M16 and many other military-grade weapons. And as seen in the Charlie Gallant case, sometimes M16s go missing from those armories.

The informant stated the weapons were still wrapped in Cosmoline. Gun manufacturers used this grease-like treatment for decades for many purposes, including as a corrosion and rust preventative on military firearms.

When agents heard these stories of M16s wrapped in Cosmoline, we were often skeptical because it was something seldom, if ever, true. But we younger agents went gaga when we envisioned capturing a cache of stolen automatic rifles.

The man, who I will call John, allegedly had these guns where he lived on China Lake, about 180 miles from Boston, northeast of Augusta, the Maine state capital. What really helped energize us and make us believe the veracity of the story was John's uncle recently sold stolen firearms to an undercover ATF Agent in Rhode Island.

My recent information was separate and distinct from the information that led to the RI investigation. The correlation of two men in the same family having illegal firearms gave the story greater validity.

A background check on the two men revealed they both had felony convictions, but no firearms arrests. This factor also assisted in our decision to pursue this case further.

We met with the informant to make plans to meet with our gun guy. I was the prospective buyer. The CI tried to get John to meet me in Massachusetts, but he was leery of carrying guns to MA with their tougher firearms laws, in the event police stopped him for a traffic violation while transporting the firearms. That would have been the least of his problems. So we arranged a mid-week rendezvous with him in Maine.

We were going to have a full surveillance team, including our airplane. I was to wear a wire so they could monitor the entire meeting. Technicians equipped my car with a radio transmitter built into the dashboard. It worked by pressing the high beam button that used to be on the car floor by your left foot.

But then the plans fell apart. The CI couldn't reach John the day before we were to meet. The only phone number we had was for his house. There was no place else to call in those days.

Supervisor Dowd and I discussed the situation and complications. I'm not sure how it happened, but I probably said I could handle this.

Jack gave me the okay to drive to Maine with the informant on Friday, stay at a hotel, and attempt to locate the target first thing Saturday morning. If, and when we located him, I was to attempt reaching local Maine agents to cover me. Looking back on this, I realize how unusual and foolhardy this plan was.

So, on Friday, I drove up past Augusta with the informant. We had dinner and got a couple hotel rooms off Route 95, planning to be on the road by 8 a.m. the next day. In the morning, using a map (pre-GPS era), we found our way into the very rural China Lake region. Somehow, we located John's supposed address. We hadn't tried calling him again because we didn't want to chance him blowing us off after we had driven three hours to make this happen.

The CI and I both approached the front door of a small unkempt house surrounded by overgrown bushes and grass. No sooner had I knocked on the door when John opened it. Over his shoulder, I could see a woman, John's common-law wife. He was perhaps in his late 30s and as disheveled as his surroundings. He was a hairy, beer-belly scratching gruff character. His woman was shifty, skinny, not-too-healthy looking.

After the CI and John exchanged greetings, the CI introduced me to John, who glared at me with a suspicious eye. In a less than friendly manner, John spouted out in my direction, "I know what you're here for. Let's take a ride so I can get to know you better."

The four of us piled into my dark green Chevy sedan that my office loaned to me for this weekend trek. John and his woman sat in the back seat. It was shortly after 9 a.m.

There was no way I could contact one of the Maine ATF Agents. Even if I had managed to pull over to a phone booth and reach one, where would I have told him to catch up with us? We were constantly on the move, plus I couldn't even arrange a meeting spot because I was totally unfamiliar with the area. So much for that plan!

John directed my every turn since I had no idea where I was or where we were going. Then, he told me to pull over when we approached a gas station with a convenience store. "Just want to get a couple six-packs. Any preference?" John asked.

"I'm good with anything," I replied. I wasn't particularly keen on drinking at this time of day, especially since I was driving and I had to keep my wits about me. Upon his return to the car, John passed around the beers, each of us popping them open. I sipped mine as slowly as I could.

Again, John told me to keep driving; he would let me know if he wanted me to turn. If I had more experience, maybe I would have taken more control of the situation, but I was hindered by fear and the desire to make this a successful trip, come hell or high water.

We drove endlessly all over backcountry roads while talking about nothing really important, just getting to know each other. Whenever I tried to steer the conversation toward guns, John would admonish me, saying he didn't want to talk about guns yet.

Shortly after noontime, John instructed me to pull into a roadside tavern for lunch. As we sidled up to four seats at the bar, John ordered drinks. I stuck to another beer, which I slowly drank and inconspicuously partially poured onto the floor under the edge of the bar. We ate, drank and bs'ed some more before piling back into the car. And then we drove some more.

I was never comfortable with this entire scenario. This was getting to be too much. My youth and inexperience with something like this caused me to lose control of the entire situation. The desire to make a case and the fear of pissing off this guy in the back seat, who may have a gun on him, all made for a sorry state of affairs.

Since it was early November, the sun started dipping into the chilly western sky rather early. Dusk was upon us just after four in the afternoon. We still hadn't spoken about guns. John finally said we were going to his uncle's house to talk business. When he mentioned his uncle by first name, I realized with some trepidation his uncle was the same guy who already sold guns to our Rhode Island undercover agent.

We pulled deeper into the woods until we reached a double-wide trailer situated between the woods and the China Lake shore. In the house, John's wife obediently went into the living room while we four men sat around a small dining table. To my left, closest to the door, was my CI. He had done well all day, engaging John and his wife in conversation without getting trashed. John sat directly across from me with his uncle to my right. A small country-style chandelier hung from the ceiling between us, washing the room with dim yellow light.

The conversation finally turned to guns, but no mention yet of military rifles. I let them know I could use some weapons in Massachusetts because the strict gun laws made the market so tight back home. And I told them I had some guys who needed the guns for some "work."

About 15 minutes into the conversation, out of nowhere, John blurted out, "I saw that look! You're either a cop or a Fed or something. I don't know why he brought you here," referring to my informant.

I'll never forget that moment. I was completely dumbfounded, taken by surprise, not understanding what caused him to snap. I had to reply quickly, "What the fuck are you talking about?"

He began loudly shouting directly into my face. My heartbeat quickened, keeping pace with my fear, but I tried to maintain a poker face. I stood up and stated plainly, "I don't need this shit. You don't want to deal, I'm out of here." I told my shocked informant we were leaving. We both made it outside, but John followed us.

He and I were face-to-face in the driveway, hollering at each other. I really wanted to get out of there sooner rather than later. My little five-shot .38 S & W revolver was tucked into my pants close to my right hip. I was more than ready to react and use my weapon if I felt any further threat.

It was now pitch-black outside. Another couple minutes passed with John cursing and arguing before my CI and I managed to get into my car. He and I spoke little as I drove, mostly silent during much of the drive.

As during much of the day, I didn't know where I was or where I was going. It was even worse in the darkness, weaving along the curves of the roads in the woods. My mind kept thinking about how we could easily have been buried out in these woods forever if this had escalated any further.

Apparently, my "senseless direction," a term I coined for my absurd ability to find my way to my destination, had kicked in. When we finally found the hotel, we grabbed a bite to eat, then went to our rooms. There, I proceeded to the bathroom and puked my guts out. The results of the day-long adrenalin rush, the scare from the day's events, and drinking all day, all took their toll.

We never made a gun case against John, but his uncle got arrested for Federal firearms charges. John was interviewed as part of the case, so as not to give up the informant or me in case some future opportunity arose to approach him. He provided no information on any crimes. Not all investigations were successful.

CHAPTER 5

More Guns in Walpole

May 10, 1977, was my first day ever in Walpole, Massachusetts. Weather-wise it was amazing. On the previous day, the biggest spring snowstorm ever to hit New England dumped about 20 inches in the greater Boston area. Thousands of trees lost their tops, which, along with branches, were strewn all over the country roads. The weight of the damp snow on trees with new leaves caused so much damage scarring the trees for years to come. But the 10th was a sunny, warm mid-spring day with rapid melting.

I had an appointment at the Walpole Police Department. This little suburb town southwest of Boston had more illegal guns than one could ever imagine. It was three years later when the largest gun seizure in Massachusetts occurred here in Walpole.

Detective James "Jimmy" "Dunny" Donahue had a problem. His name was Stephen Allen Klosieski. This gun and drug dealer was a thorn in the side of Walpole residents. Only in his early 20s at the time I became involved with the investigation, Klosieski had already created a track record. Often there was a drive-thru business going on at his parent's Washington Street house, where Stephen still lived.

Dunny was an affable Teddy bear, with smiling blue eyes, a weathered face and a full head of sandy-colored hair that already showed signs of the silver-gray which would dominate in a few short years. We hit it off right away. Over the course of the next 10-15years, we would spend thousands of hours together, both working and playing.

My only complaint with Dunny was his near-constant habit of cigarette smoking. I grew up in a house with parents who smoked. My strong dislike for cigarette smoke started at a young age. Whenever we went on a stake-out or rode around together to conduct investigations, I always went home smelling like a stinking cigarette butt.

Dunny had heard about and had seen the action in and out at Klosieski's house. Young punks, many known to the police, would stop at the house, go inside, and then leave the premises minutes later. The problem for the police was they could never get inside or get someone to inform on Klosieski. They had verified information but nothing resembling usable evidence or even probable cause for purposes of securing a search warrant.

By June 1977, my one-year anniversary on the job, Dunny and I decided we would conduct surveillances on Klosieski, starting with fixed surveillance on his house. The Klosieski family home was an early 1900s two-and-a-half-story wood-frame single-family house. It sat only a few feet off busy Washington Street, which extended all the way from the Rhode Island border through Boston, some 20 miles to the northeast. Across the street from the house was Bird Middle School, where my two daughters went to school a dozen years later.

To the right side of Klosieski's house, through a patch of thick bushes and trees, down a long driveway, was a machine shop. This place was soon to become our observation post (o.p.).

About 100 feet behind the house was another stretch of woods. The very first night we started watching the Klosieski house, we positioned a few feet into those woods. It was dusk. We were hoping for some action.

Eventually, during my career, I concluded there were hundreds of fruitless hours spent watching people and places. Only about one percent of the time spent on surveillances resulted in useful information. But that one percent could certainly prove to be the impetus propelling an investigation toward a successful conclusion.

Thirty minutes later, shortly after dark, we saw the tall, skinny shape of Stephen with his long, stringy hair come out the back door of the house, illuminated only by the interior lights. I pulled a pair of binoculars up to my eyes to get a better look at him.

BANG! BANG! BANG! It only took us that long for Dunny and me to hit the ground. Damn, it looked like he was shooting in our direction! But Klosieski never said a word. He just turned around and went back into the house. We had already both pulled our guns out, but then returned them to our holsters when we surmised he must have been test-firing his gun. Apparently, he had no idea we were hiding in the woods.

Detective Donahue could have arrested Klosieski right there for firing the gun in the neighborhood, but we knew right away we were on the right track for something bigger. Knowing Stephen was a drug dealer, and with the rumor he also dealt guns, this incident helped confirm he had a gun.

Klosieski already had a felony conviction. Under Federal law, I could foresee a case where he could be charged as a felon in possession of a firearm, in violation of 18 U.S.C., Section 922 (g)(1). We even had probable cause for a search warrant. In the morning we could seek search and arrest warrants if we so desired. See how 1% of time spent on surveillance could turn out to be fruitful? Our very first night out looking at this guy and we already had the makings of a case.

We never used that same spot as an o.p. again. Over the next days, weeks and months, we tried a couple different locations in which to conduct our surveillances. The first spot we chose was behind a parapet wall on the roof of the one-story machine shop next to Klosieski's property. It provided an excellent vantage point. However, weather changes or if we wanted to become mobile to follow Stephen if he went somewhere, this location created some difficulties.

We then shifted to using an old ATF surveillance truck, similar to a step van formerly used as a bread company vehicle. Parked in the machine shop parking lot, we had superb views to his backyard, part of his driveway and one side of his house. Although it could get warm or cold depending on the season, it offered many rudimentary Spartan benefits, like being able to have some privacy while urinating into a coffee can. Mobility was a plus.

One late weekday afternoon, Klosieski took off in his old beat-up car. We followed or at least attempted to follow him.

Since it was a Federal vehicle, I was the driver. We took a left on Washington, and a left on the country road to Route 1 (the main road from Maine's Canadian border to southern Florida before construction of Route 95), where we took another left heading northbound. The mobile surveillance started well, but with rush hour traffic and a generous smattering of traffic lights, we fell behind our prey.

I didn't want to lose the eyeball on his car, so I lost my senses. Dunny was standing in the rear compartment of the truck where he could see above the traffic. As I wildly swung to my right into the breakdown lane, Dunny bounced off the truck walls until he gained a secure position. I increased our speed, passing everybody in the two lanes to our left. Five minutes later, I lost him in the traffic, stuck behind a light at a busy intersection. Oh, well, live to work another day.

*   *   *

During this period, Dunny and I often grabbed something to eat at the Mug n' Muffin, a small local spot next to the police station that served meals all day. One day, as Dunny bantered with our friendly cute brunette waitress, she looked me over and quipped, "You must be a cop, Fed or bad guy, which is it?" Within weeks we were dating. A year and a half later, Aileen and I married, with Jimmy Donahue being one of my groomsmen. Aileen is the mother of our two beautiful daughters. We divorced 12 years later, although we remain friendly to this day.

*   *   *

Lots of nights I spent with the Walpole cops. I became friendly with many of them, including Officer Rick Stillman (who, years later, became the Chief) and Officer Scott Bushway (who became Deputy Chief). One night, well after dark, there was an armed robbery at a Ground Round restaurant, part of the Howard Johnson family, on a busy corner of Route 1.

Responding to the scene with Jimmy Donahue, we scoured the woods behind the restaurant for the culprits. Stillman and Bushway were also in the woods with us. Nobody used flashlights which could have helped our search but could have hindered our safety. We split up to search the woods behind the parking lot. In the pitch dark, we only occasionally saw each other. This was before police or ATF had jackets with billboard size lettering identifying the wearer.

I came across a tall stack of granite curbstones piled there by the highway department. I climbed atop the six-foot-high stack where I laid flat, giving me a place where maybe I could see or hear movement. Within minutes, I heard the chilling warning, "Freeze, police!" Off to my side, I had heard no motion. About 10 yards away, Scott Bushway had seen my silhouette against the white granite. He had drawn down on me.

I freaking froze in place. "Scott, it's Wayne Miller," I yelled as loud as I could. When he responded he understood what I said and I again confirmed it was safe, I hopped down from my perch. After not locating any "bad" guys, we abandoned our search. Catastrophe (defined as officer down by friendly fire) averted.

*   *   *

In the spring of 1978, our investigation of the criminal activities of Stephen Klosieski heated up. We borrowed an undercover cop from outside the immediate area. Ernie was solely doing undercover (uc) work around the eastern part of the State. He had the gift of gab both on and off the job.

We put Ernie in a position where he contacted associates of Klosieski, many of them only 18 to 20 years old. The 30-plus Ernie talked his way right into the group. He made a couple of hand-to-hand gun buys from these guys. Tracing the guns by using their serial numbers revealed they all were stolen.

Ernie was a bit of a cowboy, running roughshod. Most of his outstanding work outweighed his negative qualities. One thing that bothered many of us was he let Klosieski call the shots too often. For instance, they scheduled a gun buy for Easter Sunday afternoon. The timing ruined any family life for the day. However, we all wanted to make a case against this guy. Maybe Klosieski was testing us since a cop might not want to play on a holiday. The good news is Ernie made the deal.

The bad news is that, for reasons I can't recall, the US Attorney's Office declined to prosecute a case against Klosieski and his little posse. However, more good news, the Norfolk County District Attorney's Office issued warrants for him and his pals.

More bad news, Klosieski took off to parts unknown for a while. It took months to locate him. When we did, the D.A's Office wasn't willing to spend the money to bring Klosieski back for prosecution in Massachusetts, figuring he was somebody else's problem now.

Stephen Allen Klosieski was murdered on March 14, 1986, in Volusia County, Florida in a drug deal gone wrong. He never changed over the years. He was forever 30. Case closed.

CHAPTER 6

Family Bombing Case

The year 1993, which had already seen the terrorist truck bomb explosion inside New York's World Trade Center killing six people, and the six-year mail bombing reign of the Unibomber, now had an explosive conclusion. The year closed out with six improvised fragment explosive devices sent to a girlfriend's family members causing five deaths within 90 minutes in one of the most bizarre bombing schemes imaginable.

Michael Stevens and Brenda Lazore Chevore were an older dating couple who lived together. Brenda, a nurse, had a strong Mohawk Indian heritage. She had two previous failed marriages, and she had a seven-year-old son who lived with them. Michael came from an immigrant family. He, too, was divorced. In his mid-fifties, he was two decades older than Brenda. They also had their own son, two years old in 1993.

Stevens had a checkered past. He dropped out of high school but eventually completed his degree. Stevens attended college for two years before quitting and becoming quite a fraud, a schemer and a scammer. In the late 1980s, his conniving ways got him imprisoned for two years. After his prison release in 1989, he and Brenda met.

Their relationship was volatile with many domestic fights that brought the police to their doorstep four times in three years. In 1991, one argument grew so heated Brenda stabbed Stevens in the head with garden pruning shears. Yet, the two continued as a couple.

Brenda's family had serious misgivings about her relationship with Stevens. Her sisters felt he was strange. They thought of him as a liar. They saw his violent tendencies and how he often vented his anger. Her mom expressed her fears that Stevens was dangerous and even shared he might even kill their entire family.

Little did she know what Stevens was capable of. He and Brenda invited her parents and her 16-year-old brother to their house for Christmas dinner. There was tension in the air throughout the gathering. Besides her family being less than fond of him and always uncomfortable around Stevens, he loathed them. He stewed, and he planned, and he stewed some more. Whether their slights were real or perceived, Stevens' hatred had him planning a deadly scheme for Brenda's family. Witnesses reported Stevens had a peculiar smile on his face throughout dinner.

✻   ✻   ✻

Earl Figley was the best friend of Michael Stevens. He was quite bright. For many years, he was a schoolteacher. He had a Master of Science degree. Despite his background, he could not keep a job because he was a longtime alcoholic. Some referred to him as a harmless drunk. At 56-years-old, he was on welfare. He was easily recognizable since a car accident many years before left him blind in one eye with a glass eye and a ragged scar on his cheek. Not so visible was the damage to his brain, a portion he lost in the crash.

Now, in 1993, his friendly relationship with Stevens took on an extra dimension. He became more than a hanger-on in need of a place to live; he developed into a loyal follower, a true disciple of his felonious friend. After Stevens' release from prison, Figley moved into his buddy's house, but when Brenda moved in, Earl took up residence in a local motel for two years before moving back into the couple's house. Over Christmas, Figley held onto several presents that Stevens had made for his girlfriend's family.

*   *   *

They put the plan into its ultimate phase three days after Christmas. Earl took six cardboard boxes to delivery service companies, scheduling each package for delivery as close to simultaneously as possible. A courier service delivered four of the packages. One was transported by taxi, and another was sent through the US Postal Service. The scheduling was no small feat as the address destinations were many miles apart.

The idea was to give the appearance of Christmas gifts delivered a few days late. Brenda's mother, Eleanor Fowler, opened her box in the late afternoon. In the box, she found a plastic fishing tackle box. As she opened it, it was the last thing she did on this earth. Fortunately, her son, Jonathan, was at a friend's house when the package arrived.

Her brother, William Lazore, suspected something when he saw the package delivered to his house. Nobody is exactly sure why he felt this way, but he was an Indian medicine man who talked to the spirits.

In a strange move, he took the tackle box outside, tossed it on the ground, and poked at it with a rake. He prodded one latch, then the second one open. The device exploded, sending metal shrapnel fragments into his leg. William's son suffered an injury and their dog died in the fusillade. If he thought it was a bomb or at least something that would hurt him, why did he challenge the package?

Brenda's sister, Pamela, couldn't wait to see what was in the package that was just delivered. It arrived right around 6 p.m., shortly after her daughter ran out to the store. Her live-in boyfriend, Richard Urban, sat in a kitchen chair, hunched over to open the cardboard box. Pamela stood, watching the action from over Richard's shoulder.

Upon opening the tackle box, the resultant explosion instantly killed both individuals. The force of the blast pressure, combined with the shrapnel, shredded Richard's torso, leaving him naked except for his belt. Richard's body shielded most of Pamela, but she lost her entire jaw assembly.

The bombing barrage continued. Eleanor's husband, Rocky, received his package at the armored car business where he worked. About 6:30 p.m., he opened the tackle box while in a vault. Rocky died instantaneously, along with a second employee. The blast injured a third employee.

A fifth bomb was delivered to the home of another of Eleanor's daughters, Lucille, and her husband, Scott. When they opened their parcel, they survived because the device failed to detonate. They immediately tried several times to alert Eleanor by phone, but nobody ever answered their calls. Police rendered the IED safe.

The delivery service brought the sixth and final package to the Lakeview Correctional Facility, but they refused delivery because Scott Kemp wasn't working. Once made aware of the contents of the package their man carried, the delivery service radioed a message to him in his vehicle. In a panic, he raced away from the truck and vomited by the roadside. A bomb squad also defused this device.

The normal peace and tranquility of Christmas week in this region was physically and emotionally shattered within a few short instances. Violence never seen before in these areas destroyed the usually quiet and idyllic six neighborhoods. Suddenly, the residents took on an unknown fear their night terrors never could have imagined.

It was now up to the first responders, including the fire and police personnel, and other law enforcement investigators to calm their fears. Local Police Chief Bruce Chamberlin stated it well when he said, "What was important about this case...was that before the 11 o'clock news, we pretty much knew what was going on. If we hadn't been able to do that, then I think you would have had a lot more fear...And fear is probably as destructive as the crime itself."

✳　　✳　　✳

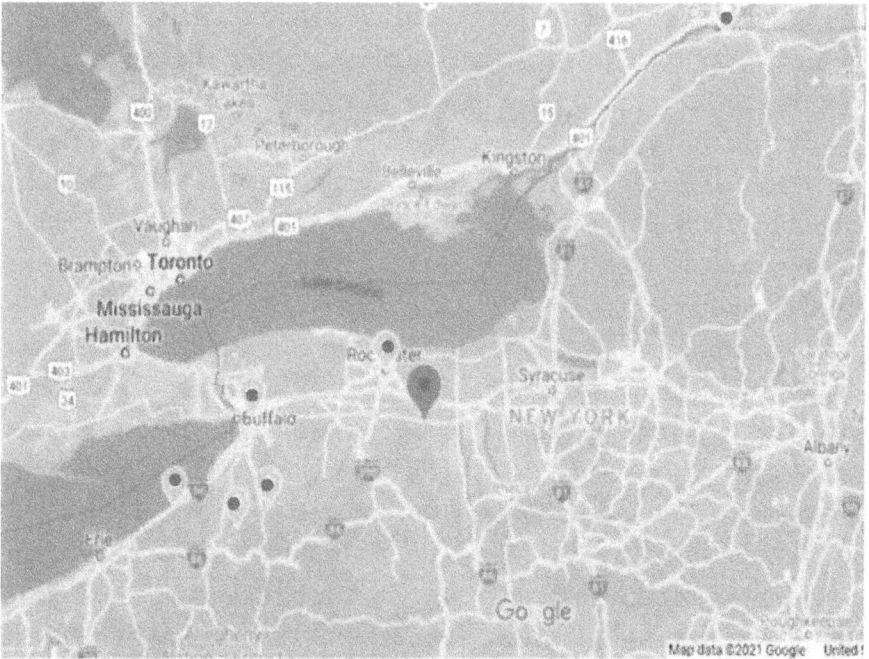

The six gold stars are the locations where Figley and Stevens sent the bombs.
The red pin represents the Canandaigua motel where Earl Figley lived with
the bombs before he shipped them. (Google Maps)

Imagine the large-scale investigation facing investigators. Each of the six cities and towns was a separate crime scene. All the scenes were within an hour of each other, except one over 300 miles away from the others.

Initially, each municipality didn't know of the other bombs. They thought their incident was a solo, unique event. First responders from each local fire and police department rushed to the scenes. They, of course, reached out to the State Police with their bomb and arson investigators.

Then, word of the multiple devices and the multiple fatalities rapidly spread throughout the state. Because of the large scale and breadth of the fatal crimes, the locals and state requested assistance from ATF. The Bureau has the personnel, equipment, money and expertise to handle situations like this.

Considering all the explosive devices detonated between 5 and 6:30 p.m., the investigation swiftly ramped up. By mid-evening of Tuesday, December 28, 1993, as I was enjoying Christmas week off, my home phone rang. It was the Northeast National Response Team Supervisor, Robert Graham.

ATF formed the NRT's in 1978 to assist state, local, and other federal agencies to investigate major fire and explosion incidents. The four teams, including those from the West, Southeast, and Midwest, could send a cadre of agents to a major explosion or fire incident scene within 24 hours of an event.

The Supervisor informed me there had been several bombings with several fatalities and injuries in Upstate New York between the northern tier cities of Rochester and Buffalo. I was to report to a meeting location in Rochester by the following afternoon.

As soon as I hung up the phone, I packed some clothes and checked to be sure all my gear was ready. Call-outs can take several days, so it was best to prepare for the long haul.

Although I always felt torn when leaving my family for these trips, I justified my feelings to my wife and daughters, and to myself that some other family was hurting in a more tragic way.

✳   ✳   ✳

By 1993, I had worked on several explosion cases, including those involving dust, natural and propane gas, combustion and other high-order bombings, including the one that killed a Boston Police Officer while maiming another, written about in another chapter. Investigators can readily tell the difference between the gas vapor explosions and those from explosive devices.

In bombing cases, the greatest damage is often at the seat of the blast, characterized by a crater with damages decreasing away from that point. However, in fuel gas explosions, the large rapid release of energy with quickly expanding gas molecules exerts the greatest pressure on the outer walls of a compartment, be it a room or a building. You may have seen natural gas-related explosions on TV. The blast obliterates some of those buildings, completely shattering structural components into small pieces, while others have entire walls pushed outward, but nearly intact.

＊　　＊　　＊

During my 38 years working fires and explosions, including with ATF and 18 years on the private side, I was part of over 100 explosions, including at the 1996 Olympic bombing in Atlanta. I was one ATF Agent, of many, who thought Richard Jewell was not the bomber. The Northeast and Southeast ATF NRTs were part of a large, multi-jurisdictional task force assigned to the Olympics. We were there for seven weeks, including orientation and familiarization with the venues. Our wish was for a peaceful few weeks. When the games started, we worked 12-hour shifts.

On the night of the bombing, I had just gotten off my shift at midnight. The blast occurred shortly before 1:30 a.m. A phone call from my wife woke me. She said her son saw a TV alert about an explosion at the Olympics. Her call beat the one from my supervisor. By 3 a.m. we started collecting the evidence from the extremely large blast site.

At 10 a.m., I was standing in the Fulton County Medical Examiner's morgue attending the first autopsies of my career. I was there to maintain the chain of custody of evidence removed from Alice Stubbs Hawthorne's body, who died from nails serving as shrapnel built into the device. I also witnessed the autopsy of a Turkish reporter who died from a heart attack as he ran toward the blast site to cover the story.

＊　　＊　　＊

First thing in the morning after the four New York explosions, I hopped in my G-ride for the trip to Rochester. With blue lights turned on once I hit the highway, the normal five-hour ride out Interstate 90 took less than four while still driving safely.

During the windshield time, I thought a lot about what I was to encounter. The Team Supervisor advised the scene he assigned me to had two fatalities. I thought about some procedures we would follow to properly conduct the forensic analysis of the scene. We needed to be sure to collect all the evidence necessary to convict the monsters who caused this death and destruction.

Upon arrival in Rochester, I learned lots of details of the 18-hour old investigation at the meeting with state, local, and New York area ATF Agents. They explained what they already knew about each explosion, the victims, and early interview information. The biggest surprise was they had developed suspects already.

Investigators initially went to Stevens' house to protect him and Brenda because the bomber targeted her family. Much to their surprise, when the Police arrived at Stevens' house, they found Brenda, Stevens and Figley there.

When identifying himself, Earl Figley pulled out his red wallet, the same color wallet later described by witnesses from the package deliveries. Additionally, surviving family members told investigators about the family problems and concerns with Michael Stevens, the investigation began to focus.

Shortly after the bombings, investigators learned from the delivery companies a man with a glass eye had delivered the packages. Now, investigators were laser-focused.

By the time we sat in our briefing, other police and ATF Agents were questioning the three of them. Interestingly, when they got to Stevens' house that morning to question them, Brenda, Michael and Earl still were together at the house. Within hours, Figley had signed a 43-page confession. Authorities then charged Figley and his leader, Michael Stevens. But they let Brenda return home.

Family members thought she was likely involved or knew of the plans. They no longer wanted her around. She didn't go to the funerals.

It was still our job to collect the evidence, determine exactly how the devices detonated, and prove a Federal case beyond a reasonable doubt independent of Figley's confession. All confessions need corroborating evidence. What if his confession gets thrown out in court? Unless we followed the evidence, we could lose the case against the suspected bombers.

At the expansive Rochester apartment complex, the seat of the explosion was in 55 Snug Harbor Court where Pamela Epperson, nee Lazore and Richard Urban (AKA Urbanski) perished. After the Rochester Fire Department completed their work at the scene the previous day, the Rochester Police secured and protected the site.

ATF Special Agent Anthony Bartello, an experienced affable guy from the Buffalo office, headed the NRT investigation team with Rochester Police Captain Mike Leach, who led four officers and two police photographers. Bartello assigned ten other ATF Agents as schematic artists, evidence technicians and interview teams.

He delegated me as the origin and cause specialist for ATF. An ATF Explosive Enforcement Officer and an ATF Chemist rounded out the team. It takes a trained army of specialists to do this type of job properly.

A neighbor who had first-hand knowledge saw the delivery of a large parcel possibly weighing 10 to 20 pounds shortly before the explosion which the witness described as making a loud crack similar to a shotgun blast accompanied by a bright flash emanating from the first-floor front kitchen windows.

Let me try to paint the picture of the scene for you. This unit was one of six within the building. Side-by-side townhouse-style apartments all had entrances on the first floor, both in the front with a glass sliding door in the rear. The front faced north. It was the third unit in from the end of the building.

Former site of the Snug Harbor Court apartment.
(Google Maps)

Rochester blast kills 2

Other bombs claim 4 victims in Western N.Y.

Rochester newspaper announcing the bombings.

The wood-framed, two-story unit measured 15 feet wide by 29 feet long. Exterior siding was wood shingles with a gable roof covered with composite asphalt shingles. There was a full basement with a concrete block and poured concrete foundation.

A walk around the entire building revealed exterior damage confined to Unit 55, with the front and rear first floor walls bowed outward. The glass of the rear slider was broken, but the front kitchen window and other debris had blown outside onto the grass and driveway with some glass over 100 feet away. Amazingly, the second-floor windows remained intact.

Inside, on the second-floor, aside from the bowed front and rear walls, the only other sign of the explosion was furniture and contents in disarray from the blast pressure pushing upward on the floor from below.

From there, we examined the basement. The downward blast pressure split and severed several wood floor joists, mostly under the kitchen and first-floor front hallway. There was a three-foot circular hole in the basement ceiling below the kitchen. I saw the jagged, splintered wood around the hole with the remains of blood and fleshy body parts. The combination kitchen stove/oven sagged through the hole.

We sifted through a large quantity of debris. We found metal battery fragments, machine-stamped metal fragments, several plastic fragments, a black rubber end-plug, and a crimped metal fragment both from an electric detonator. Despite what many bombers believe, investigators find most of an improvised explosive device (IED) after an explosion during a careful post-blast scene examination

We also sifted and collected evidence on the first floor. Besides finding similar items as we found in the basement, we recovered shredded newspaper, tape and a brown cardboard box. The box had a mailing label on it addressed to Pamela Epperson.

We collected everything. You never know what evidentiary value some random item might yield. A bomber could leave a fingerprint, especially on the newspaper when purchased or read, or even on the first piece of tape that remained after wrapping Christmas presents.

Some bombers don't wear gloves when assembling their device, figuring nothing would survive the blast. With today's forensic science capabilities, investigators and lab technicians often find DNA on the device or packing material.

The kitchen scene was gruesome. The bodies of Pamela and Richard were still in the kitchen where their lives ended. Large sections of sheetrock from the ceiling plus the upper kitchen cabinets and other debris covered the bodies. Richard's right arm and much of his face were gone.

The stamped metal fragments the bombers added to the device functioned as designed, shredding his entire torso. He was in the face-up position in front of the stove.

Except for the gaping bloody hole where her chin and neck had been, Pamela was relatively intact. Still fully clothed, we found her face down in front of the sink and stove, which hung in the three-foot crater in the kitchen floor. Dried blood and body fragments were on surfaces throughout the kitchen.

The police photographed everything down to the smallest detail. Then the Medical Examiner removed the bodies. At the morgue, the ME x-rayed the bodies seeking the fragments within the victims' bodies. Again, investigators collected evidence throughout the kitchen. We shipped these items to the ATF National Laboratory for analysis.

Based on the scene evidence, my report read that an electrically initiated high-explosive device detonated on the kitchen floor in front of the stove, killing the two people in close proximity to the blast. The device was packaged in a cardboard box with newspaper, a plastic container yet to be identified, with machine-stamped metal fragments, at last, one battery, an electric detonator and an unknown quantity of high explosives. The bomber built the device in such a manner to intentionally cause great bodily harm or death.

This is the type of incident ATF Agents, first responders and other investigators get called to at a moment's notice. You don't know when and you don't know where, but it will happen.

Training helps prepare you to do the job, as well as having the proper equipment. But nothing prepares you mentally for the savagery one human being can inflict on another. Those appalling images are still vivid in my mind's eye today. This scene was something I'll never be able to unsee. Anybody in a similar business knows what I mean.

Information of a 50-something-year-old man with a glass eye and scarred face who brought the bomb packages to the delivery services triggered New York-based ATF Special Agent Scott Sammis to act on another investigation with a similar suspect description. A few months earlier, someone dumped 112 sticks of dynamite behind a Ponderosa restaurant in a Rochester suburb. Agent Sammis traced the powerful explosives to the Kentucky Powder Company of Mount Vernon, Kentucky.

A man with the description of Earl Figley purchased the 55 pounds of dynamite on June 30, 1993, except that man presented a Vermont driver's license in the name of Leslie Milbury.

Stevens also obtained a Vermont license using a phony name of Roger Simpson. Investigators determined the names came from fake birth certificates. Within hours after the bombings, Agent Sammis established Milbury and Figley were the same person. That revelation meant Figley and Stevens connived to use bombs for vengeance against members of Brenda's family for almost a year.

Agent Sammis and other investigators conducted the interviews of Figley and Stevens within hours of the bombings. By the next day, Sammis had a 43-page signed confession from Earl Figley. As part of his admissions, Figley explained he and Stevens made the bombs over the summer into the early fall, but he thought Stevens had disposed of the large cache of dynamite until the day he delivered the packages. He confessed to buying the dynamite and delivering the bombs.

Figley never implicated Brenda as being a co-conspirator, but because of the intense fighting between her and Stevens, she threatened to leave Stevens with their son, which pushed him to forge ahead with his deadly plans. Figley stated, "He would have to stop them (Brenda's family) from supplying her with money or a place to live." Stevens did not want to lose her and his son.

With his statements, investigators easily traced the purchase of the fishing tackle boxes. Those innocuous stamped metal fragments which became deadly shrapnel came from the Liberty Iron and Metal Company in Erie, Pennsylvania. The bombers delivered the packages with the company return address printed on the boxes.

Within 24 hours of the explosions that killed five people, injured at least three others, and caused hundreds of thousands of dollars in property damage, the authorities arrested Stevens and Figley. The men could face the death penalty if convicted of the charges of unlawfully transporting, possessing, and using explosive devices to damage property and cause death, in violation of 18 United States Code, Section 2, 842 (a)(3), 844 (d), 844 (i), and 924 (c)(1) and 26 U.S.C. Sections 5861 (d) and 5871.

While local and ATF investigators compiled several dozen government witnesses, ATF Laboratory chemists and Explosive Enforcement Officers stayed busy going through the thousands of pieces of evidence collected from the multiple scenes. Unlike the manner of post-bomb blast evidence collection by the FBI where they collect, bag and tag each minute item as separate unique evidentiary items making tens of thousands of pieces, we at ATF did it differently.

We mark off grids within the scene, whether it's a room or a field. Unless there was some extraordinary item found within a grid, we had several evidence bags per grid.

In this instance, one bag from a grid contained the cardboard from the box. Another had shredded newspaper, while in another we only put the stamped metal fragments, and so on. This method makes the evidence more manageable while still following rules that enable admissibility of the evidence in court.

It's amazing to see the accomplishments of the lab personnel who not only identify the explosives and all other device components but literally rebuild the device. They also build a mock-up device to show the jury exactly what the device looked like and how it functioned. These dissectologists (one who enjoys jigsaw puzzle assembly) deserve a lot of credit for their patience and tenacity.

The bombs created by Figley and Stevens were simple devices. Inside the plastic fishing tackle boxes, they used two or three sticks of dynamite detonated from electric blasting caps. They used a switch with a battery that closed the circuit when someone opened the box. The bombers added pounds of the stamped metal fragments with the intent to inflict great bodily harm.

Faced with considerable damning evidence, in early February 1995, Figley pleaded guilty to conspiracy to making and mailing the deadly bombs in return for a 20-year sentence at a minimum/medium Federal prison. As part of his plea agreement, he had to testify in the trial against his former friend, Michael Stevens.

I'm sure many people reading this believe Figley should have gotten the death penalty or at least life in prison for his major role in the five deaths, the injuries and the heavy damages. This is the same sentiment I repeatedly hear relative to the nine defendants in my first book, *Burn Boston Burn*, a case with over 200 firefighters' injuries during this crew's two-year arson spree torching 264 buildings. It is easy to understand that feeling, but a couple of things must be considered.

First, the prosecution in these New York bombings dropped the death penalty charges for several reasons they have not fully disclosed. Even more important, for those not familiar with significant criminal trials, it is often crucial to have a co-conspirator testify to boost the case against other defendants. Prosecutors have to make a deal with a prospective witness that seems unjust. They have to weigh the pros and cons of such a deal because defense attorneys always paint these criminal witnesses as liars and scum who will testify to anything seeking a lighter sentence.

Michael Stevens and Earl Figley 6/95 photo.
(Photo: Reed Hoffmann/File photo)

Figley wept at his sentencing. As with a good portion of defendants, whether they are truly remorseful or they are trying to garner favor with the sentencing judge, he apologized for his actions.

On March 6, 1995, Stevens' trial began in US District Court in Rochester. He was facing multiple life sentences if convicted. He had nothing left to lose by going to trial. Plus, he likely felt justified by his actions, once again proving how unstable he was.

And the star witness, Earl Figley, was a pathetic, brain-damaged alcoholic character who played a huge role in the bombings. As the trial opened, observers wondered how two losers could have succeeded in so easily gathering the materials, then building and delivering multiple deadly bombs.

While incarcerated awaiting trial, Stevens solicited several of his fellow inmates to assist him to establish an alibi and also kill the government's star witness, Figley. Seven of these inmates became witnesses against Stevens. He and his mouth often became his own worst enemy. Stevens even petitioned to act as co-counsel at his trial. The judge refused this request.

Evidence presented at the trial clearly portrayed Stevens as the mastermind of this reprehensible plot, even though his disciple, Earl Figley, carried out some of the most crucial aspects of the conspiracy. Figley did a reasonable job of testifying. He took his hits for his part in the bombings. The prosecutor inquired, "Do you know who was supposed to open the packages?"

"Relatives of Michael Stevens' girlfriend. He was intending to eliminate her relatives." Figley said Stevens used the bombs to "fight back" against her family. "They didn't approve of him, or the relationship of Brenda with him."

Figley testified to another very interesting point about the packaging for the bombs. Stevens wanted to throw investigators off their trail by having Figley go to Buffalo, where he bought a pile of Buffalo newspapers as packing material around the tackle boxes. These were the shredded newspapers we found at the bombing scenes. Figley testified everything was to come from outside their home area of Rochester. It was supposed to appear as if all these bombings took place because of a family vendetta linked to Buffalo.

Stevens' approach to his defense was to blame Figley for devising the murder scheme after hearing his friend complain incessantly about his girlfriend and her family. It is incomprehensible to understand how the dispute among family members could escalate to the level of killing your girlfriend's family just so you can comfort her and have nobody left to urge her to quit the toxic relationship.

It would be easier to believe Stevens was so delusional to think this plan could possibly work. How could any rational person believe Brenda would be all right with the subsequent loss of her family and not put two and two together? One would also wonder how the jurors couldn't help but think Brenda played a role in planning the slaughter of her family.

During the trial, the prosecution called 72 witnesses, including me. I testified as an expert witness to the findings at the Rochester bombing site. Although this was my first testimony in a bombing case, it all went smoothly. The defense attorney didn't challenge me much on the scene examination, the evidence, or my conclusions. The Rochester incident was a straightforward bombing that killed two people. The defense had to tread lightly when referring to what caused the victim's deaths. He didn't want to dwell on that point, emphasizing it before the jurors.

The defense attorney called no witnesses. His chief argument was his client wasn't the one responsible for most of the planning or delivery of the bombs since the intelligent, but devious Figley made and delivered the bombs.

The defense argued a specific motive for Figley, stating Figley's 1971 divorce left him "deeply wounded and embittered," and when Brenda moved in with Stevens, he had to live elsewhere. Figley then focused his anger on her. Defense argument continued, "Something went wrong in Earl Figley's mind. He went mad. Figley can't be trusted. It's obvious you cannot convict a man based on his testimony." This is the typical argument heard in trials all over the land. Sometimes it is true, sometimes not. It is the jury's duty to weigh the testimony, considering all the other evidence.

During closing arguments, prosecutors refuted the defense argument stating, "Earl Figley was the ultimate patsy." They added Stevens used Figley to do most of the dirty work to insulate himself from culpability. Stevens had the motivation, plus he planned, designed and built the bombs he learned from how-to manuals.

His trial lasted three weeks. By April Fool's Day, it took the jury only three hours to find Stevens guilty of all 16 counts against him. The jurors also had to deliberate a second time to consider whether Stevens should face multiple life sentences.

This case was an outstanding example of excellent work by law enforcement on all levels, from the local and county police to the State Police and the Federal Bureau of Alcohol, Tobacco and Firearms.

In short order, police identified the courier service that delivered one bomb and learned of other devices en route to other targets.

A statewide bulletin informed other departments when bombs exploded in their jurisdictions that a wider investigation was underway into a bombing onslaught. The quick action by police readily identified this offensive as a targeted attack, not a random event.

The immediate coordination of the multiple agencies brought a highly concentrated effort resulting in the speedy arrests of the perpetrators. Because of the superb efforts of the entire team, the residents of all the communities shaken by this dramatic bombing siege could feel more secure in their surroundings. People from northwestern New York will not forget this notorious case for many years to come.

*　*　*

The last I knew, Michael Stevens was still in a Federal prison in Arizona serving his life sentence, however long his life may be. He is now in his 80s. He has challenged his conviction, to no avail. Stevens even represented himself when he could find no attorney to represent him.

While Stevens awaited trial, his girlfriend, Brenda Chevore, despite what he did to her family, continued to visit Stevens and still lived in their house. Now, that's blind loyalty. Her life after his conviction is unknown to this author.

In June 2011, Earl Figley was released from prison when he was 80 years old. His whereabouts after prison are unknown.

May Eleanor, Pamela, Richard, and Rocky rest in peace.

*　*　*

Bibliography

Bombing Suspect Had History of Delusion, Self-Destruction with PM-Package Bombs, Bjt, David Germain, The Associated Press, 12/30/93

2 Arrested in Bomb Blasts That Killed 5 in New York, John J. Goldman, Associated Press, LA Times, 12/30/93

Plea Bargain in Mail Bombings That Killed 5 Upstate, Lawrence Van Gelder, New York Times, 02/09/95

A Conviction in Case of 5 Deaths by Bombs, Associated Press, New York Times, 04/01/95

Tale of Vengeance And Betrayal Likely At Mail Bomb Trial, SFGate, Ben Dobbin, Associated Press, 03/06/95

Bad Blood Simmered Long Before Bombings in Upstate N.Y., Washington Post, David Germain, 01/02/94

Austin bombings a flashback to series in Upstate New York in 1993, Steve Orr, Democrat and Chronicle, 03/21/18

One Defendant Pleads Guilty in Package Bombings Case, AP News, Ben Dobbin, 02/09/95

Police Arrest Pair in Parcel Bombings, Motive Behind Five Deaths Remains Unclear, St. Louis Post-Dispatch, 12/31/93

Quiet N.Y. Region Copes With a Crime's Aftermath, Christian Science Monitor, 12/31/93

CHAPTER 7

The Bombing Murder and Maiming of Boston Police Officers

Thomas Shay Sr. suspected something wasn't right about the box he saw in his driveway that day. Could the dispute he had with a couple young guys escalate to a more dangerous situation? After all, he was already involved in a lawsuit involving an explosion.

When Shay returned home from running an errand, as he backed into his driveway at 39 Eastbourne Street, Roslindale, he heard a loud clunk from under his black 1986 Buick Century. Many low-profile vehicles would bottom out on that lip but his car never did. He parked in the driveway because his live-in girlfriend's car was parked in his usual spot on the street in front of his house. Once parked, he checked under his car for the source of the clunk sound. He saw nothing there.

Later in the day, she went out for a few hours so Shay pulled his car forward down the crest of the driveway to take his spot on the street. As he came over the crest of the drive again, he heard a similar scraping banging noise under his car. After parking, he saw a black wooden box on the narrow grassy strip between two concrete ribbons which formed his driveway. The box rested at the crown of the slight incline of the driveway. The grass was slightly dug up where the box scraped the soil.

Shay picked up the strange-looking package and tossed it near his front bushes. A short time later, Shay thought better of leaving the package there. In this tightly packed Boston residential neighborhood of well-kept older homes, he didn't want any kids to pick up the box.

He walked the box up his driveway, placing it on the ground outside his small unattached garage behind his house. Then, he went back into the house, mulling over the strange package.

The next morning, Monday, October 28, 1991, Mr. Shay drove a couple miles to the Boston Police Area E station in West Roxbury to report the suspicious package. After he described the package as a possible bomb to Detective Robert Maloney, Shay was advised to return home where he would be met by other police officers.

Officer Denise Corbett, a rookie cop, on routine patrol took the radio assignment to report to Eastbourne Street for a potential bomb. While en route, she also heard dispatch request the Bomb Squad respond to the scene. Shay met Officer Corbett outside the house and showed her the box. She looked at the package carefully without handling it. The strange black rectangular box covered with magnets caused her stomach to tighten. Once she retrieved her notebook, she started interviewing Shay in the house.

Minutes later, BPD Detective Sergeant Thomas Creavin arrived to support Corbett. Not seeing her right away, he walked up the driveway toward the garage at the rear of the property. Between a 1983 18-foot General Motors walk-in van and a 1969 Pontiac GTO in front of the garage, Sergeant Creavin saw the black box with two different-sized round objects affixed to the top facing surface. As he returned toward the street, Bomb Squad Officers Jeremiah Hurley and Francis Foley pulled up in front of the house. They asked Sergeant Creavin to show them the suspicious package.

Officer Foley had 24 years with the Boston Police. In his last five years, he worked as a Certified Bomb Technician with the Bomb Squad. Officer Hurley was only in the unit for just over a year. Once dispatch notified them they were needed to look at a suspect package in Roslindale, Officer Hurley drove their Ford Bronco to the 39 Eastbourne Street location. It was his turn to drive, which also meant it was his job to handle the suspected device. Officer Foley's job would be to handle the administrative work as well as assist his partner as necessary. They would switch responsibilities when the next call came in.

Dressed in black utility fatigues, they had only the usual police gear with them, their weapons, walkie-talkies and flashlights. The Bronco had no specialized equipment for the bomb techs. If they felt the need after inspecting the package, the large truck with their protective suits and the bomb pot where an unexploded device is placed would respond. But the box hadn't piqued their interest to the point of calling the truck to gear up with their heavy protective vests and helmets.

All three men walked to the front of the garage, visually examining the black box partially tucked under the car's left front fender. It measured about eight to ten inches long by four to six inches wide and approximately two or three inches deep.

Because Jerry had a bad back, Frank reached for the box, moving it a few feet in front of the car. The box weighed three to five pounds. It had some heft to it. He wasn't concerned about moving the box because Mr. Shay had already explained he had moved the package several times, even turning it over and tossing it onto the ground. To Foley, that meant there was no mercury switch in the box. A mercury switch, like in old thermostats, when moved to a certain position, completes a circuit, causing ignition of the device. Also, since the package had been discovered more than 24 hours earlier, it most likely had no timer because it would already have functioned.

Some unusual objects were stuck on the outside of the box. Attached to the box was a large heavy circular metal donut magnet along with several identical, but smaller magnets. These were extremely strong magnets, formerly speaker magnets. Still, the officers were unconcerned by what they saw. Officer Hurley scraped the outer surface of the box with a knife, dislodging two of the small magnets. He placed them on the bumper of the truck where they stuck to the metal. Returning to the front of the house, the bomb squad officers asked the homeowner about his discovery of the box and why he thought it was a bomb.

Shay explained how he had a dispute with two guys from an auto body shop. One of the men put an explosive, equal to a half stick of dynamite, in a metal barrel. When it exploded, Thomas Shay was nearby. It caused him physical and emotional trauma.

After he heard this explanation, Officer Hurley retrieved something from the Bronco. Then, he and Officer Foley returned to inspect the package. Jerry told his partner he thought he saw a switch. Kneeling down and putting on his glasses, Foley saw through an opening of a smaller attached box. He inquired, "Is that a servo, Jerry?"

A servo is an arm on a remote control. As he focused his attention on it, he saw the servo arm move. Then...

Kaboom! The thunderous detonation blast shook the entire neighborhood, heard by everyone near and far. A gray-whitish smoke filled the area. Officer Francis Foley, standing behind Hurley, had been looking over his shoulder. Shrapnel and the ear-splitting explosive percussion battered him, violently knocking him to the ground. His injuries were serious. Jerry Hurley's trauma was far more serious.

Frank Foley saw the ball of fire with white smoke, but, to him, the sound of the explosion was muffled. He thought the left side of his face was gone as he lifted his left hand to touch his face. His right arm wouldn't move. A warm wetness covered his legs. Foley thought he had to stay conscious or he would undoubtedly die.

Jerry was yelling for people to stay away from the area. In spite of his severe injuries, he was still alert enough to fear a secondary device could be triggered. It is not uncommon for a bomber to plant a second bomb that would detonate when a crowd of bystanders or first responders flock to the scene.

You can only imagine how dreadful this moment was for the officers' families, friends, brothers and sisters of the Boston Police Department and police everywhere, and for the people of the neighborhood and throughout the city. This type of bad act hurts so many so deeply for so long.

But it is also the time for others to react and respond to the scene. The two officers who originally saw the explosive device were uninjured, only stung by the blast.

Creavin and Corbett ran over to the screaming bomb techs. Sergeant Creavin put his arm around Jerry Hurley, consoling him, while Officer Corbett did the same to Frank Foley. Creavin yelled into his radio calling for ambulances. He also screamed at neighbors who reacted to the explosion to get towels to quell the bleeding from both officers.

Denise Corbett first saw Foley lying against a fence next to the garage. His face was partially gone with one eye missing. She observed Hurley lying partially under the truck with most of one leg missing as well as one hand.

They witnessed a horrific scene. Both officers did the best they could to comfort Officers Foley and Hurley until other first responders could take care of them. Both injured officers were still conscious. The shock had not yet set in. Each man inquired as to the condition of the other. Each man asked those comforting them to tell their wives and children they loved them. It was only minutes before ambulances arrived. And shortly thereafter, they transported Hurley and Foley from the site. Investigators had to stay with the officers to collect any evidence retrieved from the officers.

Simultaneously, additional responding officers and firefighters secured the scene. Sirens blared, vehicles of many descriptions with lots of people in various uniforms or street clothing, jammed the dead-end neighborhood street.

This crime scene extended far beyond the yard bounded by the Shay house, the neighbor's house, the garage and the street. To secure the scene required every civilian from nearby homes to leave the area.

Police must do this immediately, not only to preserve the integrity of any evidence thrown from the blast but there is always the concern of a second bomb still active in the area. Some bombers aim to maim or kill first responders.

Emergency units whisked both officers to nearby hospital trauma units. Officer Hurley's son, David, rushed to get his sister. Leanne was a senior at St. Clare High School. He told her, "Something happened to Dad and we need to get to the hospital."

At the hospital, doctors said there were hopeful signs. They asked the family if they would like to see him before taking him into surgery.

Leanne didn't think they should see him in his present condition. She felt he was coming home. "I put my foot down. Eighteen years old, still in my St. Clare uniform. And I refused to let any of my family go see him. He wouldn't have wanted us to see him like that. He would have been mad," Leanne recalled over two decades after that devastating day.

She didn't know her Dad's severe injuries included the loss of half his face, plus a partially severed arm and leg. Doctors pronounced Jeremiah Hurley dead after failing to stabilize him.

Leanne anguished over not saying goodbye for many years. But her brother, David, thought differently. He reflected, "I'm glad they didn't go in. Their last memory would have been the blood, the trauma. You want to remember him as the vibrant guy he was, laughing, smiling. That's what you want to remember."

Officer Hurley, only 50 years old, left behind his wife, two daughters, two stepsons and two grandchildren. He served with the Boston Police for 23 years. End of Watch was Monday, October 28, 1991.

Hurley's partner, Officer Francis X. Foley, was left maimed for life. He suffered severe burns and loss of his left eye. Doctors operated on him multiple times to repair his right arm. Plus he had several skin grafts. The emotional toll never fully ceased, no matter what Frank did. A veteran with years on the department, this was his last day on the job.

*   *   *

The crime scene needed processing. With the great relationship between ATF and the Boston Police Department, they immediately requested assistance from our National Response Team.

The Team had boots on the ground the following day. By the afternoon, Boston Police and ATF investigators inched forward on hands and knees, conducting a straight-line pattern search. I was one of those ATF Agents. Others concentrated right at the epicenter of the blast.

BPD had already set a perimeter extending several houses away. The fourth building to the southwest down Eastbourne Street from the bomb site was the Mozart Elementary School. There was no school that day because agents found pieces and parts in their playground.

During a bomb scene search, the typical rule of thumb is to increase the distance of the search perimeter by 50% past the last evidentiary item located. For instance, in Roslindale, when searchers found bomb fragments two houses away from the Shay property, the perimeter was moved to the school. No evidence was ever located beyond the north side of the schoolyard.

After we clawed our way through the grass in one direction, we repeated our line search at a 90-degree angle from the original pattern. We marked items associated with the device and the blast with evidence flags. The evidence technicians photographed the scene, then collected and cataloged the evidence.

We looked in the bushes surrounding house foundations. Investigators easily located half a blasting cap sticking out from the wood shingle siding of the residence to the right of Shay's house. This type of blasting cap was a small, thin metallic tube, inches long, with wires extending from one end. It is a sensitive primary explosive device used to detonate a larger, less sensitive explosive such as dynamite or plastic explosive.

Several other pockmarks in the siding were examined for device remnants. Once we completed the crawling portion of our hunt for evidence, agents scoured the same territory with metal detectors seeking the smallest metallic debris. Some investigators used ladders from Boston Fire to check nearby rooftops and rain gutters.

This type of thorough scene examination usually provides excellent results. And it did here. We found battery parts, the magnets, wiring, the blasting cap, the shrapnel used to kill and maim plus additional items. Investigators identified the toggle switch remains as Radio Shack brand, product number 275602. The evidence revealed adhesives on some components and residues on others which confirmed where the bomb builder placed some of these objects. The ATF chemist confirmed a small silver sticker was identified as the label for a Futaba brand mini slide switch. Contacts and screws also came from a Futaba component.

Investigators found evidence of the explosive used in the device. The ATF Lab confirmed dynamite repackaged from its original stick form was used.

While the scene processing occurred, other teams of investigators conducted interviews. Thomas Shay Sr., one of the first to be interviewed, was an interesting person to interview. He was evasive, never answering questions directly. His story often changed. Investigators believe a truthful story is usually consistent when retold, whereas lies are easily forgotten with an ever-changing story.

Shay Sr. told investigators how he discovered the package. When asked what made him suspicious of the package, he recounted an ongoing disagreement with two guys who ran a garage. These men became the first persons of interest.

Investigators located the two men. After their initial interviews, both agreed to take a polygraph exam. Interestingly, one man passed his test, but the other guy failed. That's where a second interview becomes crucial. The man explained why he failed the polygraph.

He was nervous about his involvement in other criminal activities. Both men were cleared of participating in the bombing.

Although Shay Sr.'s actions were strange, no new evidence was ever developed to connect him to the bombing.

Within a couple days, with the scene processing complete, my duties with the investigation were also done. Or so I thought. I had one more small part to play. And it ended up being a major contribution.

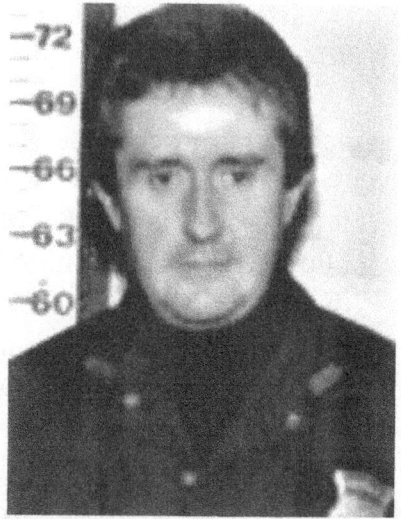

Officer Jeremiah Hurley
National Law Enforcement Memorial
photo

*   *   *

Map of Eastbourne Street, Roslindale, MA area Notice the driveway, the garage and the school (Google Earth 2021)

During the first week of November 1991, I had an investigation that took me to the Quincy, Massachusetts Police Department, just south of Boston. Over the first half of my career, I had developed several close contacts from the Quincy PD.

I met with a senior investigator, Detective Bill Lanergan. Bill was a big old lug, kind, yet crusty, and dogged sleuth. He knew more about crime in the streets than I ever imagined.

During our meeting, we discussed the Boston bombing. When I described the device as seen by Shay Sr., and the two first responding BPD Officers, plus the bomb components we found at the scene, I saw the light bulb illuminate above his mostly bald dome.

"That sounds a lot like a case I had a few years ago," Detective Lanergan enlightened me. His verbal illustration of a bomb from a 1986 investigation seemed so similar to the Roslindale bomb. He dug through a file cabinet, coming up with a case folder.

Bill explained the case to me. The comparison from his bomb description to the present device seemed too coincidental to have been built by somebody unrelated to the 5-year-old Quincy bomb. Quincy Police arrested the builder of the bomb in that case. His name was Alfred Trenkler.

I couldn't believe this happenstance connection between the two bombing cases. As a young buck investigator, the possibility of getting an early unexpected break in the cop killing bombing sent chills throughout my body. Fortune or luck often put me into big cases like being the case agent on the 46 machine gun case and "the largest arson case in the history of the country."

As soon as I could, I called the office, eager to share the news. The case agent, Special Agent Jeff Kerr, and others greeted the update with both enthusiasm and skepticism. To them, it seemed implausible the two cases were linked by the same bomb maker. Yet, the true investigators as they were, they delved into the information. They turned over the stone under the stone.

When Special Agent Jeff Kerr was a rookie, I tried to get him interested in arson investigations. He wasn't having any part of it.

When this bombing occurred, Jeff was a member of a gun group working Boston, only on the job for about four years. He was now the assigned case agent of a complex, high-profile investigation.

His situation reminded me of my same position in 1980 when the machine gun case fell into my lap and again in 1982 when I became the case agent on the Boston arson case involving 264 fires. I was only an agent for a few years when those investigations arose.

But we worked for an agency full of experienced agents, and we all worked with other seasoned investigators from other departments. That's why we worked as a team. Our supervisors assigned the best veteran agents to work with less experienced agents. Senior Special Agents Tom D'Ambrosio and Dennis Leahy worked closely with Jeff, offering guidance as needed.

Agent Kerr and Boston PD detectives met with Quincy Detective Lanergan. The similarities between the two devices intrigued Kerr and the others. Lanergan released the 1986 report to them so the bomb technicians could make a closer comparison, but the physical evidence was no longer available as it had already been destroyed.

✳   ✳   ✳

Thomas Shay, Jr. had a troubled, unstable background. (For purposes of this story and during the court cases, the father and son Shays were referred to as Sr. and Jr. However, the elder Shay's name is Thomas Leroy Shay while his son is Thomas Arthur Shay).

Shay, Jr. was born in the Brighton neighborhood of Boston, the youngest of 14 children, the only boy. His parents divorced but lived in the Boston area. At age five, the Department of Social Services took custody of Shay because he had a history of juvenile fire-setting and he frequently ran away. Shay bounced around in the system. For reasons unknown, he also had several psychiatric hospitalizations.

Shortly after his release at 18-years-old, police arrested Shay, Jr. for possession of a stolen motor vehicle. While in custody, an evaluation revealed longstanding gender identity issues, which caused bouts of depression. A judge released Shay with probation. He didn't have his high school diploma. Shay worked sporadically as a masseuse, and he did volunteer work for an ambulance company. Shay Sr. threw his son out of the house because he stole cash from him and family heirloom jewelry from Shay Sr.'s live-in girlfriend.

In 1990, Shay Jr. participated in a local TV show *People Are Talking*. The episode dealt with gay youths. In keeping with his ambiguous sexual identity, Shay described himself as "gay but not proud." This is how Shay Sr. learned of his son's sexuality. Shay Jr. allegedly witnessed the death of his male lover in a gay-bashing incident. Then in 1991, Shay fathered a baby girl.

When only 20-years-old, local police arrested Shay on charges of Falsely Reporting Location of Explosion (Bomb Scare) and Being a Common Night Walker (Prostitution). While awaiting trial on those charges, Boston Municipal Court ordered an evaluation of Shay regarding his competency to stand trial.

Let me just add my own comments here. My only qualifications to do so are my experience as an investigator with some connection to profiling criminal minds. Two items from the brief history of Shay Jr. raise red flags which could link him with the bomb. He was a juvenile fire-setter, and he had called in a bomb scare. Although these are not strong evidentiary points, they are the type of history in a person's background that can be found in a murderer's (or bomber's) past.

In Massachusetts, the courts regard a defendant competent to stand trial by displaying sufficient ability to consult with an attorney with a reasonable degree of factual understanding, plus a rational and factual grasp of the proceedings against him.

Shay's evaluation comprised five hours of interviews and several other components. The evaluating doctor wrote Shay seemed friendly, even pleasant, but he was "clearly annoyed by his evaluation, which he seems to view as a frivolous waste of his time." Shay even planned to publicize his belief the evaluation was a waste of taxpayer's money.

With the seriousness of the bomb scare charge and the ongoing investigation of the bombing incident at his father's house, Shay didn't express concern. Instead, he relished the attention from the media, saving news clippings that mentioned him. He even bragged reporters offered him money for an interview. Shay loved the notoriety he received.

The doctor reported Shay, Jr. expressed no feelings for the tragic death of Hurley or the severe injuries to Foley. His childish, self-centered behavior was a sign of a poorly developed, immature personality driven by an insatiable need for attention, but not a product of mental illness. Despite the personality and emotional difficulties, the doctor concluded Shay, Jr. was competent to stand trial.

✳ ✳ ✳

After investigators eliminated Shay Sr. and the men with whom he had a dispute as suspects in the bombing, they started looking at Shay Jr. as a potential suspect. Besides the red flags in his past, his behavior focused attention in his direction.

The investigative team held a meeting in South Boston. There, they reviewed a diary they had gotten from Shay Jr. They noted Shay rated his gay guy friends with a one or two. Knowing Alfred Trenkler was also gay, Special Agent Karen Carney, a tall Boston-raised blonde, who was present at the meeting spoke up, "It would be interesting if Trenkler's name is in the book."

At that suggestion, Special Agent Thomas D'Ambrosio thumbed through the address book, first looking under the last name for the letter "T." Nothing there for Trenkler. Moments later, as they turned another page or two, Agent D'Ambrosio realized the book was listed alphabetically by the first name. Under "A," Al Trenkler's name and phone number appeared. That was the first identified connection between the two men.

Evidence was mounting against Shay Jr. to charge him in Federal court with conspiracy and aiding and abetting the attempt to blow up his father's car. With the heat on, as investigators got closer to arresting Shay Jr., he fled the area. The hunt to find him began.

After searching information from Shay's list of young male sexual partners, investigators interviewed many of them, hoping to get a lead on Shay's whereabouts. One of those guys, who ran a small clothing store in southeastern Massachusetts, became helpful. Shay had mailed him a postcard from San Francisco. The shop owner gave this to the investigators.

After laying out a plan, four investigators including Special Agents Jeff Kerr and Dennis Leahy plus Boston Detectives Brendan Craven and Frank Armstrong took the search to the Golden State. Once there, they all split up, covering different areas of the city.

They concentrated on certain gay areas, asking around and showing Shay's picture, trying to get a lead on him. One of them covered the Castro Street neighborhood. This area was known as the place where gay couples hung out.

Jeff worked Polk Street, where the gay pickup joints lined the street. This was old gumshoe work, walking up and down the streets, talking to as many people as possible. With his strapping build and boyish good looks, as Jeff frequented the bars, he got hit on every time he turned around. One guy even grabbed his crotch. Jeff jumped, startled by the brash attention.

One place Jeff frequented, The Motherload, was a transvestite bar. He became friendly with the manager and the bouncer. For several evenings, Jeff stood with the bouncer at the entrance to the club. As Jeff eyed some beautiful women passing by their position, the bouncer laughed and told Jeff they were all guys in drag. Flabbergasted, Jeff couldn't believe his eyes until he heard a man's voice coming from another gorgeous "woman."

After showing Shay's picture to the clientele, a few said they had seen Shay in the neighborhood. Within a couple days, one patron who had Jeff's business card called him to tell Jeff he knew where Shay was frequenting.

Jeff met with the guy and headed toward where Shay allegedly hung out. Within minutes, Jeff's work paid off. Standing on the side of the road, the common streetwalker was trolling, trying to pick up anyone willing to play. When Jeff spotted Shay, he pulled over a short distance down the street from him.

He enlisted the help of his passenger to ensnare Shay. The guy ran over to Shay telling him the dude in the car wanted to have sex with him. Shay, willing to check out the situation, got into the good-looking stranger's car.

They started for the Sheraton Hotel, where Jeff was staying, and where the other investigators were likely to be. Shay asked a lot of questions, either inquisitive or protecting himself. Jeff told him he was a salesman. Suddenly, Shay asked, "You're a cop, aren't you"?

When Jeff admitted he was, Shay didn't seem fazed. He didn't fight, complain, or try to run. Jeff explained he was under arrest and after being lodged at the San Francisco PD, he was to be transported back to Massachusetts.

Once at the PD, Jeff called Agent Leahy and the two Boston cops with news of Shay's capture. In the interview room, Shay didn't want to read his Miranda rights, but Jeff read them to him, anyway. Shay was talkative, even flirtatious, but, during this trip home, he never confessed about his part in the bombing.

Back in Boston, Shay still refrained from implicating himself in the bombing. But he was willing to provide information that incriminated his friend, Alfred Trenkler. He said Trenkler made the bomb and placed it under his father's car.

Shay told investigators he threw incriminating items related to the bombing into the Quincy Quarries for Trenkler. In the 1800s, these quarries became the first large-scale quarrying operation in the United States. The Bunker Hill Monument in the Charlestown neighborhood of Boston was built with granite from the Quincy Quarries. Closed after a century in operation, the 20-acre rock formations filled with water, deep enough to hide most anything.

ATF called for help from the U.S. Navy and the Oceanographic Institution of Woods Hole, Massachusetts. They used a small submarine with sonar and cameras to search for the components Shay disposed of in the quarries. Nothing relating to the investigation was ever found.

✳   ✳   ✳

The investigative team learned that on October 18, 1991, at 2:36 p.m., a white male fitting the description of Shay Jr. purchased several items from the Radio Shack store on Massachusetts Avenue in Boston directly across the street from the Christian Science Center where Al Trenkler was working on a large project. The items purchased included the same remote control servo, the same batteries and the same Futaba battery holder found during the blast scene search.

An ATF Explosive Enforcement Officer, who had many years of experience with explosive devices, analyzed the components from the 1986 device and the evidence from the remains of the Roslindale bomb. Although the devices were vastly different, there were also many similarities suggesting the same person built or manufactured, both bombs. For instance, both devices used round "speaker-type" magnets. Both used switches. Both had the wiring connections not only twisted, which is often sufficient, but the connections were also soldered and taped in order to secure them. This was a unique feature, something known in the business as a "signature" of the bomber.

Investigators also determined Trenkler and Shay Jr. knew each other for at least a couple years through their gay community and they had several contacts over that time. Finally, they determined Trenkler built the first device in 1986 for a friend to avenge a wrong, and he likely did the same for Shay Jr. who wanted to kill his father for various reasons, including his hatred of him and for financial gain.

During a consent search on November 4, 1991, investigators, including Special Agents Dennis Leahy and Thomas D'Ambrosio spoke with Al Trenkler, who talked freely with the agents. They discussed the

1986 device that Trenkler admitted making, but he downplayed the severity of the incident. At one point, he asked if they were going to arrest him because he made the earlier explosive and he had electrical engineering education and training. The agents advised he was not going to be arrested at that time.

The agents asked Trenkler if he were to make an explosive device with dynamite, how would he wire it. Trenkler obliged the agents by drawing a schematic wiring diagram. In it, he drew wires from batteries to two blasting caps wired in series which functioned via a remote control device. This was extraordinary since none of the device details had been divulged to the public and none of the investigators mentioned the components to Trenkler.

Here is where Agents D'Ambrosio and Leahy made a critical error in judgment. When they saw Trenkler's details, they made eye contact. They realized Trenkler's drawing was significant, but they failed to take the drawing with them. During the consent search, they removed 14 items to be tested and compared with the exploded debris, but they never asked if they could take the drawing. Both agents had 15 years' experience and should have had Trenkler sign and date the drawing. They reasoned they wanted to keep Trenkler friendly and talking. Their concern was he would stop talking and get an attorney before they could investigate further. That decision came back to haunt them later.

The next day, the investigative team discussed Trenkler's drawing. The agent's inquired of one of Trenkler's friends who said Trenkler was not apprehensive about his drawing, but he destroyed it. They met with Trenkler again and asked if he would make another drawing, but he now refused.

Based on much of the above information plus additional evidence listed below, Alfred Trenkler was indicted and arrested for manufacturing the explosive device with injury and death resulting.

Trenkler's legal team filed to sever the trials of the two defendants, which the court granted. His mother's brother, who was the CEO of a major financial investment company, provided a large influx of money for his nephew's defense. The monetary supply for Trenkler's war chest was endless.

✳   ✳   ✳

During Shay's trial, the government argued Shay conspired with Trenkler to kill Shay's father by blowing him up in his car. The prosecution team, consisting of Assistant United States Attorneys Paul Kelly and Frank Libby, relied heavily on incriminating statements made by Shay Jr. after the bombing to prove their case.

A Boston police officer testified Shay Jr. commented shortly after the bomb blast, "He was sorry about it and wished he could turn back the hands of time and make it not have happened." The government used this statement as proof of Shay's guilty conscience.

In another instance, Shay Jr. spoke with reporters, consistent with his need for attention and being in the limelight. He told them investigators questioned him about whether his father was capable of making a remote-control device. There was only one major problem with that comment. Nobody had questioned him about the remote-control detonator until after he spoke to reporters. This meant Shay Jr. had knowledge only an insider to the bombing would have.

Again basking in his notoriety, Shay Jr. told a TV reporter he was only guilty of learning who built the bomb after the bombing. However, he claimed Trenkler said to him before the bombing he was planning a "surprise" for Shay Jr., which was the bomb. Shay Jr. also admitted buying the toggle switch and double "A" battery holder Trenkler used when building the bomb.

While awaiting trial in jail, Shay Jr. told his cellmate, "I'm boom boom. Don't you know me? You have to know me. I'm the one who killed the Boston cop." He also told him he and Trenkler built the bomb together and attached it to the underside of his father's car.

Combine those statements with other evidence presented during the trial. Information developed by investigators showed Shay Jr. and

Trenkler were casual friends for at least three years from 1988 to 1991. Because of Trenkler's electronic background, he possessed the skills to build a bomb. Investigators found gray duct tape at Trenkler's parents' house consistent with the tape used in the bomb.

Other evidence included the discovery of the purchase ten days before the bombing of a toggle switch and "AA" battery holder like those used in the bomb. The buyer purchased them from a Radio Shack directly across the street from Trenkler's workplace in Boston.

Radio Shack routinely kept records of the purchasers. Their records listed the purchaser of these items as "SAHY", a misspelling of "Shay." An identification number used was "3780" which was the last four digits of Thomas Shay Sr.'s home telephone number transposed to read, "7380".

Although not a necessary element for proof in this case, the motive is something every jury wants to know. The government argued Shay Jr. had a love-hate relationship with his father, having suffered undefined abuse during his childhood. To make matters even worse, the younger Shay came out as gay on a TV program. This totally pissed off his father. Shay Jr. also figured he would collect a substantial inheritance if his father died.

Investigators found no fingerprints underneath the car where the bomb was placed or on any components. There were none on the store receipt either. DNA was not an option at the time.

Except for the Radio Shack components, investigators struck out when trying to locate the source for the dynamite, the magnets, the container and the blasting cap. Often, tracing of these components provides solid leads to identify those involved with the device.

In 1992, Thomas Shay Jr. was convicted in Federal court of the aiding and abetting charge plus conspiracy. Judge Zobel sentenced Shay to 15 years. He served his time in Ray Brook Federal Correctional Institution in upstate New York. This was the same prison where I visited Robert Groblewski, the Boston cop imprisoned for his part in setting 264 building fires that were part of my first book, *Burn Boston Burn*.

*   *   *

Thomas Shay (Boston Globe photo) Alfred Trenkler after years in prison.

FBI Hazardous Device School (HDS)
Bomb Technician Memorial in Huntsville, Alabama.

The trial of Alfred Trenkler commenced in Boston Federal Court in late October 1993. He faced three counts: Count One – Conspiracy to Receive Explosives in Interstate Commerce with the Intent to Injure or Kill, and to Damage or Destroy a Vehicle used in Interstate Commerce, Count Two – Received an Explosive with the Knowledge and Intent to Kill Mr. Shay, Sr. and Damage or Destroy Property, and Count Three – Attempted Malicious Destruction of Property used in Interstate Commerce. If convicted on all counts, Trenkler faced life in prison.

One of the early key witnesses was an ATF chemist who worked the crime scene and conducted additional testing and analysis of the evidence once back in the ATF National Laboratory in Rockville, Maryland. Besides some of the items already described that were found at the scene of the explosion, she testified about several other items used within the explosive device. There were four Duracell AA batteries and five 9-volt batteries wrapped together with duct tape.

Dynamite residue was found in the blast crater (the point of explosion origin) and on other components. She determined the bomb builder used two to three sticks of dynamite which had been unwrapped from its original wrappings, then wrapped in a "muscle magazine" which was wrapped in layers of tape before being placed within the wood box.

The chemist explained there were remains of two Austin Rock Star brand millisecond delay electric detonators (also known as blasting caps) with their colored leg wires, tube and end plug. The leg wires from one blasting cap to the other were wired together, wrapped in tape and soldered.

She also testified about the fresh scrape marks on the underside of Shay Sr.'s car and on the magnets, with red paint transfer to the car from the button magnets. Investigators recovered two large blue ring magnets and 10 red button magnets. Finally, she spoke about a roll of three-inch wide silver duct tape and black electrical tape found during a search of Trenkler's parent's garage. A 15-foot strip 1 7/8" wide had been removed from the roll. This tape was consistent with that found in the device remains, but the largest section recovered measured 1 9/16". There was nothing remarkable about the black electrical tape; it was a common brand.

Remnants of a muscle magazine were in the recovered debris. This was interesting because testimony during the trials showed Shay Jr. had a strong interest in men's muscle magazines. But, testimony also showed Shay Jr. was totally inept mechanically, so it was highly unlikely he could ever make an explosive device with the sophistication observed with the component remains.

During the Trenkler trial, Thomas Waskom, an ATF Explosives Enforcement Officer testified about the Roslindale device and the 1986 bomb made by Trenkler. ATF's EEOs offer unequaled technical expertise in the bomb disposal and explosives field.

Waskom testified the bomb builder designed the device to function by remote control within the black painted wood box. His analysis of the components indicated the wood was cut from a template and built using two-penny nails and glue to painstakingly construct the box. He determined there was a receiver, antenna, on/off switch, a servo motor, batteries, and wires.

Waskom found the wiring knotted together, soldered and taped at connections. The bomber wired two electric detonator leg wires in series to initiate the dynamite. This unusual method was called dual priming. The detonators often referred commonly as blasting caps, had aluminum housing with red and yellow conductors extending from the cylinder through a red plastic plug. He testified the blasting caps required an electrical charge from the batteries of 250 to 350 milliamps. Later testimony from a battery expert revealed the 9-volt batteries were more than sufficient to power the detonators, even if their charge was largely depleted.

The EEO further testified a smaller box was attached to the large one. There was a hole in the box so the bomber could reach a slide switch to arm the bomb when it was in place. The servo motor arm would move when the bomber activated the remote control. The particular remote control used in the device worked by line-of-site only. This means the bomber had to be close by when the device detonated because Eastbourne Street was a dead-end side street crowded with houses.

The EEO analyzed everything about the two devices. Items compared in this case included the type of explosives, the electronic components such as batteries, wiring, and initiator, whether remote control, mercury switch or some other type. The container, shrapnel and items such as the magnets used to secure the device to the underside of Shay Sr.'s car were all scrutinized. The experts even analyzed how the bomb-maker connected the wires.

During the trial, when questioned about his conclusion relative to the person who made both devices, the EEO testified he, "had no doubt whatsoever the same person built both bombs." The signatures of the bombs were so similar only one person could have built them. The defense would later challenge the EEO's testimony and another important piece of government testimony on appeal.

ATF has a computer database of bomb characteristics amassed over many years. An Intelligence Research Specialist performed a series of computer queries trying to identify the bomb maker.

The Specialist affirmed the search revealed the Boston bomb had several features in common with the earlier bomb made by Trenkler. Elimination of those bombs that didn't share certain characteristics produced startling results. The Specialist's testimony included, "a series of inquiries narrowed the file of reported incidents in the database from 40,867 to seven." There was only a 0.017% chance someone besides Trenkler built the two bombs.

Among the interesting testimony during the trial was that from an automotive engineer. His testimony centered on the holding strength of magnets. It is one of those topics not many people would think needed expert testimony, but it goes to show all of the intricate moving parts of a trial.

Part of Trenkler's defense was he couldn't have mounted the explosive device under Shay Sr.'s car within the day or so before it was discovered because he allegedly had an alibi covering that time. And they emphasized the box most likely would have fallen off while the car was being driven on the rough Boston area roads if it had been on the car for any significant length of time.

The engineer did some testing on the power of the magnets used to mount the box to the car. He concluded a 6.5-pound box, including the weight of the magnets, could easily be held by the two large round magnets which need a force over 13 pounds each to separate it from the same type of surface as the underbelly of the vehicle. He further opined each button magnet needed 3.5 pounds of force with the total holding power of 42 pounds (12 x 3.5). But being on an uneven surface under the car, they didn't completely hold. He stated the evidence showed the small magnets had been applied first because they were painted differently than the large magnets. It appeared the bomb maker experimented with the smaller magnets first, then went with the greater strength of the large magnets.

Another issue he considered is how the device became dislodged in the driveway. The defense wanted the jury to believe Shay Sr.'s story was a lie. He must have planted the bomb himself in the driveway because, in their opinion, the car would have crushed the box if it was knocked off by scraping in the driveway.

Not so fast said the expert. The physical evidence alone supports that the box scraped under the car in one direction when Shay Sr. heard the noise as he backed up his driveway. Then, the box scraped again as it dislodged when he drove down the driveway hours later. He also did testing in Shay's driveway to examine this. Two other factors influenced his conclusions. The build and shape of the vehicle and the driveway caused the device to become dislodged on the way down rather than when he first backed up the slope. The sturdy box construction was not crushed because it was centered over the grass and dirt section of the driveway between the two concrete ribbons where the tires roll.

On the eighth day of the trial, the prosecution called Thomas Shay, Jr. to testify. The Government granted him immunity from further prosecution relating to anything he said during his testimony. However, Shay Jr. couldn't wrap his head around this Government gift. After much wrangling, he refused to testify because he feared being charged with perjury. Lying under oath was not covered by the immunity pass.

One was left to imagine how this certified storyteller's testimony would have gone. At the same time, his words could have either guaranteed Trenkler's fate of guilt or innocence.

Another witness, a Boston Police Detective, shows how the puzzle pieces started to come together. His short testimony concerned Shay Jr.'s unexpected voluntary appearance at the Detective's office the day after the bombing. This sometimes occurs when a guilty party wants to talk to investigators hoping to learn about the details of their investigation. It also fits with Shay Jr.'s need for attention. He didn't say anything of significance during that meeting, but he consented to a search of his travel bag he was carrying. Inside the bag was his black address book, the one containing the name and phone number of Al Trenkler. The police ended up arresting Shay Jr. that day on an unrelated outstanding warrant. At the time, only Shay Sr. and the two auto guys with who he had a dispute, were suspects in the bombing.

Shay Sr.'s attorney testified briefly. He testified he gave Shay Jr. a ride to his deposition appearance regarding his father's lawsuit on that explosion that caused him trauma. During the ride, the attorney explained to Shay Jr. the lawsuit would continue if his father should die and part of the proceeds would go to Shay Jr. He also related the senior Shay had an insurance policy with a substantial amount of money going to the younger Shay. The importance of this during the Trenkler trial was it established a financial motive for Shay Jr. to go along with his hatred for his father. And, by association, some of this money would go to Trenkler for his part in making the bomb. The prosecution used several witnesses to show Trenkler was financially strapped. He had two failed businesses already and his living conditions for a man his age were on the lower end of most scales. On the other hand, the defense tried to prove Trenkler's business had a bright financial future.

One other aspect of the attorney's testimony focused on Shay Sr.'s cooperation during the hours and days immediately following the explosion. Although he was extremely upset by the incident, he answered every question from the investigators. He also consented to multiple searches including checking his clothes and hands for explosive residues. No trace of explosives was found.

The Government used multiple inmates from different institutions who had contact with Shay Jr. or Trenkler while also incarcerated. For various legal reasons, the Government was restricted in the testimony from these witnesses. They could not shift the testimony from Shay Jr. to include any other person from building or planting the bomb. It was the Government's plan that the totality of the evidence would show the connection between Shay Jr. and Trenkler during this alleged joint venture.

In one instance the witness now lived in a sober house. He had no prison time hanging over his head, so there was no request for leniency from him. The witness met Shay Jr. in the Plymouth House of Correction. He was very sick and in bed at the time so Shay would come over to talk to him. Shay asked him if he knew who he was. The witness replied, "No, I don't. And I don't want to know."

But Shay told him very matter-of-factly anyway, "I'm the one who killed the Boston cop." Shay loved to talk. He told the witness how he hated his father with a desire to get even with him, plus his father had a big insurance policy. His comments, including he knew how to make a bomb, but he didn't make the bomb that killed the cop, and it was the cop's fault he got killed, deeply upset this non-violent convict who was in jail on drug-related charges.

The witness waited until he was paroled to come forward with information because he would have put himself in peril. Nobody in jail likes a snitch!

The Government tried to present evidence that Trenkler was parked at the end of Eastbourne Street in his car when the bomb detonated. A neighbor reported he saw a car by the elementary school where and when it should not have been. Ultimately, their evidence was weak, and the defense countered with sufficient argument to counter the prosecution's efforts.

Special Agent Dennis Leahy testified on some key issues. First, Thomas Shay, Sr. was a prime suspect for two to three weeks, but there were eight to ten persons of interest during the course of the early investigation until evidence mounted pointing toward Shay Jr. and Trenkler. This was not a rush to judgment as the defense wanted the jury to believe.

My knowledge of the case and the ATF Agents involved is that they were methodical and honest. Any pressure from outside sources to make an arrest would not have deterred these guys from making the best case they could, based on the evidence they uncovered. I know from way too much experience that mistakes happen, too. One can only hope those mistakes didn't develop into fatal flaws that affected an innocent person or caused a guilty person to go free.

S/A Leahy testified Trenkler initially became a suspect on November 4, 1991, when they became aware of the 1986 device and Shay Jr.'s address book. He said when they told Trenkler they knew of the 1986 device, he asked if he was going to be arrested. While interviewing him, Trenkler also discussed shunts and wires used as an antenna. A shunt is a piece of metal that connects two ends of leg wires to prevent stray currents from causing accidental detonation of an electric blasting cap. Trenkler admitted frequenting the Massachusetts Avenue Radio Shack three or four times.

When Trenkler came to the ATF office to retrieve some of his belongings, Agent Leahy testified Trenkler asked, "If we did it, then only we know about it. How will you ever find out if neither one of us is talking?" This was the same day Trenkler talked and talked even though Agent Leahy tried to have Trenkler leave when he didn't offer anything of substance.

This is another trait of a guilty person. An innocent person most often flatly denies any involvement in a crime and says to investigators they're way off base, "I don't know what you're talking about," and they are out the door. They don't hang around to face question after question about their involvement and their guilt.

Agent Leahy further testified Trenkler was not consistent where he was on the day of the explosion. He gave three different stories. Trenkler also was inconsistent about Shay Jr. being at his apartment and about providing rides for Shay.

Finally, on a separate but closely related topic, Leahy said when they arrested Shay Jr. in San Francisco, he volunteered, "I'm not the guy who built it. I'm not the guy who got the dynamite. I'm not the guy who placed it." Although he didn't implicate Trenkler, his remarks were consistent with others he made that support he conspired with someone else to make and deliver the bomb.

Quincy Police Detective Lanergan testified about his investigation of the 1986 explosion. He said during his second interview with Trenkler, Al calmly confessed. He said some guy asked him to make the device for him and he was to get paid for making the device which was only designed to scare and intimidate fish company owners. Later, he admitted it was a woman who retained him to make the explosive.

Lanergan recounted the device components. It had four AA batteries and two 6-volt batteries. Trenkler said components came from Radio Shack. He added he tested the device with a toggle switch and a small light bulb. Trenkler explained there was a six-inch speaker magnet to stick the device to the fish company truck. The package included everything bound with duct tape and a remote control that could function up to a half-mile.

One witness reported knowing the device contained some of the same items listed above. Of more importance, this witness testified he recalled Trenkler talked of attaching the device to the underside of the truck. This was of utmost importance when testimony of device signature was presented.

ATF Intelligence Research Specialist Stephen Scheid testified about the most contentious aspect of this trial, the ATF Explosives

Incident Data Base known as EXIS. It is a computerized system of bomb and arson particulars, including the intended targets and the device components. The system intends to provide investigative leads to state, local and federal investigators. Since 1975 data was collected from those same agencies. The output can show trends or patterns between two or more incidents. Scheid also analyzes the forensic lab reports and interview information to input data into the system.

By the end of 1991, almost 41,000 explosive incidents were in the system, but many of those were theft of explosives and other incidents, leaving 14,252 bombings and attempted bombings during the 16 year collection period. Scheid testified his query of bombing incidents involving cars and trucks revealed 2,504 incidents, 18% of all such incidents. The next search indicated 3%, or 428, of those events, involved devices placed under vehicles. Nineteen (.1%) of the 14,252 incidents involved a remote control and then, seven of the 19 had magnets involved (.05% of the total). The computer search spit out only two incidents of all the bombing cases with the same characteristics, the 1986 Quincy explosion and the 1991 Roslindale bombing.

Scheid did additional checks within the database. Only the Quincy and Roslindale events, when queried subsequent to the previous searches, revealed exclusive use of duct tape, solder, AA batteries, a toggle switch and round magnets.

The results of this database search were very impressive and convincing; at least until the defense team took their shots at it. There are two sides to every coin.

The database relies on state, local and federal input. Sometimes, bombing incidents weren't reported for one reason or another. Information from the 1986 Quincy explosion was one of those never reported. Scheid input the data well after the 1991 bombing when Trenkler and the 1986 case came to light.

One of the defense attorneys, Scott Lopez asked if the Roslindale bombing had certain characteristics and/or components, 18 in all, which were present in the 1986 explosion. None of those were part of the 1991 bombing. Scheid admitted he was the one who developed the encoding for the items inputted into the database.

When asked if he only queried car bombings, Scheid admitted the Quincy truck bombing would not have popped out. And Scheid was the one who decided to add trucks to his inquiry. He could have just queried vehicles, but he didn't code the system with that word.

Attorney Lopez made points when Scheid admitted if he had queried the system differently, the results would have been vastly different. For instance, if instead of narrowing his inquiry every time the data showed a match between the 1986 and 1991 incidents, he still queried the entire database, more similar events would have resulted. So, despite the remarkable connection of the two incidents out of all the bombing incidents contained in the system, the defense appeared to place some doubt on the veracity of the methodology of the inquiries.

The Government recalled ATF EEO Tom Waskom to testify on a different subject than his earlier testimony. He was called to offer his opinion as to "signature analysis," the personal technique or the personal touch by a bomb maker in the design and construction of an explosive device. Waskom stated the totality of the way the 1986 and the 1991 devices were constructed with similar components, he opined both devices were built by the same person. And since, Alfred Trenkler confessed to building the 1986 device, he must have built the 1991 bomb.

He listed the similarities. Both had wires twisted together, soldered and taped. They both had round magnets, the fusing system held by duct tape, and a toggle switch. Back in 1991, there was no source showing these specific techniques and components altogether. Also, both devices were tested in the same manner, i.e., using a small test lamp.

Waskom said the placing of the device under each vehicle showed the mindset of the person. Both explosives were the product of a conspiracy. The intended target was tied to one party in the conspiracy.

The builder of the device on each occasion had someone else purchase the components, both in a Radio Shack. Finally, these two very similar devices exploded within 10 miles of each other after having originally been affixed to the undercarriage of a vehicle.

After Waskom's testimony, the Government called another man who was briefly incarcerated with Trenkler. Once the two men started talking, they found out they had a lot in common. They both came from Milton, Massachusetts, both even living on the same street, although at different times. According to the testimony, Trenkler and he bonded over these ties.

Trenkler initially denied being involved in the bombing, but as they spoke about the case against him, he made statements damaging to his interests. When Trenkler admitted some of the bomb components were purchased at a local Radio Shack, the witness told him it was careless not to go out of state to make those purchases. He testified Trenkler agreed with him on that point and said it was regrettable.

When discussing the 1986 bomb he made, Trenkler said the 1991 bomb was far more powerful. As he continued talking, he told the witness even if he did build the bomb, I didn't place it on the car. Then, shockingly, he plainly admitted, "I built the bomb. I don't deserve to die or spend the rest of my life in prison for building this device." Trenkler expressed no remorse at all when he stated the bomb squad officers were foolish not wearing body armor when they inspected the bomb. It served them right for what happened. It wasn't his fault.

The two men even discussed remote control devices when Trenkler stated the remote control worked up to 50 yards. When speaking about Thomas Shay, Jr., Trenkler agreed with the witness about Shay not having the technical ability to change the batteries in a flashlight.

When the prosecution rested, they knew they put on the best case they could, based on the cards they were dealt. They presented no direct physical evidence against Trenkler. There were no fingerprints connecting Trenkler to the device. No tools or components or explosive residue connected Trenkler to the bombing. DNA, GPS tracking, security cameras at every turn and cell phones were not yet available for investigative tools. They had no eyewitness who testified seeing him with the explosive device. This truly was a circumstantial case. The prosecution spent the entire trial building the blocks, stacking them one atop the other so the jury could make an informed decision.

It was now the defense team's chance to destabilize the stack of blocks so the jurors couldn't connect the pieces against their client, Alfred Trenkler. The defense put on one expert witness and several fact witnesses. The latter witnesses were basically used in an attempt to establish multiple alibis for Trenkler to cover various time frames, and to show Trenkler's financial future was looking good. Their testimony appeared weak after cross-examination by the prosecutors.

The expert, a retired FBI Agent, had extensive bombing investigation background, almost exclusively with terrorist groups. This fact was pointed out by the prosecution because the terrorist groups bragged about their deeds whereas "lone wolf" bombers who rarely made multiple bombs wanted to be as secretive as possible. The signatures of terrorist bombers were likened to a calling card, very different from a sole bomber where their device was often "singular and unique." The defense witness felt the Roslindale bomb was not "singular or unique." He could not conclude there was a connection between the 1986 bomb and the 1991 explosive.

On cross-examination by the prosecution, this witness stated he never regards circumstantial evidence as part of his signature analysis. He looks only at the physical evidence, the forensics of the remains, to tie one incident to another, but the Government insisted circumstantial evidence, such as the target of the bomb and the motive for the bomb-maker should also be considered. I agree that a broader interpretation of signature can yield significant results when bombings or a series of arsons are analyzed and connected to a subject of interest.

*   *   *

After the witness phase of the trial, Judge Zobel discussed motions and her expected charges with the prosecutors and the defense attorneys. The defense requested the conspiracy charge be dismissed for lack of evidence. Judge Zobel ruled there was sufficient evidence for the charge to go to the jury. She cited the testimony of another inmate wherein Trenkler admitted to making the bomb and other statements about Thomas Shay Jr.'s situation.

Other issues discussed included whether the jury would believe the testimony of the ATF EEO who concluded both the 1986 device and the 1991 bomb were made by only one person, Alfred Trenkler. Or would the jury believe the defense expert, a retired FBI agent, who stated he could not make any connection between the two devices? There was a lengthy discussion among the two competing parties and Judge Zobel about the nuances surrounding what the Court should instruct the jury relative to the two bombs being, as AUSA Libby suggested, "sufficiently similar" or as the defense expert said on the stand, "single and unique."

Motive was another issue the three parties debated. Did Alfred Trenkler make the Roslindale bomb to target a third party, Thomas Shay, Sr., for a friend who wanted to avenge a wrong? That would be similar to his motive for building the 1986 device when a friend asked him to make the explosive device because she felt wronged by owners of a fish business.

AUSA Frank Libby delivered a superb powerful closing argument appealing to the jury to find the defendant guilty on all counts. He began by reminding the jury of the day the bombing occurred, telling them for the bomb techs, it is a perilous job. Each scene, each person they deal with and each device is unfamiliar. "It is their job to evaluate the scene, to assess the object or device, and ultimately render it safe for every one of us."

He explained the three main components of the device. AUSA Libby listed the main charge, the fusing circuit with the Futaba receiver and the firing circuit with the toggle switch and the servo motor. Again, he pointed out the slide switch on the outside of the package so the bomber could arm the device when he placed it so it could receive a transmitted signal.

Several points were emphasized. The device was intended to kill its target, the occupant of the car, Thomas Shay, Sr. And, the device had to have been planted over the weekend because the car had been in use before that by a third uninterested party. The five 9-volt batteries were wired in series with snap connectors soldered, and taped, and tested with a small light bulb.

AUSA Libby recounted how the investigation turned when investigators learned Detective Bill Lanergan's case with the 1986 Quincy bombing tied in with Shay Jr.'s address book connecting him with the admitted perpetrator of the 1986 incident. Evidence confirmed Shay Jr. purchased the exact components used in the device from the Radio Shack directly across the street where Trenkler was working. Remember the transposed letters on the receipt, S-A-H-Y and the telephone number of 3-7-8-0 instead of the last four digits on Shay Sr.'s business card. Was any of this just a coincidence? Those items were purchased just 10 days before the devastating blast.

AUSA Libby told how vulnerable Trenkler was in jail when he found a kindred spirit, an inmate with shared common background and experiences. He was under great tension at the time, and, he took to the felon "like a moth to flame."

The jury heard again how Shay Jr. had no special skills, no engineering skills to the point where "he couldn't even put batteries in a flashlight." And Libby repeated the testimony that Trenkler agreed about Shay's ineptitude. So, who made the bomb? There is no evidence to suggest any other person than Alfred Trenkler.

The argument let the jury know about Count 2, Receipt of Explosives in Interstate Commerce since the blasting caps originated in Austria. Count 3, Attempted Destruction of Property used in an Interstate Activity Affecting Interstate Commerce, to wit, Shay Sr.'s car that he used in business.

As AUSA Libby neared completion of his closing argument, he continued, "Now, verdict is a Latin term which means to speak the truth. And I will leave you with this: From all the evidence you've so attentively listened to over the past few weeks, there are two fundamental truths in this case. One is two families have suffered grievous losses, and the City of Boston lost the valuable, invaluable services of two highly skilled bomb technicians. The second is there can be no fault associated with those two dedicated, brave men. The criminal responsibility, however, lies with that man (pointing toward Trenkler) the defendant in this case. The United States respectfully asks that you return a verdict of guilty on each of the three counts in the indictment."

Defense Attorney Terry Segal also countered with a forceful closing argument for acquittal of his client. He wanted the jury to think the Government's case was purely guilt by association. Segal pointed out that his one defense expert, the retired FBI Agent, testified in every case he investigated, the physical evidence found linked a person with the device, but *not in this case.*

Attorney Segal wanted the jurors to think hard about the alleged bomb wiring diagram made by Trenkler for two ATF Agents, but they neglected to collect it as evidence. Did the Government manipulate EXIS by inputting the 1986 bombing into the system after the 1991 bombing? Or did they input facts in such a way that the system popped out the only two cases in the United States with similar components?

Segal quoted Mark Twain, "There are three kinds of lies: lies, damn lies, and statistics." He argued the EXIS search was skewed. His expert testified there were 13 differences between the two devices. If queried differently, the results would have been different.

The Government tried to show Trenkler would have financially gained by helping Thomas Shay, Jr. Would he risk his business by helping him with the bomb? He didn't choose to risk himself when he was intimidated by a friend to build the 1986 bomb.

Attorney Segal told the jury there was no physical evidence to connect his client to the bomb. The Government has not met its duty to prove the case against Trenkler beyond a reasonable doubt. He quoted from an inscription on the Justice Department building in Washington, D.C. "The United States always wins when justice is done to its citizens."

"I respectfully submit, ladies and gentlemen, when you return a verdict of not guilty in this case, you will be doing justice."

The Government offered one possibly significant point. When Trenkler said to Special Agent Leahy, "I know you found nothing with the sniffer," referring to the device that detects explosive residue in the air after an explosive was present, it was because he knew he didn't make the device in any of those locations that the investigators searched.

✳   ✳   ✳

Now, it was time for Federal Judge Rya Zobel to give her all-important instructions to the jury. The instructions are often challenged, and higher courts can overturn a case on improper instructions. One of the issues she needed to clarify for the jury was direct versus circumstantial evidence.

"Circumstantial evidence, is, in law, just as good as direct evidence." She continued, "Circumstantial evidence means nothing more than drawing inferences from evidence you have. It must be reasonable based on common sense." And it must be "consistent." She implored the jurors to give equal weight to both direct and indirect evidence. "Proof beyond a reasonable doubt is not, is *not*, proof beyond all possible doubt."

After explaining the difference between motive versus intent. "Intent refers to a state of mind with which an act is done. Motive is what prompts a person to act, a reason a person acts." Although the Government is not required to prove motive, it may help to prove intent.

Judge Zobel explained the verdict slip. The foreperson fills in each of the three counts, guilty or not guilty written on each. At 12:45 p.m. on November 22, 1993, Day 17 of the Trial, the jury was excused to begin deliberations.

Deliberations continued on Day 18 and on Day 19, which was the day before Thanksgiving. The jury would not be seated again until Monday, November 29, 1993, Day 20 of the trial. On that afternoon when the jury came into the courtroom at 2:33 p.m. with a question on direct versus indirect evidence again, the judge laid out some examples. The jurors went back to the deliberation room.

At 5 p.m., the jury delivered their verdicts. On Count One, Guilty. On Count Two, Guilty. On Count three, Guilty.

The Federal jury, which carefully weighed the evidence, convicted Trenkler on all charges. Manufacture of the explosive with death resulting carried the possibility of a life sentence. That's what Judge Zobel handed Trenkler.

❋   ❋   ❋

In the United States, Appellee, v. Thomas A. Shay, Defendant-appellant, 57 F.3d 126 (1st Cir. 1995), Shay Jr. and his attorneys appealed his conviction. The appellant is the party who appeals a lower court's decision in a higher court. The appellant seeks reversal or modification of the decision. By contrast, the appellee is the party against whom the appeal is filed.

Shay presented a three-pronged attack. His attorneys argued evidence supported his father, Thomas Shay Sr. built the bomb, Shay Jr's statements about the bombing were unreliable, and the remainder of the government's case failed to prove Shay Jr's guilt.

The defense declared his compulsive need for attention with grandiose stories, often false and ever-changing, were signs of a personality disorder. Further, Shay Jr's statements conflicted with the truth about the bomb, including that they used C-4 as the explosive in the bomb.

The appeals court ruled, "For the reasons described herein, the case is remanded to the district court for further proceedings consistent with this opinion. We retain jurisdiction to review the district court's conclusion whether it should permit Dr. Phillips to testify."

Improper rulings, errors in procedure, or the exclusion of admissible evidence may result in a lower court's decision being overturned and sent back for further action. Both parties in a legal case can appeal a lower court's final decision. The appeal itself doesn't necessarily mean there will be a new trial. In Shay's case, a new trial was ordered.

Because of his earlier cooperation, the Feds let Shay out of jail while awaiting the new trial in 1998. However, he pleaded guilty in return for a lesser sentence, 12 years, instead of the original 15-year sentence.

In August 2002, Thomas Shay was released from prison after serving 10 years in prison. The court mandated Shay stay in Massachusetts to fulfill his probation.

Again, two of those affected so dearly by the 1991 blast showed their genuine spirits. Hurley's widow, Cynthia, now president of Massachusetts Concerns of Police Survivors reasoned, "At the time {of the trial} you think that it's years away. Definitely, he didn't get what he deserved, but… it's coming, whether you like it or not."

Retired Officer Francis Foley offered these thoughts, "I wish he had gotten more time. But I'm not going to sit around and worry because of him."

Since his release, Shay continually violated the terms of his probation supervised release. Conditions required him to stay out of trouble. In 2005, a judge sentenced Shay to four months in prison for leaving a halfway house and assaulting a Northeastern University Police Officer. This charge came after Shay tore the badge off the detective, who was part of a sting operation to catch a man posing as a physical therapist who gave students inappropriate massages. Shay certainly was innovative.

Again in 2006, police arrested Shay in Massachusetts for selling drugs to a teenager and theft from another. Shay fled the jurisdiction to avoid prosecution and being sent back to prison for violating the terms of his Federal probation. The court issued a fugitive warrant for Shay.

For a year he was on the run. U.S. Marshals looked for him throughout New England and in the Chicago area. Fox TV's "America's Most Wanted" was about to do a piece on Shay when his freedom run suddenly ended.

On a Sunday in mid-July 2007, the Quincy Police visited the Shay family home three times. Two adult sisters of Thomas' were fighting. One was drinking too much. She attacked her sister. Then she attacked a police cruiser.

As the police arrested her, she tried playing a trump card. She feared her arrest would lead to the state taking custody of her 2-month son. Already with a history of violent crimes and skipping court appearances, she was right to be fearful. The woman told the police she would tell them the whereabouts of her fugitive brother, serve him "up on a silver platter" in exchange for continued custody of her child.

The U.S. Marshals went to the Shay house the following day. Everyone at the house lied, saying Thomas Jr. wasn't there. A quick search of the home finally found him sleeping in a second-floor bedroom.

On the same day of his capture in July 2007, the Boston Herald received a letter from Shay, Jr. taunting investigators searching for him. The two-page letter was postmarked from Portsmouth, New Hampshire. In part, Shay goaded, "Guess what guys, today I spent the day with binoculars watching the U.S. marshals who are looking for me, Ha Ha!"

The Herald quoted Supervisory Deputy U.S. Marshal Jeffrey Bohn, referring to Shay, "He has been cross-dressing to avoid capture."

But now they had the 35-year-old fugitive in handcuffs leading him into Federal court.

Shay further mocked, "The police are upset about the sentence I got. The government can't find the most notorious gangster Whitey Bulger, so let's go after the fag, the cross-dresser Thomas Shay. That will make us some headlines." He later denied disguising himself as a woman to avoid detection.

When Shay initially fled the state, Federal Judge Rya Zobel ruled he could remain free because of an unusual motion from his defense team. They convinced Zobel that doctors diagnosed Shay with a rare disorder "pseudologia fantastica" which caused him to tell tall tales.

A letter penned by Shay appeared to prove this out. "I am up here with the Browns, giving my support to a noble cause." Shay also stated he hung out with Randy Weaver, who allegedly visited the Browns, tax evaders holed up in their New Hampshire compound. Weaver's wife and son died, along with U.S. Marshal Bill Degan during a siege at Ruby Ridge in Idaho. Shay claimed, "Randy lent me some voice listening equipment, so I got to hear what you {Marshals} were saying, planning."

Shay wasn't laughing when the court held him without bail while he awaited a decision on the revocation of his probation. The court sentenced Shay to 33 months at a Memphis, Tennessee prison. He also pled guilty in state court to the 2006 charges for which he received another 6-month jail sentence to be served after his Federal time.

The state took his sister's baby for safety purposes.

✳   ✳   ✳

This case was about to become the yo-yo of criminal sentences. Rulings over the next 15 years went back and forth, bringing the families up and down with each decision. On April 4, 2007, U.S. District Judge Rya Zobel vacated Trenkler's life sentence. She sentenced him to 37 years in prison. Trenkler, then 51-years-old, would have to serve about 23 more years. He already served 14 years.

After reviewing arguments from Trenkler's defense team, Zobel agreed that, at the time of his original sentence, federal law dictated only the jury, not the judge, could give a life sentence. There was no such order from a jury; Zobel sentenced him without the proper authority. In 2005, Trenkler wrote to Judge Zobel after he learned of another case with a similar sentencing error.

Joan Griffin, Trenkler's new attorney, requested a 10-year maximum sentence for her client. This would have resulted in Trenkler's immediate release. She reasoned the bomb detonated accidentally. Since it was a remote-controlled device and he didn't detonate the device, he shouldn't get a life sentence. "I am not aware of any case where something detonates accidentally, where that is then first-degree murder," Griffin contended. This argument sounds like an admission Trenkler built the bomb.

AUSA James Lang countered. He called the bombing a "deliberate, diabolical act." Lang asked Zobel to reinstate the life sentence or, at least, give him two 45-year consecutive sentences. Prosecutors missed two deadlines to respond to Trenkler's re-sentencing motion. U.S. Attorney Michael Sullivan said his office would appeal Zobel's ruling.

No longer on the job, Francis Foley implored Judge Zobel to keep the life sentence. "I consider him a terrorist. I consider him a coward. To me, any sentence other than the original one you originally imposed on him is unacceptable."

Hurley's family, including his widow, Cynthia, was also present in the courtroom. Over 200 police officers lined the street outside the court. They saluted her and the family as they passed. Sixteen years after Hurley's death, they have not forgotten.

✳   ✳   ✳

Also in 2007, the other defendant in the case, Thomas Shay, Jr. filed motions in the Federal court to withdraw his guilty plea contending the U.S. Attorney's office coerced his confession. That motion went nowhere. Shay was again released from federal custody in 2009. There has been no further news about his life.

In August 2008, the First Circuit Court of Appeals reinstated the original double life sentence of Alfred Trenkler. One court giveth, while the other taketh. In its 32-page decision, the Court ruled Trenkler waited too long to challenge his life sentence, originally imposed in 1993. The Appeals Court ruled Judge Rya Zobel overstepped her authority when she reduced his sentence.

The United States Attorney Michael J. Sullivan said in a press release, "I can only hope this will bring some measure of peace for Officer Hurley's family and for Officer Foley."

At the time of this ruling, Trenkler, age 52, was serving his sentence in the Federal Medical Center at the old Fort Devens site in north-central Massachusetts. For now, it appeared Trenkler would be in prison for the rest of his natural life. Or would he?

The saga continued. In a highly unusual move, in 2009, the Boston Police Department took another look at this case, 18 years after the catastrophic explosion. This review came because of renewed support for a new trial or release of Alfred Trenkler based on potential fresh evidence, a flawed original investigation, and allegations of prosecutorial misconduct.

Trenkler had a zealous advocate. In his 570 page book, *Perfectly Innocent - The Wrongful Conviction of Alfred Trenkler*, author Morrison Bonpasse, with Trenkler, lays out a detailed presentation espousing Trenkler's innocence. Highlighted herein are a few of his claims (My comments are in parentheses.):

Of 24 latent fingerprints found during the investigation from Thomas Shay, Sr.'s car, none matched Trenkler or Shay, Jr. (Not knowing all the details of the prints, this is explained easily by the wearing of gloves while making and placing the device.)

Early in the investigation, ATF Agents identified Thomas Shay, Sr. as a suspect based on his evasive, uncooperative manner, and his "inconsistent, largely unbelievable story." (This is typical in an investigation. Hypotheses are formed as part of the scientific method. As evidence is developed, some suspects are eliminated while new ones are identified. If Shay, Sr. hadn't been looked at, people would say investigators rushed to judgment.)

These and other materials were not made available to the defense at the time of trial. (If items are exculpatory [evidence that may justify, excuse, or create reasonable doubt about a defendant's alleged actions or intentions], they should have been turned over.)

Trenkler's conviction was based on circumstantial evidence. (There is nothing intrinsically wrong with circumstantial evidence. Circumstantial cases rely on indirect evidence. They are often weaker than direct cases, but circumstantial evidence can still prove a case. When relying on circumstantial evidence, conclusions must be reasonable and natural, based on their common sense and life experience. The evidence, weighed by the jurors, was found to be credible. Thus, they found Trenkler guilty.)

An ATF explosives expert testified Trenkler was the same person who built a bomb in 1986 (for which he was convicted) and the Roslindale bomb. An appeals court ruled this testimony should not have been allowed in trial. (Makers of explosive devices often make them the same way each time. It is their signature. Depending on the details, experts can clearly identify the device as being made by the same person.)

A career criminal in jail with Trenkler testified Trenkler confessed to making the bomb. It is alleged the government gave the witness a deal for a reduced sentence after the trial, which was not disclosed in Trenkler's 1994 appeal. (If the government promised the witness a reduced sentence for his testimony, this is inappropriate, or at least must be disclosed. If the government decided after the testimony to reduce the sentence because the witness did a credible job, this has no bearing.)

Five of those jurors who read the book now believe the case should be reviewed. Some believe he deserves a new trial, at least.

Others believe he is innocent. Have you ever watched one of those shows on TV or listened to a trial?

The evidence presented by the prosecution can seem lopsided, overwhelmingly convincing for guilt. Until you listen to all the evidence from the defense, then the case frequently becomes more even. These jurors sat through the trial 18 years ago. It is not surprising a treatise like this in-depth book swayed their opinions years later. Even retired Boston Federal Judge, Nancy Gertner, implored Judge Rya Zobel to reconsider this case. The five jurors all wrote to Judge Zobel. She was aware of the letters at the time she denied Trenkler a new trial.

Cynthia Hurley showed her graciousness when she considered this issue. She said every time Trenkler seeks a new trial, it tears her apart, but she said to a Boston Herald reporter, "I do not want anybody in prison who doesn't belong there. If there is evidence, let's find it. Let's hear it."

She met with two Boston Police command staff who read the book. After their explanation, Mrs. Hurley said, "I came away thinking there was something out there."

However, after review by the United States Attorney's Office, the U.S. Attorney at the time of the review, Carmen Ortiz told the Boston Herald, "We have found nothing undermining our confidence in the guilty verdict." All the points of contention were properly scrutinized with all concerns dispelled.

Retired Officer Francis X. Foley, forever maimed physically and mentally by the blast, still believes the "terrorist" Trenkler is guilty. He feels Trenkler will forever try to get out of prison.

That explosion affected other people in many ways. One of those so haunted by the bomb blast was Boston Police Officer Denise Corbett. She was one of the officers who responded first to the senior Shay's call to Boston PD when he suspected something about that package he found in his driveway.

Corbett was a rookie on that fateful day in 1991. Officer Corbett witnessed the devastating detonation. She and her partner were the first to attend to Officers Hurley and Foley. The gory, traumatic experience left her with an internal pain that never left. Denise Corbett committed suicide in 2006.

This case never seems to go away. In January 2021, after spending 28 years in prison, convicted murderer Alfred Trenkler filed a motion for a compassionate early release because of his poor health and the continuing Covid-19 pandemic. The Government opposed his motion, as did Hurley's four children, who saw the motion as a gimmick to get out of prison early.

In a statement made to Bob Ward of Boston 25 News, one of Officer Hurley's daughters, Lisa Quinn, said, "Everyone has a little compassion here and there, but there is no reason for this man to be out of jail, especially on a Covid-19."

The Sentencing Reform Act of 1984 established a provision for compassionate release. Typically, there are "extraordinary and compelling" grounds, such as being terminally ill with a life expectancy of fewer than 18 months.

The Coronavirus has caused an onslaught of motions for early release since the virus has spread throughout many prison populations.

Trenkler's attorneys claimed Trenkler, now 64-years-old, suffers from a serious heart condition, making him especially vulnerable to death if he contracts Covid-19 while incarcerated in his Tucson, Arizona federal prison cell. At the time of this comment, Trenkler had not gotten his vaccine, even though it was available.

But Hurley's children continue to suffer the painful loss of their hero father. One of his sons, Donald Powell, stated, "There's a vaccine, people are getting it. He would be safer in an isolated federal prison than being out on the streets exposed to the general public."

A few months later, on May 7, 2021, US District Court Judge William E. Smith vacated Trenkler's life sentence again. But his ruling was not for a compassionate release relating to his failing health and Covid-19. Trenkler was now vaccinated and the Arizona prison where he was incarcerated had no virus cases.

Rather, under the sentencing reform passed in 2018, the First Step Act, Judge Smith found an "extraordinary and compelling reason" to negate the life sentence, giving Trenkler a chance to live outside prison walls. He gave Trenkler a 41-year sentence. Noting the bomb could have killed more people, he said, "a sentence of 41 years would be one reflecting the seriousness of the offenses, promotes respect for the law, and provides just punishment." Since his 1993 conviction, Trenkler has served 27 years in prison. Trenkler, age 65, with good behavior credit, could be eligible for release in about eight years.

The US Attorney's Office, the Boston Police and the victim's children all expressed disappointment with the ruling. Frank Foley's son, a Boston firefighter, stated to the judge in a previous hearing, "He's riddled from fear. Not from Trenkler, but people like Trenkler. My Dad lives with these nightmares of his friend."

In one of those poignant aspects of life, Leanne and her brothers, Donald and David, became members of the Boston Police Department. David wears his father's badge number. Each officer has over 20 years of service.

Leanne reminisced about her father, "He was humble. Very proud of what he did. Very good at what he did, and I'd just love for people to remember him for the solid guy he was."

❋ ❋ ❋

Fifteen bomb technicians have been killed in the line of duty. Jeremiah Hurley is the only one from New England. A plaque in his honor rests with the others at the FBI Hazardous Device School (HDS) Bomb Technician Memorial in Huntsville, Alabama. Dedicated in 2007, the memorial honors all public safety bomb technicians who died in the line of duty while performing a hazardous device operation or response.

Very special thanks to ATF Special Agent (retired) Jeff Kerr for his invaluable insights and information on this case.

https://www.nbcboston.com/news/local/children-of-late-bomb-technician-follow-fathers-legacy-at-boston-police-department/48496/; Ally Donnelly, April 5, 2018.

http://archive.boston.com/news/local/massachusetts/articles/2007/07/17/fugitive_bomber_is_caught_napping/-TheBostonGlobe, Shelley Murphy, Globe Staff 07/17/2007.

Hazardous Device School Bomb Technician Memorial — LEB https://leb.fbi.gov/image-repository/hazardous-device-school-bomb-technician-memorial-in-huntsville-alabama.jpg/view

Dress-up Cop Killer Caught https://roslindale.wickedlocal.com/article/20070717/News/307179576; Michele McPhee, July 17, 2007.

https://www.karenfranklin.com/comp/thomas-a-shay/;

The Commonwealth of Massachusetts, Dept. of Correction, Bridgewater State Hospital Competency Report; Paul G. Nestor, Ph.D.; December 24, 1991

https://www.patriotledger.com/article/20070717/NEWS/307179697; The Patriot Ledger, Dennis Tatz, July 17, 2007.

https://www.bostonherald.com/2009/11/22/boston-police-department-takes-new-look-at-bomb-case/; Boston Herald, Jessica Fargen, November 22, 2009.

https://www.law.cornell.edu/wex/appellant

Citing virus risk, convict in officer's bomb death seeks release, The Boston Globe, Shelley Murphy; April 9, 2021

Sentence reduced for convicted bomber, The Boston Globe, John R. Ellement and Shelley Murphy; May 8, 2021

Justia Law, United States, Appellee, v. Thomas A. Shay, Defendant-appellant, 57 F.3d 126 (1st Cir.1995)

CHAPTER 8

Chelsea Bar Fire

Boom! The back wall of the second-floor apartment blew out completely, landing in the vacant lot next to the three-story commercial building. Jack, naked, except for his boxer shorts, had escaped to the first-floor landing inside the rear door just as the blast occurred. The first arriving firefighters found him shivering in the mid-November chill outside the blazing structure. Flames were spewing out of the barroom on the first floor and from every opening on all four sides of that second-floor apartment.

After the firefighters finally quelled the flames, the Chelsea Fire investigators conducted their initial interview with Jack. A couple days later, Jack told me the same story. As I looked at him while he spoke, I tried to gauge the validity of his words.

Jack Bennett, in his later 30s, was handsome in the goofy, yet arrogant manner in which he presented himself. About six feet tall with a full head of dirty blonde hair, he appeared fit, but yet he also seemed a little worn out for his age, perhaps due to burning the candle at both ends. Or maybe from burning a building.

Jack said he owned the building for a couple of years with a partner, Steve. He ran a bar on the first floor and he had two vacant apartments on the upper two floors. He related earlier that night, he had trouble with a Columbian customer who had been dealing drugs in the bar. Around that period of the late 1980s, Chelsea, a two-and-a-half-square-mile city immediately to the north of Boston, had a large Hispanic population and a serious drug problem. Jack said he kicked the guy out of the bar, but the man cursed him the entire time.

After closing up for the night, Jack went up to the third-floor apartment to sleep, as he did about once or twice a week. When he was just about asleep, he said he heard a snap and crackling sound from the lower floor. (What, no pop?) He went down the rear stairway to investigate, thinking something bad was happening or about to happen.

On the second-floor landing, he pushed open the door to the vacant apartment. It was already ajar. He said that about 20 feet ahead, the apartment was fully ablaze. Within moments, a vast wall of flames erupted toward him. As fast as he could move, he descended to the next landing when a force from behind pushed him to the ground level

Burned out "That Place"

and out the rear doorway. That's how he ended up in the chilly night air in his skivvies.

It was at that moment the second-floor apartment exploded with fire blowing out the gaping hole. Even before I had a chance to examine the fire scene to conduct my origin and cause analysis, I had a feeling Jack was being less than honest with me.

*　　*　　*

Firefighter on second floor of structure.

This was an interesting fire scene. I worked the scene with Chelsea Fire Deputy Chief Dennis Williams, a thickly built, cigar-chomping firefighter with a silver-haired flat top. Dennis was well known in the fire investigation field. His protégé, Fire Inspector Joe Shai, assisted as he was learning the investigative end of fires. We had received written consent from Jack to conduct the scene inspection.

On the exterior, besides the missing rear second-floor wall, there was charring around several other second-floor windows, but no charring from any first-floor windows. We made a couple fascinating observations when we examined the large section of wall lying on the rear grassy lawn. The wall had a mid-section with two double-hung windows centered by a fixed picture window. There was no fire damage to the wall or any of its components. This showed the explosion occurred very early into the fire or totally before any fire.

It was pretty cool, as the fire investigator nerd that I am, to see the window glass had only broken when the entire section of the wall hit the ground. All the glass was right there on the ground within the parameters of the frames. There was no soot on the glass either.

Considering this point, since we were beginning to believe gasoline had been used in the building to help spread the fire the combustion process with gasoline produces copious amounts of black, sooty smoke, but since the blown-out wall and windows were devoid of soot, then the explosion was confirmed as having occurred at the outset of the incident.

Now, a quick note to explain this fire and explosion science phenomenon. In simple terms, fire is a rapid oxidation (a chemical process involving heat, oxygen and fuel) process resulting in the evolution of heat and light. Many, but not all explosions, are an even more rapid chemical process resulting in the sudden expansion of gases with pressures that can cause noise, movement and shattering of materials. When a fuel/air explosion occurs, such as when gasoline or natural gas vapors mix with air, the created pressures exert force on the exterior of the compartment, in this case, the walls and ceilings in particular.

Here, the exterior wall was weaker than the other walls. That is likely why it failed, whereas the other walls remained mostly intact. I have seen occasions where a bureau of drawers with photos on top remained in place while the exterior wall completely failed from an explosion. This also explains why people standing in a room with this type of explosion can survive.

On the first floor, there was heavy localized fire damage centered near the stairway to the second floor. The stairs were in the main lobby outside the bar/ lounge area, which had minimal burn damage.

This was the first time I had ever seen stairs completely burned away in a building that was still standing. The treads and risers had all but disappeared. Only the three stringers remained one on each side of the stairs along with a center string. All were charred so badly, I couldn't safely navigate them to the second floor.

Here is where we took multiple samples, with some of them giving off an odor similar to gasoline. These were subsequently lab tested and came back positive for gasoline residue.

During the normal progression of a fire, stairs rarely burn away to completion. As a simple explanation, when a fire starts on the lower floor at or near the base of the stairs, the hot gases and heat from the fire move upward toward the ceiling and up the stairwell well above the stairs themselves. With a roaring fire pushing upward with the natural airflow, the buoyancy of the hot gases and the chimney effect created by the open stairwell, the heat radiating down to the stair treads will scorch and char the wood surfaces, but the stairs infrequently exhibit heavy burning.

Also, the dynamics of a fire on the upper floor, even an extensive fire, don't cause the stairs to burn. However, gasoline sloshed on the stairs can keep the fire on the treads and risers for sufficient time to ignite the wood. This scenario and configuration of stairs within a closed stairwell, that is, one with walls on both sides could consume the stairs.

The second floor had the rear wall missing. The sheetrock ceilings had all collapsed onto the floor. After the sheetrock mixed with water from the firefighter extinguishment operations, there were now several inches of mud-like muck on the floor. The exposed wood studs and ceiling framework had some charring, but still had the strength to support the third floor. Here, the damage was consistent throughout the apartment, top to bottom, left to right, front to back. There was no pattern showing where fire within the apartment may have originated.

Inspection of the third-floor apartment revealed extreme fire damage throughout the area. The conditions were so bad that it was unsafe to examine the third floor except on ladders extending to the wall openings. Captain Williams and I headed outside to confer. The Captain told me that we could eliminate the third floor because firefighters observed the fire on the second floor extended into the third floor.

Since this was the day before Thanksgiving, the daylight was fast fading. The scene needed additional work, but since we had now believed this fire was incendiary, we contacted the U. S. Attorney's Office after the holiday to seek a search warrant. We called it quits for the day. But before we left, we secured the building to keep intruders out.

On Friday, an anonymous phone call came into our Boston ATF Office. The caller had an older man's voice. He stated Jack intentionally set the fire, but he offered no other details and, before he hung up, he refused to identify himself.

With a little research and footwork, we were nearly certain the caller was a man named Ed who had worked with Jack and his business partner, Steve. On Monday, we located Ed, a septuagenarian who didn't like arsonists. He was a feisty, wiry, bespectacled, mostly bald guy who liked to tell stories.

After confronting him, with very little nudging, Ed gave up quite a story about the fire. He had been friends with Jack for years, doing a variety of jobs for him. Jack had told him about the phony Columbian drug dealer story to cover his burning of the building. He detailed how Jack went to five different gas stations filling five 5-gallon plastic pails with gasoline. Ed further explained Jack poured a pail of gasoline down the front stairs from the top to the bottom while the other 20 gallons were partially poured within the second-floor apartment with some liquid left in all four pails. Ed added Jack bought a flare gun at a fishing supply or sporting goods store south of Boston.

Jack stood on the rear second-floor landing and fired the flare gun through the gasoline-soaked apartment. The fire immediately flashed into a ball of fire expanding toward Jack's position. He had barely escaped down the stairs as the explosion blast wave helped push him out the first-floor exterior door.

There was one other significant piece of information provided by Ed. Jack's partner, Steve, co-owned the bar and the building. He was unclear how involved Steve was in the bar and the fire, as he was a developer who spent most of his time redeveloping older three-decker homes in Boston into condominiums. At the moment, we had nothing on Steve, but maybe if we did our due diligence on the investigation, something might turn up that we could use.

Well, at least Jack had been truthful about two things, the fireball that nearly fried him and the pushing force behind him that shoved him to the outside. Jack's statement to me about hearing the snapping and crackling while he was in his third-floor apartment was pure b.s. That sound is associated with the burning of combustible fuels such as wood, not gasoline. Wood was not the first fuel that was burning during this fire; it was the gasoline vapors.

Armed with the first fire scene observations and the information from Ed, we drafted an application for a search warrant. The Assistant United States Attorney concurred with our efforts. A Federal Magistrate approved the warrant.

Our goal was to find additional evidence that not only supported that this fire had been intentionally set but also to find items, like the remains of the plastic pails used to transport the gasoline. This would corroborate Ed's information. Then, we could proceed from there to further investigate if Jack was, indeed, the arsonist.

The next day, a cold early December day, we returned to the loss site to complete our scene examination. Besides Dennis Williams, I recall being accompanied by young Special Agent Jeff Kerr, a tall strapping kid, to assist me with the scene work. This was Jeff's first fire scene, and last. He hated everything about it, particularly the still smoky nature of the atmosphere, which he found to be highly nauseating.

We concentrated our efforts on the second floor within the slippery sheetrock slime. With rakes and shovels, the most useful of low-tech tools at a fire scene, we methodically scraped from room to room, although we surmised the living room would produce the best results since the greatest damage from the vapor explosion had occurred there.

Our labors were fruitful. Hidden under the mud, we first found a curved metal handle from a 5-gallon pail, but we couldn't locate the melted remains of the plastic pail itself. However, over the next hour or two, we recovered two more handles without pails until we finally uncovered a handle that was stuck within the flattened re-solidified remains of a pail. We continued to search in vain for any remains of a flare gun even though we had no information what Jack had done with it from the time he fired it into the gas-laden apartment to the moment he escaped to the exterior of the blazing structure.

The arson was confirmed. We had the gasoline samples from the stairs. The remains of that melted plastic pail had also trapped gasoline residue within the plastic when it re-solidified. The handles and the pail remains helped substantiate the information provided by Ed. But we needed more evidence before we could make a case.

There was not even enough information to support probable cause for a search warrant. What exactly would we be looking for and where exactly would we look? We had no information Jack had anything in his car or at another location that was associated with the arson. Aside from confronting Jack with allegations that he had set the fire, we needed to do something else to bolster the case.

We approached our new informant, Ed, about wearing a wire, doing an undercover stint while he wore a recorder and a transmitter. He readily agreed. Our plan was for him to engage Jack and possibly Steve in conversation about the explosion and fire.

Working with Ed, we set up a loose script for him to follow so it provided the best opportunity for Jack and Steve to make admissions about their involvement with the crime. We even had hopes Jack would admit exactly where he had purchased the 5-gallon pails and the flare gun.

Over the course of the month following the fire, we even checked Jack's credit card purchases, but he had apparently paid cash for everything he used to set this fire as we found nothing useful. It certainly would be nice to get that admission as the more evidence we could get on Jack, the better. There was never enough evidence when it came to prosecuting most arson-for-profit cases.

Shortly after the New Year, the day came when undercover Ed was scheduled to join Jack and Steve in South Boston. The ruse used by Ed to get their attention was the Feds had knocked on his door, pushing him for information on the fire. Ed and Jack were the first participants at the meeting. Initially, Steve was a no-show.

I, along with a small team of ATF Agents, sat in a car around the corner from the rendezvous. We listened to the discussion. Every word was heard loud and clear. Jack was very easy, rather gullible, and not suspicious at all of Ed's story. The two men began by wondering how and why the Feds got onto Ed in the first place. He wanted to know if Jack had covered his tracks well before and after the fire.

Jack explained his preparations before the fire, including the acquisition of the gasoline at several different gas stations and the purchase of the flare gun someplace on the South Shore, meaning anyplace south of Boston. Jack didn't bite when gently pushed by Ed for specific information about the location of the store. He retold how and where he had spread the nearly 25 gallons of gasoline and how he almost got caught in the fire, barely escaping with his life.

Jack laughed nervously at his overuse of the gasoline that caused his near-death experience. Thank you very much Jack for validating Ed's information and confirming our fire origin and cause determination. But Jack failed to give us more specifics on the locations of his purchases.

Just as Jack admitted Steve knew the details about the fire, Steve walked in the door. Even though Ed continued to talk about the fire, a shrewd Steve steered away from the conversation. He never said one word that could even be construed as an admission of guilt or even that he had prior knowledge about the fire. Neither undercover Ed nor the naïve Jack said anything that caused Steve to implicate himself.

We uncovered no additional evidence over the next few days, so we confronted Jack with the tape recording. Before we did so, we spoke with Ed, who was all for our plan. He had no fear either of these guys would ever hurt him. Within minutes, Jack folded. He confessed to the entire arson, but he wouldn't say anything to incriminate Steve.

Presenting the same tape recording to Steve, his arrogance was off the charts. He irked me to no end. Steve simply said there is nothing on the tape that involved him with the fire. There was no evidence whatsoever against him. He added, "If you have anything on me, then arrest me. If not, leave me alone."

Steve was right. We got nothing we could use against him. Jack pled guilty in Federal Court. He received a four-year prison sentence. Case closed.

CHAPTER 9

Major Mill Blaze – An Electrical Ignition, or Was It?

Real estate developer Nissim Mizrachi from Long Island knew a good deal when he saw it. The Mohasco Mills site was over 200 miles from his usual territory. It was on the north side of the Mohawk River in Amsterdam, New York, about 40 miles northwest of Albany, the state capital. The Mills offered a tempting investment. But maybe not your typical investment!

This complex of 16 mill buildings was originally built in the mid-1800s. In 1920, the Mohawk Carpet Mills occupied several of the buildings until they merged with other mills to form Mohasco Mills in 1956. The buildings totaled over 800,000 square feet on 25 acres, making it one of the largest mills in the United States.

Mohasco manufactured textiles, including canvas and blankets, for the US Military during World War II. However, Mohawk Carpets couldn't keep up with changes in the textile industry. They also outgrew the buildings for the newer equipment. In 1968, the Mohawk manufacturing operations moved to the southern states. By 1987, the Mohasco Mills in Amsterdam was completely abandoned.

Mizrachi borrowed about $4,000,000 from a German bank to purchase the Mohasco property and to make site improvements.

The purchase price was a remarkably low $692,000, far less than one dollar per square foot. This 1992 loan and real estate transaction was an early sign of banking malpractice that eventually led to the later crises in the real estate and banking industries. The stock market crash of 1987 may have also played into the events that followed at the mills.

The new owner sent some men to start renovations at the property to create the illusion redevelopment of the mills was underway. Mizrachi allegedly spent about $50,000 on materials used in the initial overhaul, a mere pittance when compared to the massive work needed to get these buildings shipshape. Where did the rest of the loan go?

According to an article from *Upstate NY Photos*, dated September 16, 2016, and from court records, Mizrachi made several extravagant personal expenditures including cosmetic facial surgery, art, Persian rugs and luxury cars. He also had the arrogance to secure a $14,000,000

The original For Sale or Lease Pamphlet

fire insurance policy, over 20 times the purchase price, written with the help of a close associate. All of Mizrachi's actions relating to this property were classic deeds in preparation for an arson-for-profit scheme.

*   *   *

Three months after the policy took effect, on the night of August 28, 1992, the weather in the City of Amsterdam was pleasant, a little cloudy, with a moderate breeze flowing past the Mohasco Mills out of the southeast. Shortly before midnight, the Amsterdam Fire Department received a box alarm reporting a fire at the mill site. First due firefighters observed fire venting from the first floor A/D corner of the five-story brick Building One as they pulled off of Forest Avenue into the parking lot. Their observations would later prove invaluable.

The fire grew exponentially, engulfing the upper floors rapidly before the firefighters got a handle on it. Within 28 minutes, the roof and upper walls of the 75,000 square foot building caved in, collapsing to the lower floors, causing the total ruin of the initial fire building.

Flaming brands floated aloft with the buoyant heat currents, and radiant heat from the firestorm ignited combustibles of other nearby mill buildings. Within a short time, a major conflagration overwhelmed the firefighters, rapidly turning into a General Alarm response.

The buildings spewed tons of black smoke visible for miles because of the city lights and the glowing fire within the smoke. With the heavy smoke and the darkness of night, visibility on ground level was extremely poor. The shimmering brilliance of the yellow, orange and red flames that leaped above the crumbling structures provided the only light.

Because of the closeness of the buildings, plus an 80-foot cliff behind some structures and others running along the 40-foot-wide creek, firefighters had limited access in which to attack the burning mills. Fire crews with every available piece of apparatus traveled many miles to fight the onslaught of the flames. The fire presented as a formidable foe in the long, drawn-out battle before relenting to thousands of gallons of water and the relative lack of available fuels after the fire consumed most combustibles.

Amsterdam Fire Lieutenant Walter Martin was on vacation the day the fire struck the city. However, when he learned of the fire he responded to the scene to assist with the "all hands on deck" situation. Once at the site, Lt. Martin was put in charge of one of the volunteer fire departments who had answered the mutual aid call-out along with 26 other departments and almost 150 firefighters.

Martin's unit positioned on Lyon Street behind Buildings 8 and 36. There was no fire there for the longest time as the blaze was concentrated on the opposite side of the small creek devouring the mills surrounding Building 1.

As the inferno spread, a Chief ordered Lt. Martin to move his crew to put out some hot spots. Two young volunteers looked at him wide-eyed. One said, "We've never seen anything like this, but you have probably seen something like this every day."

The Lieutenant quipped, "Son if I've seen a fire like this every day, there would be no City of Amsterdam left." They did some mopping up, but eventually, they made their way back to the creek side of Buildings 8 and 36. As they stood in front of an open overhead door at one end of the small bridge over the creek, his crew had a superb view of the burning, collapsing mills only yards away across the waterway.

Altogether the fire destroyed 7 or 8 buildings, including Buildings 1, 7, 7A, 7B, 11, 26, and 33, totaling about 350,000 square feet, many with multiple floors that collapsed. Another handful of structures were also damaged, but an aggressive interior attack saved five buildings from total destruction. Firefighters sprayed fourteen million gallons of water to quench the fire's appetite. The site truly looked like a war zone with several bombed-out structures. At least 12 firefighters suffered injuries during the conflagration. By luck or the Grace of God, none died from the raining down of bricks, stone and timbers.

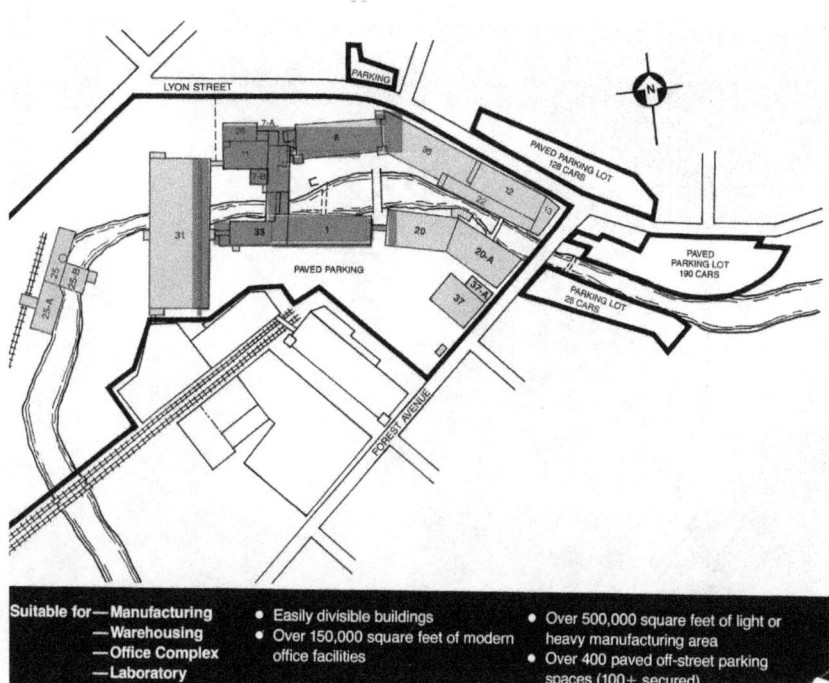

LYON STREET

PARKING

N

7-A

8

36

PAVED PARKING LOT
126 CARS

11

7-B

2

12

31

33

1

20

20-A

PAVED PARKING LOT
190 CARS

PAVED PARKING

37-A

PARKING LOT
28 CARS

25-A

37

FOREST AVENUE

Suitable for—Manufacturing	• Easily divisible buildings	• Over 500,000 square feet of light or
—Warehousing	• Over 150,000 square feet of modern	heavy manufacturing area
—Office Complex	office facilities	• Over 400 paved off-street parking
—Laboratory		spaces (100+ secured)

Damaged and destroyed buildings are highlighted in red.

When daylight unfolded over the smoky aftermath, the need for a large-scale investigation was clear. This fire was the worst in Amsterdam's history, and it ended up being the largest fire in the State of New York that year. The Amsterdam Fire and Police Departments, along with investigators from the New York State Police and the Fire Prevention and Control Bureau, invited the ATF National Response Team (NRT) to help with the origin and cause analysis and any subsequent follow-up.

The NRTs consist of 10 to 12 members, including fire and explosion trained Special Agents, chemists and Fire Protection Engineers. State and local authorities invite the NRTs if there is a large dollar loss, many injuries or deaths related to a fire or explosion.

Little is left standing of the former Mohasco complex in Amsterdam destroyed in
an arson fire on August 28, 1992. (September 5, 1992, The Leader-Herald)

The advantage of bringing ATF in to assist with an investigation
is the ability to provide full-time fast-hitting investigative efforts
supported by trained personnel, the backing of Federal money and the
luxury of time to concentrate on the investigation. Usually, the team

Daylight view of fire-damaged mill buildings.

members respond to the scene of major incidents within 24 hours unless there are special circumstances.

Since this fire occurred on a Friday night and the site continued to smolder throughout Saturday, the Response Team met with the state and local investigators late Sunday afternoon. Team members, led by Assistant Special Agent in Charge Jim Adamcik, came from all over the Northeast. Once the meeting and briefing on the fire were complete and the Team Leader made all assignments, we broke for the night so we could begin the scene examination and the interviews first thing in the morning.

By 8 a.m., Monday morning August 31, the investigators assigned to work the fire scene were on-site, ready to go. The landscape absolutely resembled a World War II European city after a bombing run. Building 1 was a vast pile of bricks from the collapse of five floors and three walls.

Only the D wall stood tall because an enclosed catwalk that connected the third floor of this building with the adjacent Building 20 supported the wall. Twenty-five feet separated the buildings. That four-story mill was missing its roof and part of the fourth floor.

Behind Building 20 and across a small creek, there were varying degrees of devastation spread over six more former mill buildings, many with large sections, roofs and walls collapsed.

If this had been an active mill site, the damages would have been in the tens of millions of dollars. Lots of jobs would have been lost. Now, it was just an enormous mess waiting to be further demolished and carted away.

Heavy equipment, including a large crane capable of reaching to the top of the remaining standing walls of several of the destroyed mills, stood at the ready waiting for directions on where to begin. My assignment was to assist with the origin and cause determination.

By this time I had been a Certified Fire Investigator, sanctioned by both ATF and the International Association of Arson Investigators for a few years. I had previously examined over 300 fire and explosion scenes.

As part of my job here, I was to direct the crane operator so we could minimize further damage to the area of possible fire origin since firefighters had advised us only the first-floor A/D area of Building 1 was burning when they arrived. I volunteered for this assignment because I had previous experience with other heavy equipment operators.

After our initial visual assessment of the entire site, just on the outside of the buildings, several of us took a seat on the loading dock in the catwalk's shadow to stay out of the sun. We had to wait for the crane to position so we could remove the catwalk and remaining wall of Building 1.

With our backs to wide open rolling doors to the first floor of Building 20, the scent of gasoline wafted by us with the slight breeze drifting between the buildings. We all noticed the distinctive odor.

A member of the federal Bureau of Alcohol, Tobacco and Firearms investigating team takes a break amidst the charred and twisted rubble Monday afternoon during the probe of the weekend fire at the former Mohasco complex on Forest Avenue.

Recorder photo: Lisa Major

Me sitting in rubble of Building 1 waiting for heavy equipment to re-position. (Not taking a break!) (Recorder Lisa Major 9/01/92)

I said aloud, "We'll find it once we get in the building" as I was looking inside the doorway to an enormous pile of collapsed brick.

Minutes later, another alert ATF NRT member piped up, "What's this bundle of zip cord?" We all turned around toward the large solid wood handle of the rolling door.

Wrapped around the handle was a large coil of brown, probably 18-gauge AWG wire many of us see on home extension cords or lamp cords. We often refer to this wire as zip-cord because it is an electrical cable with two or more metal conductors held together by an insulating jacket that can easily separate by pulling the conductors apart.

The agent continued, "Look, the wire continues out into the parking lot," and moments later, upon further inspection, he added, "And it also goes into the building!"

These wires were, at the very least, strange. I remember thinking what the heck was this all about. As a trained investigator, the agent walked into the building through the open doorway to investigate the wire further. About 80 feet along the concrete floor path, the wire continued under a stack of pallets. The agent flipped the pallets over. What he uncovered astonished him. He yelled for the rest of us to come in and see.

There was no fire damage on the first floor of this structure. The large, cavernous room held old contents to the left and right of the wide alley where forklifts had once maneuvered goods.

As we walked to the pallets, we all shook our heads in incredulous amazement. The brown zip cord was visible in a small clearing. We took photographs to document the findings.

The familiar overpowering tang of gasoline was prevalent in the area. A 5-gallon white plastic pail was lying on its side on the floor. The cover for the pail, also on the floor, had a small irregularly shaped hole cut into it. The wire disappeared into a wrap of white cotton rags. Gasoline soaked the rags.

As we unwrapped the cloth, the findings continued to surprise us. In the center of the material was a work light, the kind often used when working under the hood of a vehicle with the hook for hanging and the cage to protect the light bulb from breaking; except, in this case, the lamp was broken, even with the cage in place. But there was no glass within the cloth wrap, indicating someone broke the lamp prior to wrapping it in the gasoline-soaked rags. The extension cord wire was connected to the work light. There was minimal charring within the rags.

This was a failed incendiary device. So, this is how the arsonists intended the device to function. One or more arsonists wired the work light with the broken lamp, wrapped it in gasoline-soaked rags which would have been the first fuel ignited. Then, the pallets were to be a growth fuel. The fire would have rapidly grown within this perfect fuel package, basically kindling wood in a configuration in which flames would leap toward the ceiling.

What was the ignition scenario? That electrical extension cord wired to the broken lamp also extended about 50 feet into the parking lot. At that end of the wire, someone had peeled away the insulating cover to expose the copper conductors. We surmised the culprits had touched the conductors to the terminals of the car battery. To their way of thinking, the electrical current to the broken lamp would have caused arcs and sparks that should have ignited the gasoline vapors from the rags.

Once outside under the catwalk area, we looked a little further for more evidence. With little effort, the trail of evidence was easier to follow than the bread crumbs or pebbles left in a fairy tale. Under fallen bricks between the two buildings, we located additional brown zip cords. One wire entered a ground-level man door into Building 1 some 10 to 15 feet from the loading dock. However, until the equipment operator cleared several feet of bricks and other debris, we couldn't follow the wire any further.

A second wire cable continued past the doorway. And on and on it ran. We followed it to a footbridge extending across the 40-foot-wide creek dividing the mill building complex.

Through an open ground floor doorway into another multi-story mill, Building 36, we walked, following the brown zip cord. About 15 feet inside the door, again the cord disappeared within a jumbled pile of 10 wood pallets. The total length of the wire measured 190 feet long.

After removing the pallets, we found another botched incendiary device. Two more five-gallon white pails stood next to the pallets. The distinct odor of gasoline was present in the pails. This was another building with no fire damage at the gasoline-soaked rags or on the first floor. But again, there was upper floor and roof damage. These physical items made for substantial evidence.

Lt. Walter Martin watched the local news coverage of the fire and reports of the subsequent early stages of the investigation on TV. At one point, the camera on scene zoomed in to the open doorway across the creek. The large stack of pallets was visible.

Lieutenant Martin later learned about the incendiary array under the pallets. It stunned him to find out he and his team had been standing mere feet from the gasoline-fueled device with no inkling of the potential significance or danger associated with his positioning.

Up to this point, we were examining the fire scene under the auspices of the fire department's on-scene authority to investigate the fire and with consent from a company that leased Building 1. However, with our preliminary findings of evidence that this fire was incendiary and other attempts made to damage or destroy other buildings, we stopped our scene work until we sought and received a Federal search warrant from the United States District Court, Northern District of New York. With a warrant in hand, we collected all the evidence.

One of the relatively new tools used in fire investigations was the utilization of accelerant detection canines. These highly trained canines could smell and detect the smallest quantities of certain combustible liquids most commonly used to assist in the ignition and spread of a fire.

Fire investigator Mike Knowlton of the NY Office of Fire Prevention and Control used his partner, accelerant detection dog "Buddy" in Buildings 20 and 36. Buddy alerted five times in Building 20 with three additional alerts in Building 36. Knowlton took samples from each alert site. When the results from the laboratory came back, each sample tested positive for the presence of gasoline.

Immediately after finding this astounding treasure trove, we relayed the information to the team supervisors and locals. Some interview teams returned to the fire scene to view the evidence and take information from the items. They attempted to trace the point of sale for each item used in the device—the gasoline, the cotton cloth rags, the brown electrical wire, and the work lights.

Generally, most investigators wouldn't truly believe these items would have been purchased locally in a small city like Amsterdam with a population of about 20,000 souls. With an arson this elaborate, one might think the supplies needed to pull off this job would have been pre-planned and purchased ahead of time in some other location than Amsterdam. But as one of my bosses always used to repeat a James Goldsmith quote, "If you pay peanuts, you get monkeys."

The interview teams fanned out around the city. Each pair had a state or local investigator teamed up with an ATF Agent. The locals were extremely helpful in locating the gas stations and any store that possibly sold the wire cable, the work lights, and the cotton cloths.

At a convenience store gas station, the investigators made their first score. When asked about someone buying gas for something other than a car, the store clerk provided a short story about two guys, described as two white males, one about 5'3", the other being about 6'5". They were driving a compact car, but they ended up putting some 20 gallons of gas in it. The clerk expressed amazement and wonderment, thinking where all that gas was going in that little car.

Since we figured the amount of the continuous length of the brown electrical cord could only have been sold in a spool, and the electrical work lights were probably purchased at the same time, the investigators checked for a hardware store or electrical supply store that sold these items. There were no Home Depot stores or Lowes around, only small independent shops.

They soon found the store. The clerk there also described the two men who purchased hundreds of feet of wire and the lights with the same "Mutt and Jeff" description, like the mismatched characters in the early comic strip. This portrayal was nearly identical to the men who bought the gasoline. The clerk also confirmed the men said, "They were going to light up a big barn. People with no electricity do that sometimes, so it wasn't that strange."

Finally, upon checking where the many identical cotton cloths came from, the investigators found a paint store where a very tall man and a short man, both with Polish or Eastern European accents, bought a large bundle of the cloths plus several 5-gallon pails. Now, they knew how the gasoline had gotten transported.

Investigators sought to interview the owner of the property, Nissim Mizrachi, who had dual American and Israeli citizenship. He came to the US in 1959 and quickly became a successful real estate developer who flipped properties. He would seek to buy run-down properties at a cheap price, rehab them, and then sell the property at a premium. There was no information or evidence he had previously engaged in any illegal activities, including fraud or arson.

At the time of the fire, Mizrachi was conveniently in Tel Aviv while his wife and children remained at their home in Great Neck on Long Island. This can be an innocent coincidence but is often a red flag for investigators.

Obviously, he couldn't have set the fire himself, with his air-tight alibi, but that didn't clear him of having any involvement with the arson. Investigators spoke briefly with him by phone, but he was evasive and directed investigators to speak with his attorney.

Meanwhile, back at the fire scene, we deliberately and methodically cleared the tons of debris from Building 1 with the use of heavy construction equipment. When we finally cleaned close to floor level, we used hand tools to complete the delayering. At last, the meticulous work uncovered evidence of arson.

The electrical cable we had seen leading into the doorway where it had disappeared under the debris was now visible over its length. It, too, connected to a broken work light wrapped in cotton cloths. Although these were fire-damaged, the burning hadn't come from the center outward; the fire only charred the outer surfaces of the cloths. This showed the device hadn't performed as designed, so some other fire ignition scenario must have successfully functioned.

From the three unsuccessful devices, we figured the arsonists botched the job because they didn't know the basics behind Ohm's Law. Named for a German physicist, the law states electric current is proportional to voltage and inversely proportional to resistance. Simply, when the arsonists connected the wires to the car's 12-volt battery, the current was inadequate to cause an arc at the broken work lights because of the long length of the wires. The resistance created by that distance caused the current to drop, making it insufficient to initiate the arc.

As we prepared to complete the scene examination, based upon the three failed devices found within three different mill buildings, we had no qualms about joining with the state and local authorities to announce the fire at the mill complex was a deliberate act, in other words, it was arson. Amsterdam Fire Chief Jim Scheckton told the local press the fire was "intentionally set by gasoline... in multiple locations." There were only a few unanswered questions at this point. What was the final ignition source? What was the motive behind the fire? And ultimately, who was responsible for the arson?

Finally, the NRT members left for home on Friday. The local Agents, including case Agent John Morgan, continued with the state and city investigators over the next few months working diligently to put a case together. Their impressive work led to one of the most successful cases of this type ever.

Morgan and his team determined the arsonists used a rental car while in the Amsterdam area. They traced the car to one of the men fitting the description of the guys who purchased the components for the incendiary devices. This led them back to Long Island, the stomping ground of the mill complex owner, Nissim Mizrachi.

Evidence continued to emerge showing Mizrachi had felonious plans for the mill complex even before his purchase of the property was complete. While digging deeper into Mizrachi's business affairs, we discovered what became of the $4,000,000 loan from the German bank. It didn't take long to determine he had defrauded the bank by using most of the money for extravagant personal expenditures including luxury cars, household art and relics, plus cosmetic surgery. He had applied for that money using falsely inflated credit information.

Allegedly, the money was to be used to redevelop and modernize the mills, which he renamed Creek Side Industrial Park. Mizrachi was also about $30,000 in arrears on his property taxes. After the fire, in a brazen show of audacity, through his attorney, he asked the city to assist him to rehab the site with tax incentives and grants.

Investigators then uncovered two of Mizrachi's henchmen, George Buzzetta and Miroslav Zacpal, both from Long Island, had also been involved in another unrelated arson-for-profit conspiracy. The investigators arrested the men the second week of January 1993. As the interviews progressed, everybody started confessing to their involvement in the Mohasco Mills fire and started rolling over on their co-conspirators.

This was how the conspiracy unfolded. Mizrachi knew and trusted Zacpal, who had already burned his own $350,000 yacht. Zacpal said Mizrachi sometimes begged him, and other times, bullied him to burn the mills.

On August 27, 1992, Zacpal received a $9,900 down payment check from Mizrachi. Eventually, Mizrachi paid $50,000 to complete the deed. Undoubtedly, the payment came from part of the bank loan.

Zacpal then engaged Buzzetta to assist him as he previously had with the boat arson. The men planned to split the money four ways because Buzzetta and Zacpal hired two young men in their 20s, Arthur Sickler and Weslee King, to set the fire. Sickler and King were "Mutt and Jeff." The foursome studied the sales brochure to settle on which buildings to burn. There was even discussion of a bonus being paid if they successfully destroyed multiple structures.

Before finalizing their plans on how to set the fire, the men discussed several ideas, including stealing a gasoline tanker truck and igniting it with an explosive device. King had come up with the Rube Goldberg device after seeing something similar during an episode of the TV series, MacGyver. As part of their confessions, after they all traveled to peruse the site, Zacpal and Buzzetta left for Long Island while Sickler and King were busy purchasing everything investigators had already uncovered.

After dark, Sickler and King pulled into the complex parking lot to prepare the device components. Patrons at a local bar not only saw where the arsonists parked, but they also heard them yelling while they carried out their nefarious business.

The devices were all set up, but after connecting the wires to the car battery, nothing happened. It surprised the arsonists that there wasn't an immediate explosion.

After the incendiaries failed, Sickler cautiously went into the first floor of Building 1, igniting the fuel with a lighter. He also set fire in one building across the creek. Amazingly, he didn't get burned or blown up when the gasoline ignited. Within minutes after setting the

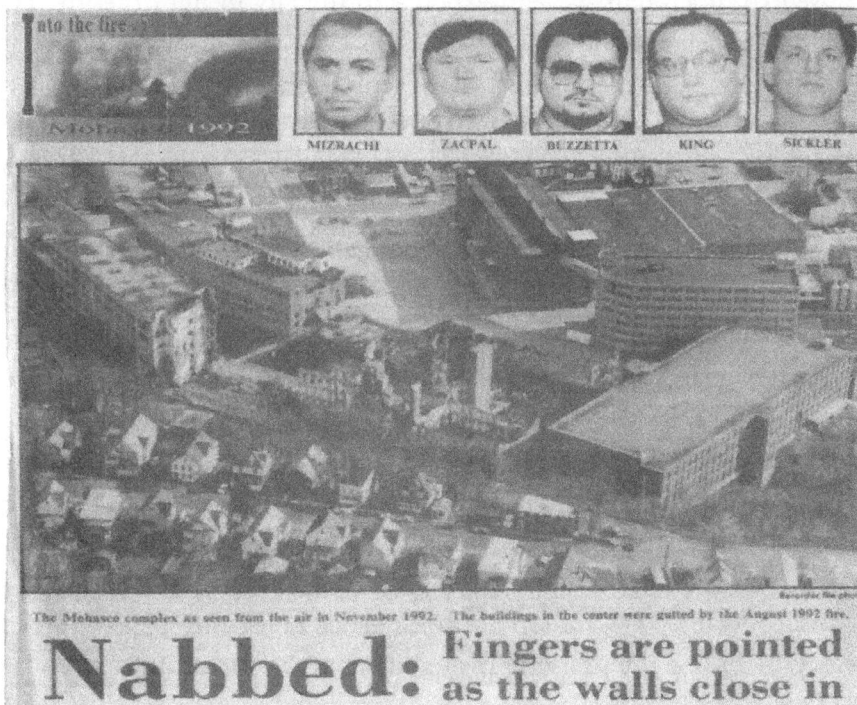

The Mohawk complex as seen from the air in November 1992. The buildings in the center were gutted by the August 1992 fire.

Nabbed: Fingers are pointed as the walls close in

Newspaper announcing the arrests. (Recorder File 9/1995)

fires, just after 11 p.m., the two men were on the highway heading back toward Long Island.

In January, Mizrachi returned to the United States from Israel filing the paperwork to collect the $14,000,000 insurance claim for the loss of the burned properties. Agents then placed him under arrest on multiple Federal charges relating to arson, mail fraud, and bank fraud. It didn't take long for him to confess. Special Agent John Morgan and Assistant United States Attorney Thomas Spina spent hours getting the details from Mizrachi, who was looking for a plea deal.

As a condition of his plea deal, Mizrachi became a witness against his underlings in exchange for a six-and-a-half-year prison sentence. That was a sweet deal considering he was the one who solicited the others to commit the arson, and he had the most charges filed against him. Because of his actions, so many firefighters were injured, plus he caused so much damage and expense to the city to fight the fire. He could have faced decades in prison.

The court probably hurt Mizrachi even more in his wallet, ordering forfeiture of $4 million and to pay restitution of $4.1 million to the defrauded bank. With all the blatant moves made by Mizrachi during the purchase, insuring and burning of the property, he must have thought he was too smart for the small town investigators. But he didn't count on the full team effort who put this case together.

Detailed information from Miroslav Zacpal and Weslee King revealed Sickler made fraudulent disability claims. When faced with these charges, he eventually confessed and cooperated. With all the men pleading guilty in Federal court, this strange arson case abruptly ended.

Weslee King received a brief prison sentence, but the other three men received sentences ranging from four to six years. In my experience, it is very rare to get confessions and guilty pleas from so many, including the property owner, in an arson-for-profit case.

As a strange twist, in 1994, prosecutors charged the wealthy Mizrachi in a scheme where he bribed prison guards with expensive handouts including perfume, cognac, and sneakers worth $150 in exchange for certain benefits including pizza delivery!

In another twist, also in 1994, an arsonist set another fire at the mill complex. However, the man arrested and who pled guilty to this arson set the fire purely for his pleasure.

The mill site remains a vacant lot to this day.

Special thanks to *My Upstate NY Photos*, *The Recorder and The Daily Gazette* (Of Schenectady, NY) for references from articles 1992-1995, present Amsterdam Fire Chief Anthony Agresta, and retired Amsterdam Battalion Chief Walter Martin for his assistance, information and photos used for this story.

CHAPTER 10

King and Queen Restaurant

The best way to burn a restaurant is by creating a friction fire –
rub an insurance policy against the building.

(Author unknown)

I couldn't let this story go untold. It was unusual and interesting. What seemed like merely an investigation of a failed arson attempt, this one ended up involving organized crime, political and corporate corruption plus international intrigue.

Who was responsible for the fire? You make the call. Whereas the last story failed to understand electrical theory while deploying a Rube Goldberg device, this case had its own massive failure.

This case involved the King and Queen Restaurant in downtown Taunton, Massachusetts. Except for a physics miscalculation, the property nearly became a gigantic crater.

Mid-morning on Sunday, June 26, 1983, Mr. and Mrs. Restaurant Owners arrived at their Greek restaurant. They parked in the side parking lot and walked up to the front door. As they prepared to unlock the door, they noticed a strong odor related to natural gas. For those few readers who don't know, natural gas has no odor itself. Manufacturers add an odorant to get people's attention, alerting them to the presence of the gas.

Picture the possibilities for the couple. If they had no part in the attempt to destroy their restaurant, the odor evokes some fear because an explosion may be imminent.

From their location on School Street, a mere look over their left shoulders provided an unrestricted view of the Taunton Fire Department Headquarters. You can imagine a brief discussion between them, but then they could make their way the 150 yards to notify the Fire Department of the possible gas leak.

But what if the owners arrived to prepare for Sunday opening, as usual, thinking the building was already destroyed by then? One can visually imagine them driving toward the restaurant, possibly confused, upset and angry that their place still stood undamaged. Did they know exactly the plan to set the fire? Or did they use a third party to arrange for the fire? Either way, as they stood with their keys in hand to open the front door, their discussion possibly got a little heated.

Since I interviewed the owners multiple times after this incident, I learned the Mrs. had the stronger personality of the two. She definitely wore the pants in the family, making most of the crucial decisions.

With that gas odor and explosion potential, their conversation might have been stressful. "What do we do now? Do we go inside to dismantle the fire set-up, risking an explosion, or do we report it to the fire department? Either way, we'll be taking a chance. Do we gamble with an arrest or an explosion?" They did, in fact, report the gas odor to the fire department.

What firefighters encountered when they entered the building certainly would piss off most anybody, definitely first responders to such a scene. The gas odor smelled so strong. Spending any time in that atmosphere can cause a person to pass out.

Most likely, with so much gas in the building, the atmosphere was too rich for an explosion. This means the ratio mixture of gas to air measured above the upper explosive range. Immediately, the firefighters backed out of the building. The FD notified the gas company, requesting a shutdown of the gas from outside the restaurant.

With the gas shut off and the building made safe, the firefighters re-entered the restaurant to locate the source of the gas leak. Some firefighters checked the kitchen gas appliances on the main floor of the single-story block building. Others headed to the basement, inspecting gas line connections and other appliances like the gas-fired water heater. What they saw forced them out of the structure again. This time they notified the power company to turn off the building's electricity. Simultaneously, the firefighters radioed for their fire investigators even though there was no fire to investigate.

However, the Taunton investigators had plenty to investigate, an attempted fire or explosion. Taunton was one of the earliest cities to form an investigative team. There, they had a Taunton Police detective join with a Taunton firefighter to investigate fires. But this duo realized the complexities presented by this scene with a subsequent criminal investigation far beyond their capability. They called the State Fire Marshal's Office and ATF to work the investigation with them.

I already had a good relationship with the Taunton investigators because they attended classes I taught. They also became members in the Massachusetts Chapter of the International Association of Arson Investigators, where I was active for many years. Welcoming their invitation to assist with this investigation, I couldn't wait to sink my teeth into this juicy case. The puzzle presented by each investigation is what I loved about my job.

However, the timing of this investigation couldn't have been worse for me. Although the massive conspiracy arson case I was working in Boston was in a slight lull, it still commanded much of my attention. Everybody else in our ATF Arson Group was busy with other investigations. In addition to my present caseload, within a month, another arson-for-profit fire piled another investigation onto my desk.

Let me paint the picture of the King and Queen for you. The interior of the restaurant looked neat and orderly. Inside the double glass doors to the right was the dining room. There was a bar area located to the rear of the dining area. Through swinging doors, a sizeable kitchen covered the back section of the building. Along the Side B wall (left side from the front of the structure) was the cooking line with many appliances, including a large multi-burner gas range. Here we found the gas leak. Someone had mechanically disconnected the gas line by detaching the hard pipe stub at the backside of the range.

This was no accident. Because of the way two gas fittings join, it is necessary to use two wrenches, one to hold each fitting in order to loosen the fittings. Perhaps the person who disconnected the line figured that with the building destroyed by an explosion and fire, nobody would discover this disconnection. And, if found, the perpetrator assumed investigators would believe this incident was accidental.

However, in reality, most investigators would know this was an intentional mechanical disconnection. Upon careful inspection, evidence of an explosion causing the disengagement is often obvious. The forceful ripping of the connection severely damaging the fitting threads is a dead giveaway. Had this attempt only involved a disconnected gas line, I would not have included this case within this book.

Taking a walk down the basement stairs revealed another true Rube Goldberg incendiary device. About halfway down the stairs, a two-inch by four-inch wood stud was partially laying on a step cantilevered outward into midair. A screw positioned near the end of the stud had a nylon fishing line tied to it. That line extended up to the open-framed ceiling, draped over a copper water line. It stretched down to a semi-clear plastic gallon water bottle that was suspended in the air along with the stud.

Another nylon filament line, also tied to the same board, again extended up and over the copper pipe. This tautly stretched line connected to a single pole light switch controlled the basement lights. The gallon bottle initially was full of gasoline. The torch made a pinhole in the bottle's bottom. Crumpled newspapers were on the stairs below the suspended bottle to collect the gasoline drippings.

The plan was for gasoline to drip from the bottle, causing a shift in weight distribution. When enough gasoline flowed from the bottle, the wood stud would shift downward, pulling on the fishing line, ultimately flipping the light switch to the "on" position. If that doesn't sound like much of a device, there was more.

There were three bare bulb porcelain light fixtures mounted on the unfinished basement ceiling. The arsonist tied several matchbooks with the matches exposed against each bare light bulb. Gasoline-soaked newspapers encircled each bulb.

Thus, when the time-delay stairway device functioned, the light switch activation energizes the lights. Once the bulbs become hot, the heat energy ignites the matches, lighting the gasoline-soaked papers. These then drop to the floor, igniting nearby combustibles.

The ensuing fire would ignite the fugitive natural gas vapors that escaped from the disconnected gas line on the first floor, causing a major fire or most likely, a catastrophic explosion. There is one prerequisite. The gas vapors must be within the flammable or explosive range. Ignition of this device would have resulted in massive destruction of the building with life-threatening conditions to anyone nearby.

Now, you can begin to understand the dilemma Mr. and Mrs. Restaurant Owners faced as they stood outside the door to their restaurant if they were part of the plan. One can also understand why the firefighters retreated from the building, making the structure safe before the investigation started.

The device failed to function because the perpetrator apparently neglected to test the device fully before enacting the plan. The gasoline in the full jug initially squirted or flowed out the small hole in the jug's bottom. But the forces of gravity, and the effects of air pressure as the liquid level decreases, caused the flow from the hole to diminish to merely a trickle. Eventually, the liquid leak dwindled to an occasional drip with virtually no liquid lost over a period of several hours. Physics doomed this intricate device.

Had this fire, and likely explosion, erupted as planned, it is doubtful investigators would find any basement device components. However, experienced fire and explosion scene investigators likely would look at all gas appliances and their connections. That's when they would recognize someone intentionally disconnected the gas range fittings.

As you can see, the scene was very unusual. It was the most unique scene I ever witnessed in my 38 years of scene examinations. One more aspect at this scene was significant and bizarre to us.

At first glance, everything in the dining room looked normal, ready for business. There were 20 tables, sized mostly to fit four customers, with a few smaller tables for two. Altogether, there were 74 chairs, those dark brown wood chairs with the curved back. The seats and chair backs all had red vinyl padding. Each chair, tidily arranged at tables, where they would be after closing the previous night, was ready for the new day's patrons.

This is where normal ended. I can't recall exactly how we discovered someone had sliced every single seat cushion with a sharp tool. The cuts were virtually identical, two slices covered most cushions in the shape of the letter "y".

Visual analysis of the cuts showed a right-handed person began with the left side of the "y", top to bottom, using the same motion to the longer right side of the letter. There appeared to have been no hesitation in the slices, just smooth duplications. Then, this person placed each chair in its proper place at the table.

This begs for some obvious questions. Who took the time to slice each chair? Why was the same configuration sliced into each chair? What was the motivation behind this action? Who would have placed each chair neatly back at every table? I felt it was more likely the restaurant owner positioned each chair in place as normally done nightly, whereas someone with vengeance on their mind would have plundered and pillaged the dining room.

We collected every piece of the incendiary device as evidence. I saved the gas line fittings for fingerprinting. The lab technicians also did tool mark analysis on the fittings in case we located the tools used to disconnect them. We also kept the water jug, the gasoline, the nylon filament, the wood stud, all the newspapers, the light bulbs and matches.

Interviews of the restaurant owners provided us with enough verifiable information, allowing us to conclude they didn't personally set up the device in their restaurant. Still, we continued having our suspicions about them being responsible for attempting to destroy their business.

Without asking, they readily and repeatedly offered their beliefs that the previous owner was the person with the sole motive to burn the building. They insisted it had to be him. Mrs. pointed to the chairs as prime evidence. After all, his first name was Yiannis, hence all the chairs slashed with his first initial. What reason would Yiannis have for wanting to burn their business?

In the year since the new owners operated the business, the revenue they took in was half of what Yiannis' books showed he made during the three years before selling the restaurant to them. The Restaurant Owners had taken Yiannis to court over this discrepancy in numbers. They alleged he kept two sets of books, cooking the numbers in one to make the business look far better than it was.

The owners stated they had changed the door locks after they purchased the restaurant. We confirmed with a locksmith the owners had replaced the locks purchasing six keys at the time. Slight problem with that last fact; the owners said they only had two keys. When confronted, the owners stumbled a bit. They located three more keys before suddenly locating the sixth key two weeks later. Yiannis did not have one of them. The firefighters found all the doors locked when they arrived at the scene.

With the locks secured as evidence, the lab conducted a forensic analysis of the interior of the cylinders. When someone picks a lock, their actions scratch marks into the metal. The key made for the lock runs over the same surface, leaving wear patterns. A tool mark examination can determine that somebody had picked the lock. The analysis, in this case, showed nobody had fooled with the locks.

Two of us interviewed Yiannis at his pizza shop. He was very forthcoming. Not appearing nervous, Yiannis answered every question satisfactorily. He stated the new King and Queen owners didn't know how to run a restaurant. Since this was their first restaurant, Yiannis explained they cut too many corners, and they had a poor chef. We also verified his alibi for Saturday night.

As the days and weeks passed, the multiple laboratory analyses from the items sent to the lab produced no other usable evidentiary value. We found it hard to believe we didn't get one identifiable latent fingerprint, even on the newspapers.

One weak piece of information we developed was the brother of one of the Restaurant Owners frequently went fishing. Maybe he was the source who provided the nylon filament line used to make the device in the restaurant. We interviewed him, but we got nowhere. We couldn't even get enough information for probable cause for a search warrant.

After a couple weeks of investigation, we put the attempted arson story in the local newspaper. We hoped a reader would respond to the article. Only days after the story appeared, an eyewitness came forward. He told us he didn't attach any importance to his observation until he read the article. His information wasn't too exciting.

This person related that after midnight on the Saturday night in question he was walking on School Street. While passing the restaurant's front door, a man started coming out that door. Apparently, this person must have spotted the passerby. The witness saw him back away from the glass, hiding in the shadows. He thought he may have seen the person's face, but he offered no additional details.

After conferring with other investigators, we tried something for the first and last time for me. We wanted to hypnotize the witness attempting to draw more details locked in his head. The United States Attorney's Office gave their blessing, although they expressed skepticism about the value and admissibility of any information garnered through this process. If the witness could describe the man's face, then we would use a sketch artist. Maybe this would lead us to a suspect.

The Boston Police Department had a detective experienced with hypnotism. He explained the entire process to us. Further, he stated he was not a miracle worker, but he added this tool may work. What would we have to lose?

But, the hypnotism session was disappointing when, again, we received no useful information. The witness only recalled seeing an olive-skinned man who wore a short-sleeved flowered shirt with dark hairy arms, but he could not describe the man's face. He added nothing further.

We offered the polygraph test to Yiannis and to Mr. and Mrs. Restaurant Owners. We explained that, if they passed the test, we would rule them out as being involved with the attempted arson and we would move on.

They wanted to know the flip side of that coin. What if the test showed they were deceptive? As with most people faced with taking a polygraph exam, they expressed nervousness and concerns about the validity of the polygraph. I explained we would re-interview them about any discrepancies in their responses.

Most courts don't allow the results of the exam. Yiannis took the polygraph exam and passed. The owners declined to partake in the experience.

Many more hours were expended conferring with people in all walks of life familiar with the Greek ways of life, including those running restaurants. I learned Mr. Owner was an illegal alien until he married Mrs. Owner, a United States citizen, a marriage of convenience.

We learned this Greek immigrant became desperate to pay his bills, falling deeper into debt because of his poor business skills. The insurance proceeds would have alleviated his problems and he could have made a profit by selling the land after the fire.

Because of knocking on doors and speaking to potential witnesses, two anonymous phone calls came into the office. The callers named two people as the arsonists who tried to burn the King and Queen. One of the calls was traced to a small college in New York City centered in the Greek community, but the callers were never identified.

We could not get good information to connect the alleged named torches to any fires. Without the benefit of the yet-to-be-developed internet, all we could do is run their names through NCIC (National Crime Information Center).

Fear of retaliation kept anyone from coming forward in person to become a witness because we learned there was an organized crime group behind burning restaurants for cash-strapped Greek owners. The group even torched other restaurants that were competitors for certain Greek restaurants.

In an effort to get more information about our fire and others, we sent a memo describing the strange incendiary device to police and fire departments throughout the United States. The Rhode Fire Marshal's Office responded. They, too, were investigating a series of fires at Greek-owned restaurants. The only problem was their fires had so much damage, they never identified exactly how the fires were set.

Because of the demands put on me and the entire ATF Arson Group by the 264 fires caused by the guys in the *Burn Boston Burn* case, only sporadic investigative time could be devoted to the King and Queen fire. Additional information developed involved bank fraud, gambling debts, IRS and US Immigration.

Now, I hate to leave you hanging, but that's exactly what happened to us and this investigation. No further usable information or evidence was developed to solidify a stronger case. We tried to interest prosecutors at both the Federal and State levels (yes, we shopped the case around.)

There were no takers. I imagine a few readers have thoughts on where the investigation could have gone. It was frustrating to be so close with so much physical evidence, but not a perfect enough case the attorneys thought worth prosecuting. With the near disaster caused by the attempted arson and the potential significance of breaking into an organized arson ring, this case should have been prosecuted. Who knows where arrests could have led? Sometimes it seems the prosecutors don't realize they are part of the investigative team, a vital part to put pressure on defendants to cooperate.

You make the call. Based solely on the information I provided, who do you think was responsible for this near-disaster?

CHAPTER 11

Serial Arsonist? Lance Lalumiere

Jefferson, New Hampshire is a bucolic hamlet of about 850 people nestled within the northern shadow of Mt. Washington, the highest peak in the White Mountains' Presidential Range. For outsiders, many know Jefferson well for its Christmas-themed park, Santa's Village. Otherwise, it is a sleepy place with only four roads traversing in and out of town.

But throughout much of 1988, Jefferson became an infamous hub of activity because of some 26 arson fires during the middle six months of the year. The area suddenly became flooded with firefighters who found themselves busier during these few months than they would normally be in six years. New Hampshire State Troopers patrolled the crossroads all night long, stopping anything that moved. Because of its small size, the town had no police department. The State Police enforced the law in town.

Fear was in the air. Residents kept lights on at their properties all night long. Many hardly slept at all. Most didn't leave their homes for fear theirs would be the next to burn. People kept their shotguns and rifles at the ready. Trespassers beware. Any moving shadow in someone's yard could become a target.

In May, Jefferson volunteer firefighter William Perkins spotted smoke coming from the Skywood Motel across the street from his house. Jefferson has an all-volunteer fire department. He ran over to assist with the extinguishment of the fire that gutted several rooms. Just three days later, as he was readying for bed, he heard a vehicle screeching away from his house. Perkins ran to investigate, "When I opened the stairway door, the flames just exploded toward me."

He barely managed to get his wife, two children, an elderly tenant, and his 76-year-old father out of the house. From that point on, Perkins stayed up nights, armed and alert.

When interviewed he said, "I'm up every night, and I will be until he's caught. I can live on a couple of hours of sleep as long as I have to. I've got a family to protect."

Another long-time Jefferson resident, elderly widow Helen Merrill, had been keeping guard from the front porch of her 100-year-old large wood-frame home. Mrs. Merrill finally relaxed when her son, his wife, and three of her grandchildren came from out of state to stay with her for a visit in August. Shortly after going to bed, around 12:30 a.m., someone set her house on fire.

When they noticed smoke, the entire family frantically escaped the house. Helen darted back into the house to get her handbag and some mementos she had stored in a bag ever since the fires began several months before, while the others stood watching the fire rapidly spread. After she returned outside, she and her family watched their home burn to the ground.

Quoted in the article, her son, Albert, said, "I looked back as flames engulfed the place and saw my whole childhood, my whole life, burning up in front of my face. We've always had a home to come to and now it's ashes, just ashes." Aside from the few items, Helen retrieved from her home, there was nothing else left. Victims of an unknown assailant. To them, and others like them, the fires were senseless acts of violence.

The Jeffersonians weren't used to crime like this arson spree. Besides being fearful of their surroundings for the first time in their lives, the people became suspicious of each other. They wondered, often aloud, who among them was the arsonist? Could it be my neighbor? The store cashier? The volunteer firefighter?

It didn't take a sharp investigator to think the torch was someone who lived in town. The targeted buildings were often occupied houses. The arsonist set nearly every fire after midnight. With over 20 fires under the arsonist's belt, without getting caught, this was a sign the fire setter knew his way around town very well. Who else knew Jefferson well enough to have the confidence, the balls or some mania to crawl around the town in the middle of the night? Everywhere one turned, the charred remnants of the fires fed the fears and vigilantism of the townspeople.

John Harrigan, the editor of the local weekly newspaper, finally ventured out to dinner with his family, after staying home nights for several weeks. When he returned home, Harrigan found the rear wall of his kitchen heavily charred. The outstanding work of the local firefighters saved the rest of his house.

Harrigan expressed further anxiety that the torch may have been watching him to know he left his house. Only a local person knew the routines of other locals. Harrigan added, "The whole town is on edge."

The Town of Jefferson, having no police department of their own, called the State Police and the State Fire Marshals to conduct surveillances, examine the fire scenes and conduct interviews. The Troopers patrolled the streets at night, hoping to spot the arsonist. They stopped vehicles so they could identify the occupants and determine their reason for driving through town. One of my friends, Dave Wheeler, was one of those Troopers.

By mid-summer, with the fires continuing, the New Hampshire Fire Marshal's Office requested the help of the Boston office of ATF. Only weeks earlier, when ATF noticed the string of arson fires, we offered assistance to the New Hampshire State Police. But initially, they said thanks, but no thanks. However, as the fire-setting persisted, they called us with their plea for help.

I was getting close to graduating from the ATF Certified Fire Investigator (CFI) program, and, by this time, I had been in the ATF Arson Task Force Group for over six years. So my supervisor assigned me to work on this case along with another member of our group, Tom Perret, the case agent. Tom had recently completed a six-month-long arson investigation in northern Vermont. He wasn't pleased he again had to be away for an indeterminate period.

We packed our bags to head to the North Country. Jefferson was three hours from my house, not a great distance, but the investigation could take a lot of long and strange hours. Upon arrival, we met at Troop F with the state and local people to discuss the case and to get us up to speed. Troop F was where we attended briefings every morning and some evenings.

We reviewed the chronology of the fires, the origin and cause determinations of each fire, and discussed future investigative steps. The Staties already had done a good job mapping the fires, trying to establish a geographical pattern. They also had a rudimentary profile of the arsonist or arsonists who were wreaking havoc on this town.

The profile sounded similar to many others. The subject was likely a white male (which was not a stretch in this part of New Hampshire since a male of color was pretty rare), probably 18-25 years old, with only a high school education and a manual, low-paying job. Although the arsonist's motive was unknown, it appeared he was striking out for some real or perceived wrong under the revenge category. They had no serious suspects.

Something was totally striking and unique concerning the cause of these fires. Certainly, these fires were all classified as arsons, intentionally set fires.

However, fire investigation books define fire cause as "the circumstances, conditions, or agencies that bring together a fuel, ignition source, and oxidizer (such as air or oxygen) resulting in a fire or combustion explosion."

New Hampshire State Fire Marshals conducted most of the origin and cause examinations during this fire spree. The physical location or point where the arsonist set these fires was often easy to define. This arsonist always set these blazes on an exterior wall, out of view from any nearby street.

But what was unique was the arsonist took an unusual amount of time setting these fires, either standing, kneeling, or sitting down while wielding some sort of torch to ignite the combustible house wall, burning a focused hole through the exterior siding.

In all of my years of fire investigation, I had never seen such a manner of setting a fire, never mind over 20 fires. This method showed some level of comfort with setting the fires. Usually, an arsonist would be in more of a rush setting the fire, then escape from the area. Was this an indicator the arsonist was a townie?

After our briefing, I teamed up with seasoned fire investigator, State Fire Marshal John Southwell. John was an affable guy, great to work with always. As a member of the Fire Marshal's Office from 1986 into the early 2000s, he eventually became the state's first accelerant detection canine handler.

Tom Perret did one thing he always did best. He organized the investigation. It was disjointed and a complete mess.

By now, there were nearly 20 fires, but Southwell had written not a single origin and cause report. To his credit, the sheer number of fires overwhelmed him. He had so much work, but so little time.

Tom had a heart-to-heart talk with him. He explained to John that if we suddenly identified a suspect, we had no crime because he hadn't completed his reports delineating the cause of the fires. John locked himself in an office to get the reports done.

When we freed John from his desk, we rode together every day I was in New Hampshire. As fate would have it, he and I were in the right place at the right time.

On the second or third full day of working the area, John took me to view several of the charred fire scenes and to conduct some interviews. About mid-day, a caller reported a house fire in an adjacent town. The time of day didn't fit the temporal pattern of the other fires set in the middle of the night.

John did all the driving since he knew the area pretty well. We raced over to the fire, arriving just as the first crew of firefighters was aiming water through a gable end second-floor window of a wood-framed dwelling. Other firefighters walked in the front door, checking for any people who may still be inside.

Aside from the fact this was a daytime fire, the origin of this fire was in the interior. Flames were blowing out a second-floor window, but there was no fire on the exterior. We quickly learned firefighters found the house locked upon their arrival. Eventually, John and I got inside and determined the fire cause was accidental.

The very next day, John and I headed to another interview. It was a partly cloudy, cool, somewhat crisp day that typically invades northern New Hampshire as the summer heat fades. It was late morning. My recollection is we were driving northbound, approaching the stop sign at the junction of the main east-west road, Route 2. It was one of those days when I even remember exactly what I was wearing. In those days, we Federal Agents always wore a shirt and tie, but the rest of my wardrobe was a summer-weight khaki suit with soft Rockport shoes.

John alerted me to a pickup truck flying toward us down a hill on a dirt road across the intersection. He immediately recognized the vehicle as belonging to the Jefferson Volunteer Fire Department Assistant Fire Chief.

Southwell said, "He's in a real rush. Let's see what's up." We crossed the intersection to intercept the Chief. He told us they just learned of a structure fire in town. He told us the address. My tour guide knew where it was, so we sped off in that direction.

A couple of minutes later we spotted a narrow, energetic column of dark gray smoke rising above the tree line. The smoke helped to direct our last couple of turns. As we headed along a dirt driveway, past a large fenced-in corral, straight-ahead we observed a neat L-shaped one-and-a-half-story log cabin. Smoke emanated from a small front porch near the A/B corner.

In firefighter parlance, the four sides of a typical building are designated by the letters, A, B, C, D, and in some places by numbers, so to have a uniform method for fire officers and firefighters to lessen confusion when speaking of a building. Usually, but not always, the front is Side A facing the street or parking area where the firefighters would approach the structure or park. We describe the remaining sides in a clockwise direction. I once investigated a fatal fire in a 5-sided building that wasn't the Pentagon. Side E was the fifth designation.

John pulled his car toward the A/B corner, well away from the house so as not to interfere with arriving fire apparatus. We were the first responders.

Between us and the front porch was a white male, in his early 20s, bent over at the waist, coughing, spitting up, and retching with slight vomit. He had on a t-shirt, blue jeans and remarkably, a pair of knee-high black fire boots. We both jumped from the car and ran to check on the guy's condition. Was he a firefighter? A victim? An arsonist?

The male wasn't able to talk at the moment, but once satisfied his condition appeared temporary and not serious, John and I flew into action. Small flames just above the floor level of the covered porch were climbing the logs within the L-shaped corner. We pushed open the front door that was already ajar. To my right, I saw more small flames on the inside wall. There was only a light hazy smoke condition throughout the open kitchen and living room areas in front of me.

Back on the front porch, I grabbed a garden hose, turned it on and directed the spray toward the fire area. John opened several windows from the inside. Just then, the first firefighters and apparatus pulled up to the site. John and I left the firefighting to them as we changed our hats going into fire investigation mode.

We interviewed the mystery man. He identified himself as Lance Lalumiere. The log cabin belonged to his brother, Michael. Lance told us he uses the house to take a shower as he lived nearby in a trailer with no electricity or running water. When he drove up to the building, shortly before we arrived, he discovered the fire. He had gone into the house to check on the progress of the fire, where he gulped down some smoke which caused his sickly condition.

I asked Lance why he had on fire boots. He replied, "I was on the volunteer fire department, but they let me go. The only things I had left were my boots." Further, I inquired why he took the time to put the boots on, to which he stated, "I had nothing else. I had to protect myself." Looking at Southwell, I shrugged my shoulders and gave him a quizzical look.

By this time, Tom Perret and a cadre of investigators arrived on the scene. They had been sitting in a local restaurant eating an early lunch when this fire call caused them to drop everything so they could

New Hampshire State Fire Marshal John Southwell and his canine, Andre.

respond. Now, Tom teamed up with a Trooper to further interview Lance.

After the firefighters completed the extinguishment of the fire, John and I spent a few minutes examining the scene. With the limited size of this fire, the origin was the area where we saw the fire when we arrived on site. Around the third and fourth logs above the porch floor, there were three distinct, pinpoint burn holes clear through the narrow section where two logs meet. The interior damage matched that of the outside, with the exception that the char damage showed the fire originated on the exterior side.

There were no inherent potential ignition sources in the area, meaning there were no competent heat sources there, such as electrical components, heating systems, candles, or even focused sunlight as through a magnifying glass. This very specific origin with three distinct and separate burn holes through wood logs required a long-term pointed ignition source such as a torch.

As any of you who have started a fire in a fireplace or campfire know, it usually takes additional lightweight fuels such as newspaper and kindling wood to ignite wood logs. We found no residues of such fuels at Michael Lalumiere's log cabin home. There were only those three burn holes that barely spread beyond the holes.

Lance had driven over to his brother's house in his old, beat-up little station wagon, which he had parked behind the house. John and I walked over to the vehicle to peer through the windows. In the rear cargo compartment in plain view was one of those handheld BernzOmatic-style propane torches. It is not something many people carry in their car.

Suddenly, we felt like we were getting close to putting the cuffs on Lance. It certainly looked like he had the opportunity and the means to set this fire. Yet, we didn't want to jump to a hasty conclusion.

Daily, we investigators discussed the motive for these arsons. One theory was the motive had a sexual connection. Tom thought this was probable. We always ask ourselves questions like, "What caused someone to set these fires? What changed in their life to cause them to act out in this manner? Why were certain buildings targeted?"

Tom was busy interviewing Lance trying to answer some of these questions. His approach with Lance was to tell him, "Look, I'm from out of town. I know nothing about this place or these fires. Tell me a story."

And Lance did. Lance said he regularly ate dinner at Michael's house, which Michael's wife of 10 years usually prepared. She also washed Lance's clothes and acted very nice and friendly toward Lance. She made him shower there because he usually smelled worse than a goat.

Lance said in the spring Michael split with his wife and he took on a new girlfriend. He did not get along with her. Lance was pretty upset about the fact Michael dumped his wife. Was it coincidental the fires began within weeks after Lance lost his "mother", caretaker, and girl crush?

Southwell and I interrupted Tom to ask Lance about the torch. In vague terms, he again described his actions that morning and his discovery of the fire. He explained he used the torch to help people with frozen pipes during the winter, and he never took the torch out of his car after the season ended.

Now is a good time to interject that Lance wasn't the sharpest tool in the shed. Besides what we could discern from speaking to him, we soon found out from his family and friends he was a bit slow with a low I.Q.

After discussing this with the State Troopers, they used a tracking dog, a bloodhound, to get someone's scent who may have cut through the woods next to the corral. Maybe that would lead us to something. We wanted to leave no stone unturned.

The State Police had access to an experienced tracker. When he arrived at the property, I spoke to him. He told me he trains his bloodhound constantly and has used him in hundreds of investigations. We decided not to give his dog the scent specific to Lance, but let him combine ground and air scents to track the scent of a person who had passed over the area.

I watched as the handler led his dog to the far end of the corral. Almost immediately, the dog appeared to alert to something because he started along a path between the corral and the woods. For a moment, it was comical watching a horse in the corral running to the fence to see what was going on. The horse lowered his head toward the tracking canine, which looked up a couple times at the intruder, but he continued into the woods out of our sight.

After about 30 minutes, the dog and handler returned. He informed us the dog tracked directly to a rickety old trailer about three-quarters of a mile away, but no one was there. The handler didn't know the trailer belonged to Lance. He divulged this revelation out of earshot of Lance, who was still hanging around shooting the bull with his old buddies from the volunteer fire department.

Southwell and I approached Lance to ask him a few more questions. We asked him if he used that trail to walk between his trailer and Michael's house. He replied he rarely used it. When asked when he may have used the trail last, Lance said it was before the previous winter, possibly November.

The handler informed me his dog could pick up a scent two or three months old. He added with the winter snows and the passage of nine to ten months, it was not feasible for his dog to track someone from that long ago.

Now we had to make a decision regarding Lance's short-term situation. Tom asked Lance for permission to search his trailer. He consented. Perret went with Lance and a State Trooper. Tom said the search was the worst he ever conducted.

With no running water in the trailer and Lance's lack of cleanliness, the inside conditions of the trailer were repulsive. The toilet ran over with piss and crap. Lance's dog never used the toilet. The trailer served as his bathroom. The smell was nauseating. Flies were everywhere. But otherwise, the search was successful.

Tom found maps with 17 fires plotted on the maps. When he asked Lance about the maps, he admitted drawing them. Any reason for drawing them? But he only answered that he was curious about the fires.

Tom asked him to come to Troop F to take a polygraph exam just relating to Michael's fire. Lance agreed. He drove himself over as he was not under arrest. Once there, we interviewed him further about Michael's fire and about the other fires that had occurred around town over the past several months.

The State Police polygrapher was Detective Dave Crawford, assigned to the Major Crimes Unit. When he arrived, we briefed him on the recent happenings. He quickly planned his shortlist of questions to ask Lance. It was a rather simple task. Did you set the fire at your brother's home? Do you know who set the fire? This was the line of questioning.

Lance failed the polygraph exam miserably. Detective Crawford, a highly qualified interviewer, had questioned many people, both innocent and guilty, involving all sorts of crimes. He interviewed Lance further, asking him about the discrepancies between the test results and his responses. But he got nowhere. Talking to him was like speaking to a brick wall.

One simple statement from Crawford elicited an interesting response from Lance. "Lance, you set your brother's fire today." Lance's verbal response was "No," while he shook his head up and down, yes. When you try doing this purposely, it can be difficult. But when done subconsciously, it is effortless. It was a subliminal admission of guilt. Tom watched this questioning through the office window. His jaw dropped when he heard and saw Lance's reply.

We needed to speak with Lance's brother, Michael Lalumiere, for at least two reasons. During fire investigations, it is often imperative to speak with the owner and/or occupant of a dwelling. This is to learn about pre-fire conditions and about the activities of any people who had been in the building, including when they were last there.

Since we determined the fire had been intentionally set, we also had to do our due diligence to learn as much as possible about who set this fire be it Lance, Michael, or some other arsonist. We wanted to explore potential motives for someone to burn Michael's house in broad daylight, outside the temporal pattern created by the Jefferson arsonist. More particularly, we wanted to know if Michael had any idea why his brother would want to burn his house.

At this point, only the handful of investigators knew these fires were being set with a blowtorch. We were soon going to divulge this little secret to a civilian.

After Michael arrived, Southwell and I sat with him in a small interview room. Once we asked him the usual questions concerning a fire, we determined Michael was a hard-working guy who had been at work all day since early in the morning. Thus, we eliminated Michael as having anything to do with setting the fire. We described to him what we knew about his fire.

Michael explained Lance's living situation to us, including his upbringing. Lance's mother had thrown him out of the house in the middle of the winter a couple of years earlier. He was mostly alone and a loner. Michael told us about his ex-wife and Lance's relationship.

We later learned from an acquaintance of Lance that Lance wanted to "jump" Michael's wife. He not only had sexual fantasies about her, but he also had powerful feelings for her. She also played the role of a mother figure to him.

Once we laid out some of the evidence for Michael, after his initial doubts his kid brother could be an arsonist, he became a believer. It was then we solicited his help to speak with Lance. Michael was fully onboard. He realized Lance was in big trouble. As a straight shooter, Michael wanted to do the right thing and get his brother to confess his wrongdoings to him.

We sat Michael with Lance in a glass-walled interview room. We watched as Michael's brotherly love was on display. They sat at a small table, virtually knee to knee, with Michael's hand often reaching out to touch his brother's hand or arm. He tried to explain the facts of life to Lance, that his life was about to change. Michael tried different tactics, love and tough love, tender and anger. But Lance never caved. He never confessed to his brother.

✳   ✳   ✳

During the weeks following Lance's interview, there were no more fires in Jefferson. We ATF Agents headed home as this investigation was now a local matter that was under control. The investigation continued to concentrate on Lance. Aside from him being present at his brother's burning house, with the torch in his car, and a motive for him to set the house afire, the evidence against Lance for setting the other Jefferson blazes was weak.

In those days, there were no security cameras capturing the arsonist's travels. There was nothing connecting Lance or any other person to the fires. Plus, there were no GPS or cell phones, which would have only provided limited information anyway since the arsonist set all the fires within this small North Country town.

As a loner, Lance most likely never spoke to anyone about these fires and acted alone. Considering hardships in Lance's life, including his mother throwing him out, the fire department cutting him loose, and losing his brother's wife, it's no wonder Lance didn't trust anyone.

This investigation took an innovative turn. Detective Dave Crawford, who conducted Lance's polygraph examination, took it upon himself to make this case. He developed a rapport with Lance, so he wanted to build on that fledgling relationship.

Over a three-week period, Dave spent nearly 80 hours with Lance. Their time together was friendly, relaxed. They even went fishing. All the while, Dave befriended Lance, growing closer to him. Lance finally came to trust Dave, confessing to 16 fires. There were 21 fires in total in Jefferson during the spring and summer.

On Wednesday, October 12, 1988, the State Police arrested 23-year-old Lance Lalumiere for setting fire to his brother's log cabin. Authorities subsequently charged Lance with setting another 15 fires during the spring and summer in Jefferson.

Police also charged another young man from Jefferson with setting a fire in a nearby town, but no information ever connected him to the other unsolved fires in Jefferson. Nobody was injured in the string of fires that terrorized the town, but property damage was extensive.

Special Agent Perret wrote a case report that delineated the totality of the evidence against Lance. The State of New Hampshire never called upon ATF to further assist with the case.

Most of the 800-plus residents of Jefferson did not believe Lance set these fires. Some said he wasn't smart enough to set these fires and get away with the crimes for so long. A fund raised money for his defense. The Jefferson Volunteer Fire department even raised money for Lance. Maybe they, too, didn't believe Lance was setting the fires. Or maybe they just felt sorry for him.

Before the trial, Lance recanted his confession. He went on trial in June 1989. During the trial, the State relied heavily on Lance's confession. The defense countered that the police coerced the confession from an illiterate and dyslexic man. The jurors wrangled over the veracity of his confession.

After the three-week trial in Coos County Superior Court, in less than two days, Lance was acquitted by a jury of his peers. Here's a short example about the type of people who made up his peers. We knew of one man who was both the father and grandfather of a child, while his son was both the brother and father of the same infant. Confusing? The man had a Canadian maid and a young adult son when he impregnated the maid. When the baby was born the father took on the role of grandfather while his adult son, who was the brother of the baby, assumed the role of the baby's father. Now that is only an example of one person. I'm not saying that all the jurors had similar stories.

Following his acquittal, townspeople expressed fresh fears over multiple issues. Would there be more fires? Will someone attack Lance? Will the police go after Lance again?

With the trial behind him, Lance moved in with another brother, Rene. Lance later married. Whether Lance had been setting those fires or some other unidentified arsonist was doing it, for whatever reason, there were no more arsons in Jefferson or the surrounding towns. Amazing!

Special thanks to retired Special Agent Thomas Perret and retired New Hampshire State Trooper David Wheeler for their help with this story.

The New York Times Archives (See the article in its original context from October 14, 1988).

Washington Post, 7/02/1989 FORMER FIREFIGHTER ACQUITTED OF SETTING NEW HAMPSHIRE FIRES,

People.com by People Staff December 26, 1988, 12:00 p.m.

CHAPTER 12

The God and Country Serial Arsonist

A light snow had coated the untreated surfaces, including the long semi-circular driveway that curled behind the large single-story commercial building. The 75-year-old security guard was still working long past his prime to supplement his income and to keep himself from going stir crazy just sitting around at home. Still on the ball, while on his rounds, he immediately noticed the dual tire tracks heading up the slight hill of the driveway.

The guard steered his vehicle onto the drive to copy the tire tracks. As he rounded past the left-rear corner of the business, the guard saw an older dark-colored car parked about midway down the length of the 200-foot building. The headlights of the guard's car highlighted a man standing right against the rear exterior wall of the building, a few feet from the vehicle.

There was nothing to indicate the man had just stopped there to take a piss. Rather, his right arm, partially obstructed from view, extended into the building through a broken window. Caught with his hand in the proverbial cookie jar, the unidentified male hurriedly retracted his arm from the opening, scurried around to his driver's side door, and drove off as fast as the traction allowed.

He got away, but not before the security guard noted the car's rear license tag.

*   *   *

Suddenly, a series of churches south of Boston were being burned. For four-plus years, from 1989 to 1993, this area had been the subject of over 30 structural arson fires. These churches were of several denominations, Baptist, Methodist, Lutheran and Protestant. Most were considerably smaller than the Catholic churches of the area. And no Jewish temples, Muslim mosques or other denominations, often targets of hate crimes, were touched.

Churches in New England were rarely targets of intentionally set fires during this time. Hatred or revenge against religious institutions in the Boston area was not common.

There was a fire at the St. James Lutheran Church in Canton. There was another fire at a Bridgewater church, and another at the Calvary Baptist Church in Hanson.

Another series of arsons also occurred in veteran organizations, American Legion Posts and Veterans of Foreign Wars Halls. The perpetrator (s) attacked targets in cities and towns spanning an area of 15 miles by 20 miles. At least 10 different towns experienced these fires.

During this period, I was working closely with the State Fire Marshal's Office, especially the South Team. Their territory covered south of Boston including Norfolk, Plymouth, Bristol, Barnstable (Cape Cod) and Dukes and Nantucket (the islands) Counties. I was fortunate to be friends with and work with MA State Trooper (later Sergeant) Michael Cherven. Mike lived in Foxborough, the next town over from where I lived in Walpole.

We had worked on many fire cases together over a 10-year period. In the Boston ATF Arson Task Force since 1982, I had developed several liaisons with State and local law enforcement and fire department members over the years. This is what we did at ATF, work with locals. Without them, we were nothing. Most fires were local jurisdiction responsibility. However, some fire investigations were beyond the state and local capabilities. My job was to work with and assist state and local investigators on fires within their communities.

By now, I had also become a Certified Fire Investigator, working within the debris, the rubble, and the charred remains of fire and explosion scenes to determine the origin and cause of the incident. Besides Trooper Cherven, I frequently worked alongside local investigators like Westwood Fire Lt. Billy Scoble (later Chief), Norwood Firefighter Bill Turner and Canton Fire Lt. Tim Ronayne (later Chief), all in Norfolk County.

They did me a favor by calling me to their fires so I could see more fires and learn from their experience. Each fire presented a new set of circumstances, new challenges. I got to see a variety of fires ranging from incipient stage fires to near-total destruction disasters.

The local guys got something out of having me present. As my training hours mounted, I shared my learning and training, plus I gave them an extra set of eyes and hands. We worked side by side through both cold and heat. We often trained together, and we occasionally had a drink or two together. Just friends with a common love for our work.

This string of arsons that hit the South Shore of Massachusetts had a lot in common. Someone set all these fires under the cover of darkness, most of them set after midnight, but before dawn. The origin and the cause scenarios were nearly identical. Whoever was setting these fires drove their vehicle right up to the target building, where they broke a rear window, poured a small amount of gasoline through the window and lit the fires with an open flame.

There was never a rock, brick or anything left behind that was used to break the windows. That meant the arsonist carried the tool or breaking object with him or her.

At the time of this investigation, profiling of an arsonist was still fairly early in its infancy. Profiling is the use of personal characteristics or behavior patterns to make generalizations about a person. Law enforcement uses these characteristics to determine whether a person may be engaged in illegal activity.

The profile, in this case, sounded similar to other persons of interest I would eventually encounter in future cases. The arsonist was likely a white male, between the ages of 18-25, who has under-performed in life. An analysis of his high school history would show very little extracurricular activity, not much in the way of sports or club credits, if any. He probably did not attend college and he most likely had a menial job, not one where he needed much skill and one within the lower pay scale. This person would also have few close relationships, having trouble connecting especially with the opposite sex.

Another interesting aspect of the profile relates to the arsonist's vehicle. Although it may not be the best of vehicles, it is usually in good running order. Why? So he can get away from his crime scene.

It seemed the perpetrator wasn't concerned with the successful burning of the structures. The act of setting a fire appeared more significant than the amount of damage or destruction.

For instance, in a couple of arsons, the arsonist poured gasoline on a non-combustible surface of concrete block walls. I recall one fire in a Lutheran Church. It was one of those fires that basically only burned the gasoline vapors, just barely scorching the interior surfaces. It fit the same modus operandi (method of operation).

This shows the arsonist's lack of care about the amount of fire, or his disorganized methodology because he didn't thoroughly plan his attacks. Simple fire-starting was not his forte.

After a few fires spaced over several months covering as many towns, Trooper Cherven and I arranged a meeting with several local police and fire departments. We discussed each fire, including the similarities of the incidents. Everybody discussed potential suspects.

One suggestion sparked our interest, a viable person of interest. This subject seemed to check those boxes of the profile. So we focused on him, learning as much as we could about him without letting him know we were investigating him.

This white male was in his mid-20s, check. He never attended college, had a low-level, underachieving job as a high school janitor, check. His being married seemed to be outside the parameter of the profile. But upon closer scrutiny, this subject spent an inordinate amount of time hanging out with a couple of high school girls, instead of being home with his wife and child. So, having trouble with close relationships, check.

When we plotted the fires on a map, his house was roughly in the geographical epicenter of the pattern of identified fires. He lived very near to the first fire. The significance of this is serial arsonists often set the first fire in a string of fires closest to where he was most comfortable, usually nearest his house or work. Then, as he grew more comfortable after successfully setting that first fire, he spread outward from there.

Besides the profiling of the potential arsonist, we also did temporal and geographical profiles. We analyzed fires according to their time of day, day of the week, and even looked into when the full moon occurred. The team hoped we could predict the day of the next fire. We looked at the types of buildings burned, plus their physical locations and appearances. This form of profiling often assisted with predicting the neighborhood of the next fire and also pinpointing where the arsonist lived.

We started conducting nighttime surveillances of this guy. At the time, my first wife and I were on a break; we had separated, with a divorce on the horizon. One Saturday night during this hiatus, I had no personal plans and didn't feel like staying home. It wasn't my weekend to have my two young daughters, now about seven and eight years old. So I decided to sit outside our subject's house, which was in one town that already had at least one fire within this spree.

Suspected arson fires

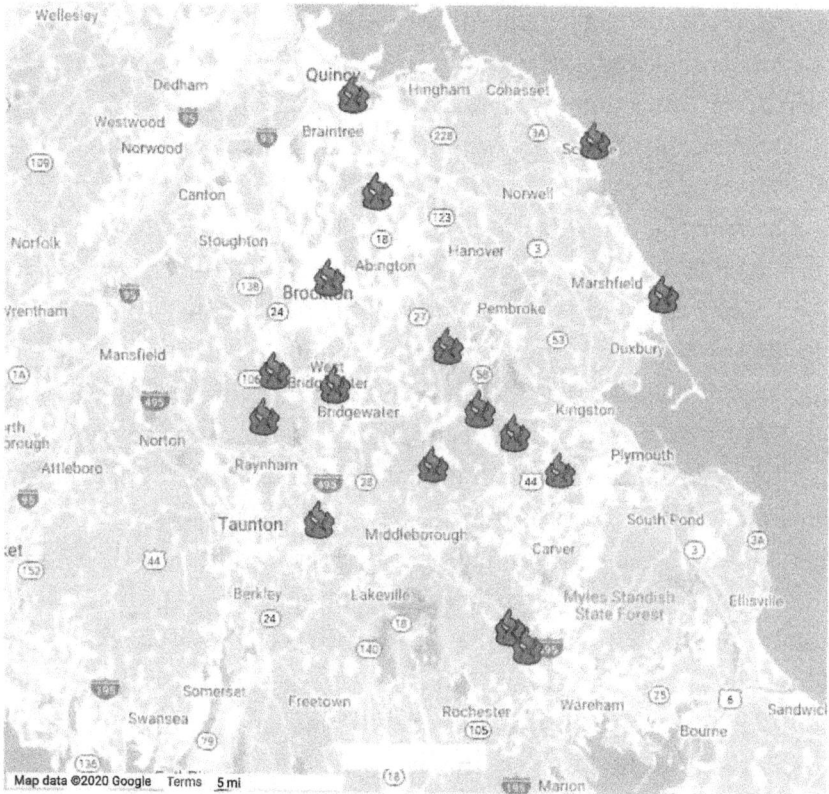

Suspected fires set by serial arsonist. (Google maps 2020)

About 9 p.m., I set up on his house, parked across the street. My enthusiasm for doing the job may have exceeded my judgment. I hadn't reached out to anyone before conducting this surveillance, not my Supervisor, not another Agent, not the local police. Perhaps I hadn't thought that through completely. I slouched down in the driver's seat of my Government vehicle. The street was quiet, although it was a cut-through between main roads. Houses built on quarter to half-acre lots lined the congested residential street.

I kept my eye on the second-floor apartment of the two-family house where the lights were on. I could see our subject occasionally moving about in the front living room. His car was in the driveway. I didn't really expect much success with this surveillance since the arsonist set the fires sporadically. Sometimes there were two fires in a week; other times there were no fires for several weeks.

After two to three hours, with no activity, a car careened around the corner from over my left shoulder. Within seconds, my driver's side-view mirror was sheared off. The vehicle sped off down the street. It took a couple of seconds before I even realized the mirror was missing.

My first reaction was, "What the fuck?!" I didn't think my car actually got hit by the other car. I jumped outside, retrieved my mirror and then noticed a large chunk of tar weighing a few pounds lying next to where the mirror had been. That's what took my mirror off, but did they throw it at my car in an act of vandalism? Or could it have ricocheted off their tires as they flew around the corner?

I couldn't wait to investigate further. Any additional delay and I would lose any chance to get these guys. I hopped back into my G-ride and gunned it, chasing after the disappearing car. As I raced from the arson subject's neighborhood and closed the gap between the escaping car and myself, I placed my bubble gum blue light on my roof and hit my siren to pull the car over. The driver readily complied.

After alighting from my car, I carefully approached the driver's side. With a flashlight in one hand, my other on my hip holstered weapon, I could see four nervous teen males. I identified myself as a Federal Agent and explained I had been parked on the road when they sped by me, hitting and damaging my car. Their nervousness was partially because of the multiple beer bottles, both empty and full, in the front and rear seats. Never mind getting pulled over in Dad's car.

They were dumbfounded when I asked them why they threw an asphalt chunk at my car. I tried to catch them off-balance. Their immediate joint reactions when I asked the question made me believe they hadn't thrown it, but it instead flew off the road in that one in a million shot.

When they provided no further answers, I grabbed their IDs and the vehicle information before advising them someone would contact them within a few days. I also told them I wouldn't call the cops right now. "Now get home before I change my mind, boys," were my last words.

So here it is, sometime shortly after midnight early on a Sunday morning when I placed a telephone call to my supervisor to advise him of my mishap. Needless to say, he was not pleased, but being a good supervisor, he took control of the situation. He told me to contact the local PD and then get my ass home. He would be in touch. This ended being the third time Internal Affairs interviewed me. We were starting to be on a first name basis.

A short time later, the investigative team doubted the subject of my surveillance was the arsonist responsible for at least 16 fires by this time. We had received no additional information on his habits, and surveillances of him yielded no clues. He was even home all night when a new fire occurred that fit the same m.o. (modus operandi, method of operation.)

It was about this same time an alert young West Bridgewater Police Officer brought a new person of interest to our attention. This is exactly why we stressed communication through meetings among local, state and federal authorities; it can produce results.

This officer, on routine patrol after midnight, came across an older maroon Dodge Aries stuck in soft sand next to the road. A white male was standing outside the car. The officer pulled over to offer help.

Once he confirmed the man was, in fact, thoroughly stuck, the officer called for a tow truck and waited with the man until help arrived. During this time, the man, a white male in his 40s, started fidgeting and pacing back and forth. The officer got a little nervous himself and inquired further.

He asked for the man's identification. The subject's license revealed he was James A. Dix of Holbrook, Massachusetts, which was about 10 miles to the north. When asked why he was there, Dix replied he had trouble sleeping so he went out for a drive. When he pulled off the road to turn around after getting lost, he got stuck in the sand.

But his anxious demeanor put the officer on higher alert. He walked around the vehicle, shining his flashlight through the windows. The car's interior was a pitiful mess, strewn with fast food wrappers and cups. He asked Dix if he would open the trunk.

When James complied, the officer observed a couple important items. The two-and-a-half-gallon red plastic gas container stood out. When asked about it, Dix stated his car's gas gauge plays tricks on him and it's not always accurate, so he carries the gas can.

What the officer noted next was so subtle, so innocuous, yet so vital. One never knows what small notation during an investigation can lead to a critical piece of evidence. He picked up "an old-fashioned wooden handled hammer." These were the officer's exact words when he wrote his report. Dix informed the officer his Dad had given him the hammer.

Why would a hammer in the trunk of a car have any importance? As you may recall, we noticed there was never any item left behind used to break the windows where the arsonist poured gas. He had to take the item away with him. A hammer was more likely to be that tool than most other items.

Why did the officer document the details about the hammer in his report? It was because we had the inter-agency meetings and discussed the details of the fires as we saw them. And that information had gotten disseminated to the boots on the ground. And we were glad it did! West Bridgewater immediately shared their police officer's report with the State Fire Marshal's Office and ATF.

Now, a gas can and hammer in a car's trunk that gets stuck on the side of a country road in the middle of the night with a jittery driver, in and of itself, doesn't mean Dix was an arsonist. However, with new additional information, plus that gut feeling, we soon focused on James Dix as the "God and Country Serial Arsonist", a name coined by Trooper Cherven.

*   *   *

Just for a moment, I want to compare this instantaneous attention on Dix with the slow interest my ATF Arson Task Force, and me specifically, placed on arsonists who were the subjects of my first book, *Burn Boston Burn*. For those of you who don't know, *Burn Boston Burn* is a true crime case about a conspiracy of nine men, including three Boston cops and a Boston firefighter. Over two years in the early 1980s, these fire buffs turned arsonists, torched 264 buildings due to tax-cutting measures which caused layoffs of hundreds of police and firefighters, resulting in millions of dollars in damages and hundreds of injuries.

Even though we had information members of this group may have been setting the fires, we didn't sufficiently focus our attention to pressure any of the subjects for nearly two years, when we finally made arrests resolving the series of arsons. Why did these serial arsonists continue to get away with their fire-setting sprees? Was there any difference with the Dix investigation once we centered our attention on him?

There were many factors and differences that affected our investigation. First, we had another few years of experience, and we had that enormous case in our background. In the present case, we had less than two dozen fires with few potential suspects, spread over eight towns in a five-year span, not the 200 plus fires with hundreds of potential suspects. In the current case, once we identified a viable suspect, we were more able to concentrate our efforts on him, but yet it was difficult to arrest him.

In both investigations, we still had no benefits of cell phones, GPS or security cameras at every turn. The downfall of both the large arson conspiracy and this case came from lucky breaks, but even those breaks came after hard work. When you have a large conspiracy, the cards fall when someone talks. But when you have a lone wolf case, there is no one to talk to except the perpetrator himself.

✳   ✳   ✳

Another few fires happened, spread over several towns. At one fire, we observed a fresh set of tire tracks in the grassy dirt behind one of the church fires. Because of the grass surface, it was not suitable for casting, so we could not make a comparison with a vehicle's tires should we identify a suspect.

However, we took detailed measurements of the width of the tracks to the inside and outside of the tire impressions. With those measurements, we researched through automobile books and vehicle experts, not through the non-existent internet. We came up with a couple of vehicle types, including the Dodge and Plymouth K-series vehicles.

Early on the morning of January 23, 1988, a fire occurred at the American Legion Post on Plymouth Street in Holbrook, Massachusetts. Trooper Cherven notified me of the fire a few hours later. I met him at the scene.

Holbrook Firefighters had done a good job knocking this fire down. They confined it to a small area of the function room just inside a broken floor-to-ceiling window on the rear wall of the building. The scene examination readily showed a char pattern on the wood flooring with minor extension up the wall. There were no inherent ignition sources within the burn pattern.

Also, the gasoline odor was still noticeable in the room. We took floor samples for laboratory analysis to verify our olfactory senses. No remnants of an ignition source, like a matchstick, were located. There was no item identified used to smash the window. Nothing had been left behind.

In my report, the cause determination for this fire read it was incendiary, intentionally set by a person (s) unknown with the use of an open flame and a liquid accelerant to assist with the ignition and spread of the fire.

About 24 hours later, in the early morning hours of January 24, the Hanover Fire Department received a call for a fire at the Hanover Middle School, about nine miles east of the previous day's fire. First, responding firefighters found flames shooting out from a large first-floor window. They quickly knocked down the fire, but the fire caused significant damage to one classroom.

Again, it appeared the evidence of clean glass on the floor showed the arsonist had broken the window prior to setting the fire. But then, the firefighters spotted something that would finally help resolve this case.

In the grass, completely covered with heavy frost, was an old fashion wooden handled hammer. It had no frost on it. The hammer was quickly and safely placed in a bag.

Trooper Cherven and I met at the scene to conduct the origin and cause investigation. Again, based on the broken window, the fire patterns, the presence of gasoline and the elimination of other potential ignition sources, we concluded this fire was intentionally set using an open flame.

We assumed the volatile gasoline vapors flashed on the perpetrator when that person applied open flame, startling him enough to drop the hammer, making him race away from the scene without recovering his tool.

It was at this fire where we took samples of the glass. We did this thinking the ATF lab could compare glass from the Hanover Middle School, the Holbrook American Legion, and any glass shards that may be embedded in the hammer's handle. Although I saw nothing on the hammer, maybe there was something there for the lab to find.

At this time, nobody on our investigative team or at the ATF lab considered analyzing the hammer for traces of DNA. The first criminal forensic cases using DNA occurred in 1986 in England and 1987 in a Florida rape case, but these cases involved blood and/or semen samples.

"Touch DNA," an alternative sampling method where skin cells are retrieved from an object and analyzed for a DNA profile, was not used in a criminal case until 1997. The FBI did not even use DNA testing until 1998. So DNA testing relative to this investigation was not even on our radar.

With Dix, we did a little background investigation on him. We also interviewed him shortly after the police brought him to our attention. This helped us to jump on the Dix bandwagon.

There were some unusual factors in Dix's background that didn't seem to fit the profile of the subject arsonist. James was 44-years-old, far older than the profile suggests, but that is a physical age, not a mental age. His educational background could really throw off the profile; he was a graduate of Boston College.

However, sometimes investigators have to look a little closer, overturn that rock under the rock. Checking Jim's high school yearbook revealed the only entry next to his name was Kitchen Helper. There was nothing at BC that distinguished him either.

Dix joined the Navy, but in 1969, just when the United States was amidst the Vietnam War, the Navy released him from further service. We couldn't find a person or further documentation verifying why he was discharged. His only job during this period was delivering newspapers to houses in the early morning hours. This "career choice" was far below his educational level. Besides the other factors, Jim lived with his Mom and Dad in their small Cape Cod-style house.

Armed with this information, I knocked on the door to the Dix residence the day after a new fire fit the pattern. The fire was less than a mile from his house. The building differed from most of the structures within this string of fires; it was a rickety old wood factory building. But the fire was set in the same manner as the others. The arsonist again broke a window and poured a small amount of gasoline to set this fire.

Since much of this case is being written from memory, I don't recall anyone being with me when I went to his house. And I don't know why that happened, except maybe we didn't want to scare him with a couple of investigators casting a shadow on his doorstep.

James' mother answered the door, a woman in her mid-60s. She was feisty, to say the least. After I identified myself and asked to speak with Jim, she said he was sleeping. She wanted to know what I wanted to speak to him about. Was she just being a mom? Being nosy? Was she over-protective or domineering? I replied I needed to speak to him about a fire that occurred the previous night.

"He didn't have anything to do with any fire. He wasn't feeling good. He was home all night," she spit out.

"Would you give me a written statement on that?" When she replied affirmatively, I immediately drew up a written statement right then, which she signed. Then I said, "Well, I still need to speak with Jim now."

With an exasperated sigh and a nasty look, she relented, awakening him, as he had been out during the wee hours of the morning delivering papers, and possibly doing other things. As the investigation continued, I learned Mrs. Dix was the domineering one who wore the pants in their family. Mr. Dix was milk toast, very weak in the face of his wife and son, Jim.

When I first saw Jim as he came outside, he looked older than his 44 years. As I judged this book by its cover, I saw he was no fireball of a person; he looked squirrelly to me. After introducing myself, I explained I was investigating a fire that occurred the previous night. He asked why I was speaking to him. I told him I had been investigating him relative to other fires he had been near when the fires occurred.

Out of the clear blue, Dix blurted out, "The only reason you are talking to me is because I got stuck in the sand one night." That was one strange correlation to my line of questioning, almost like a guilty conscience pseudo confession. Our investigators thought he likely was planning to set a fire the night he got stuck.

We talked in circles for a while, before I left with my introduction to James Dix. I put him on alert we were looking at him for the series of fires so he would keep looking over his shoulder.

Shortly after this interview, Trooper Cherven and I held another meeting with the various local municipalities to discuss the latest information. Our investigative team planned to follow Dix during his nocturnal runs. That proved easier said than done.

Dix, along with dozens of other paper carriers, would meet to pick up their supply of bundled newspapers to ready them for delivery to the individual customer's houses. This pickup occurred about 3 a.m. After Dix left that location, we began following his maroon Dodge Aries with the driver's door painted a different color.

Since his route covered many towns over a 15-mile stretch, Dix traveled on some major highways, Routes 3 and 128 (now Interstate Route 93), all south of Boston. Dix presented a problem immediately. He drove on these highways at about 45 miles per hour, far below the posted speed limits. And he did this all the time. Then, he drove even slower on the deserted town and rural roads. Several nights of following him yielded no results. And no fires occurred during this period.

One June night in 1990, around 3:30 a.m., the burglar alarm sounded at the Veterans of Foreign Wars facility in Foxborough, Massachusetts, the hometown of the New England Patriots. The racket awakened an elderly man who lived across the street. Looking out his bedroom window, he saw an older, maroon-colored car with no headlights on pulling out of the VFW driveway. Then the car headlights came on. He now observed flames coming from a window of the VFW and immediately called it into 911.

As the Foxborough FD responded to the scene, back in Holbrook, Fire Chief William Marble was awake in his bed at home. The Chief was monitoring one of his ambulances that was out on a call. Over his scanner Chief Marble, who had been at our task force meetings and privy to James Dix being an arson suspect, immediately popped out of his bed.

He jumped into his car and drove over to the Juniper Road address of Dix's home. He did this based on a hunch that a veterans' fraternal organization burning in the middle of the night could be a target of Dix.

The Chief backed into a driveway across from Dix's place. He could plainly see his driveway. Jim's Dodge was nowhere to be seen.

So the Chief leaned back in his seat, waiting for him to return. About 45 minutes later, his wait was over. Jim pulled into his driveway. He alighted from his car and walked into his house, none the wiser that he was being observed.

The next day I assisted with the origin and cause investigation at the VFW. Due to quick work by the FD, the fire scene examination was easy. Heat and smoke damage was visible on the siding where the fire had extended from the structure's interior through a large broken window. Inside the window, the function hall carpeted floor had an irregular char pattern on it. The wall to the sides of the window had surface burning only. The odor of gasoline was strong on the edge of the char pattern. We took debris samples from the area.

This fire set was unusual. There were no windows on the lower exterior walls. The broken window was about eight feet above ground level. The arsonist most likely stood on his vehicle's roof or hood in order to break the window and pour gasoline through the opening. We observed some window glass on the ground with more on the floor inside.

I walked across the street to speak to the eyewitness who reported the fire. He related his story, but he had nothing else to add. He could provide no further details about what he saw. Or, should I say, what he didn't see since he didn't have his eyeglasses on when he looked out his window at the fleeing car.

With the vague vehicle description combined with Chief Marble's observations, my next move was to pay another visit to James Dix. When his father let me into the house to speak to Jim, I found him in the first-floor living room of the Cape Cod-style home. He had converted the room into his bedroom. What I saw amazed and confused me.

He had covered the walls of the room with a combination of sheets of plywood and soft foam, the type you may put to cover your mattress. Jim was sitting on a couch centered in the room. Directly in front of him, about three feet away, was a TV with a program playing. Three feet to Jim's left was another TV, also on and tuned to the same show.

Jim still didn't know I was in the room. He had headphones covering his ears even though the TVs were fairly loud.

When Jim finally noticed me standing next to him, he took off the headphones. After I asked Jim where he was the previous night, he lied to my face. First, using the same story he used once before (and he would use it again years later), he said he was home all night.

By simply putting him on the spot, asking him if he was sure he stayed in all night, Jim changed his story, admitting he was restless so he went out for a drive. He explained he planned to go to a race at the Raynham racetrack someday, so he wanted to see where it was.

I pushed for more details of his venture, like what routes he had taken. His description placed him driving over the same secondary road twice where the VFW was located. I also asked him whether he had been in any of several towns. My list included Foxborough, but he didn't bite on that one. We still did not have enough evidence to arrest Dix. We needed to work harder or get lucky.

✳   ✳   ✳

That luck came on February 3, 1993. Shortly after midnight, 75-year-old Security Guard Alexander Peers was on duty for Tilcon Construction Company in, the City of Champions, named for its rich sports history and hometown boxers, Rocky Marciano and Marvin Hagler, about 20 miles south of Boston.

Mr. Peers approached the large semi-circular driveway that wound behind the office building. He noticed there was a parallel set of vehicle tire tracks in the fresh one-inch snowfall which occurred a couple of hours earlier. He decided to investigate.

As he slowly drove his car up the slight incline of the driveway beyond the curve to the rear of the building, he saw a blue Thunderbird parked about 50 feet ahead of him. His car high-beam headlights illuminated a white male standing between the Ford and the rear wall of the building.

At first, Mr. Peers thought maybe the guy was taking a leak. However, he could plainly see the man's arm extended through a broken rear window.

Suddenly, but without panic, the perpetrator shielded his face from view. Casually, he walked around the rear of his car, got into his driver's seat and drove slowly off around the far side of the building. But not before the security guard recorded the Massachusetts license plate. Mr. Peers also followed the subject to the front of the building, where he observed the car turn left onto Howard Street.

Returning to check the rear of the building, he found both the storm window and the interior window smashed with glass on the ground. Then Mr. Peers headed to his office at the construction portion of the Tilcon building where he telephoned the Police.

Brockton Police Officer Melvin Lightford responded to the Tilcon office within several minutes. After relating the story to Officer Lightford, together they inspected the broken windows. The storm window was thoroughly smashed, whereas only a lower section of the inner window was broken, with enough room for a hand to make its way inside.

Officer Lightford moved closer to the window. The powerful odor of gasoline wafted out of the opening from the interior office. Mr. Peers also smelled the gasoline odor.

The two men noted two sets of footprints in the fresh snow. One set of prints had a smooth appearance while the other set showed a pattern. A check of Mr. Peers' shoes showed a pattern that matched the one set of prints.

Officer Lightford also checked the license number he received from Mr. Peers through the Registry of Motor Vehicles. The registration came back to Joseph Dix of 63 Juniper Road in Holbrook, a small town next to Brockton. Lightford radioed his station, asking them to notify the driver of the car that the Brockton Police would like to speak with him.

Both Mr. Peers and Officer Lightford then went to the Brockton Police station. Upon walking through the double doors at the front of the station, Mr. Peers saw the same man from the Tilcon building standing in the PD lobby. He immediately told the Officer. Shortly thereafter, the man in the lobby identified himself as James Dix, son of Joseph, who owned the car.

After the attempted arson, the Brockton Police notified SFM Trooper Mike Cherven of the incident. Mike then called me at home, waking me from a sound sleep. When I arrived at the Brockton PD, a large masonry edifice sitting on a hill beside railroad tracks, I met with Mike, Officer Lightford, and a Brockton Detective. James Dix was sitting in lock-up, being detained for the moment.

We held a line-up. It was not the typical line-up where the suspect stands with a few semi look-alikes while a witness tries to identify the suspect as the person who allegedly committed a crime.

Here, James Dix was part of the line-up; so was I, along with four other police officers. The difference was this line-up was for the accelerant detection canine, Sgt. Hulk, handled by Trooper Cherven, to walk along the line sniffing the participants for traces of suspected ignitable liquid residue.

Mike instructed all of us to squat down and extend our hands outward. Dix was next to me in line. I watched as Hulk made his way down the line toward Dix and me. Mike had Hulk in work mode, sniffing the hands, feet and bodies of the participants.

As Hulk inched closer to Dix, I saw Jim curl his extended fingers into tight fists while his arms pulled back taut against his torso. His body language spoke volumes. His face tensed with a scared, anxious look like he was waiting for something bad to happen.

Hulk reached Dix. A couple of sniffs by Hulk of Dix's hands were all it took. Hulk alerted by sitting and looking up toward his handler. Mike instructed Hulk to seek again. Hulk repeated his alert, not just to the hands of Dix, but also to his shoes and pants.

Immediately upon completion of the line-up, Trooper Cherven swabbed Dix's hands, then he secured his shoes and pants. Later that day, Cherven forwarded these items to a laboratory to check for the presence of an ignitable liquid. Although the canines are highly trained, lab testing was vital to identify and verify whether the samples did in fact have certain residues present.

Mike and I sat Dix down in a conference room. We tried to conduct another interview with him. It was my fourth face-to-face with Jim. But as on three previous occasions, speaking with Dix was like trying to speak to him while he rode a merry-go-round. The conversation just kept going around in circles, getting nowhere. He admitted nothing.

The Tilcon Construction Company was a business that affected interstate commerce. Several other fires we suspected Dix set also qualified for prosecution within the Federal system. With those fires occurring in three different counties, we took the case to the Federal Court system.

After further investigation, much discussion, and wrangling, the prosecutors only charged Dix with the attempted arson of the Tilcon building. There was insufficient evidence, as defined by the United States Attorney's Office, to charge Dix with any of the other fires.

I don't know why the AUSA felt the evidence wasn't strong enough to connect Dix to other fires, but when Dix pleaded guilty to the one count, the prosecutor attempted to convince the Federal Judge that Dix was responsible for additional fires. For instance, he argued the blurred view of an old Dodge Aries leaving the fire at the Foxborough VFW, combined with Chief Marble's observation Dix was not home when the fire was being set, sufficiently connected Dix set that fire.

He also presented information that a plastic newspaper wrap found outside the St. James Lutheran Church fire in Canton was enough to tie Dix to that fire, although the lab found no fingerprints on the wrapper. Another piece of evidence was the set of tire tracks in the grass and dirt outside another church fire. As you recall, these tracks matched the same make car Dix drove, but we could not directly associate the tracks to only his vehicle.

How did the hammer found outside the Hanover school play into evidence put forth before the judge? The hunch of having it analyzed at the lab paid off. Sort of.

After the Hanover fire, I returned to the Holbrook American Legion fire scene from the previous day to collect glass from that broken window. We shipped glass samples to the lab.

The lab found the smallest piece of glass in the wood handle. I later saw it when the lab returned the evidence to our office. That piece of glass was only as big as a grain of sand!

When the lab compared that grain to the two known samples from the fire scenes, the techs determined it came from the Holbrook fire, tying the two fires to the same person. However, they found no fingerprints on the hammer. So how does the hammer tie Dix to the 2 fires?

With a hammer in hand, Trooper Cherven and I visited Dix's father. Mr. Dix, almost 70 years old, told us he had laid wood floors for a living. He knew exactly the hammer type it was. This specific hammer had a certain weight that was too light for his work. He said this hammer was decades old. He had given it to his son along with other tools because they were no longer useful to him.

When I asked Mr. Dix how he could definitively say this hammer was his, he pointed to the wooden wedge in the handle's top. He stated he put that wedge in there himself because the hammerhead had gotten loose. It was the same wood wedge that some of you have seen in your grandfather's hammer. The Assistant United States Attorney did his best to associate James Dix to that hammer. Do you think the hammer information was adequate to charge Dix with those two fires?

All of this circumstantial evidence didn't convince the judge. With a potential 10-year sentence looming over Dix's head for the one charge, the judge sentenced Dix to only a two-and-a-half-year prison sentence. Well, at least we got him off the street for 30 months.

Time flies when you're having fun. In 1996 Dix was released after doing his time. There is no directive requiring the Federal prison system to notify anybody a convicted arsonist is being released to the streets. And Jim hit the streets running, or should I say burning.

Jim moved back into his parent's house, except his mother had died during his incarceration. Within a couple weeks after his release, there was another fire in an old wood factory building within a mile of his house. It was the same building we suspected he hit during his pre-arrest fires.

This fire was nearly identical to the previous fire at the building. Instead of a broken window, someone forced a wooden front door partially open to this now-vacant building. A person poured a little gasoline into the opening and lit a fire.

* * *

At this point, I would like to mention something very dear to me and many others. My friend and associate, Sergeant Michael Cherven, had died. He had just finished exercising when he suffered a heart attack. Mike was so respected by the law enforcement and fire community that they carried his casket atop a fire engine to the cemetery.

I could no longer rely on his expertise or his friendship. It took quite a while for the shock and sense of loss to fade, but he will not be forgotten. Mike was no longer there to assist me with this recent Dix investigation.

* * *

The newest fire was brought to my attention. The day after the fire, I once again visited the Dix household to interview him. Jim wasn't surprised to see me. I told Jim I had to ask him about a fire that happened nearby the previous day. As with all times before, Jim denied knowing anything about a fire.

We spoke for a while. Dix finally admitted he hears voices and has for years, but he added the voices never told him to set fires. Again, he denied he ever set a fire.

I inquired about his actions on the previous day. Jim replied he rode around to celebrate his fiftieth birthday because he was in prison when he turned 50. I asked him to tell me specifically about his movements.

He detailed his routes as he drove around all day and night. North of Boston, outside of his normal territory, he visited a strip club. Then, he bought himself a birthday cake, again because he didn't have one in prison when he turned 50.

This was the first time I heard Dix associated with anything to do with women, something sexual in nature. Dix never even had a girlfriend. Or any friends, for that matter. Could the viewing of women undressing have stirred him to act out, set a fire?

Jim even brought me to his refrigerator, where he showed me the remains of the cake he bought. When he opened the box, he told me he was eating it while he was driving. The cake remains were evidence of that; his finger marks where he clawed mouthfuls of cake were clearly obvious.

His route details put him driving directly in front of the fire building twice. The problem was the building was on the primary route between the Dix residence and the highway, so it was natural for him to pass by that building. I couldn't even get a search warrant to look for evidence related to the fire.

I later spoke with Mr. Dix, father of James, at his house when Jim was out somewhere. He told me quite a few things about Jim I didn't know. Mr. Dix didn't have any medical or psychological information on Jim because there was none. First, he told me he recalled one day when Jim was yelling in the backyard. Mr. Dix said he stuck his head out the door to check on the commotion while Jim was yelling, but nobody was there. He thought Jim heard voices. He was yelling at something in his mind.

Mr. Dix said he has had no central heat for nearly two years because Jim pulled the thermostat off the wall. He added Jim would eat all his food and not contribute any money, which left him next to nothing because he lived on a small Social Security check.

Within a month after speaking to Jim, he ran afoul of the law. Two young teen boys allegedly threw an apple or crabapple at his car breaking one of his windows.

In his second instance of violence, but the first known aggressive act against a person, Dix tried forcing one boy to eat an apple laced with glass. The victim told his parents, who reported the incident to the police.

Because of the complaint, Dix's parole was revoked because he refused to take his medication for the paranoid schizophrenia that was diagnosed while he was in Federal prison. Dix could be held for an indefinite period based on doctors reviewing his progress.

In October 2010, James Dix, now 63 years old, was back on the streets of Massachusetts. I don't know what he had been up to or where he had been.

But on Monday, October 4, Dix had an appointment with his Federal probation officer. The meeting occurred at a two-story office building on the very busy Long Pond Road in Plymouth, Massachusetts, the town where the Pilgrims had landed nearly 400 years before. In an almost unheard-of move, Dix requested his assigned officer to send him back to prison. When he was told he couldn't do that, Dix demanded, "Do I have to start a fire and be standing right there in order to get some attention?"

With his outburst, Probation called the Plymouth Police. The police took Jim to a hospital for evaluation, but the doctors released him a few hours later.

Jim drove to a local gas station, purchased about $2.50 worth of gasoline, and returned to the probation office. Sticking with the same method Dix used at least 30 times in previous years, he broke a first-floor window, poured in gasoline and ignited the volatile gases. But contrary to his prior fires, James just stood there and watched the fire as it burned the office with the flames licking up the exterior of the structure.

A Plymouth officer on routine patrol spotted the flames as he was driving past the building. Pulling into the parking lot, he had no trouble spotting Dix who was still standing there.

Simply, Jim immediately told the officer, "I did this." He also eventually confessed his motive for setting the fire was because he was angry with his probation officer for not sending him back to prison.

Police immediately arrested Dix. He was sent to Bridgewater State Prison for evaluation. After being charged in Federal court for the fire, Dix eventually returned to prison again for a lengthy period. He got his wish.

Massachusetts State Trooper Mike Fagan showing where Dix set the District Attorney's Office on fire
(Photo by Stephanie Spyropoulos for the Boston Globe.)

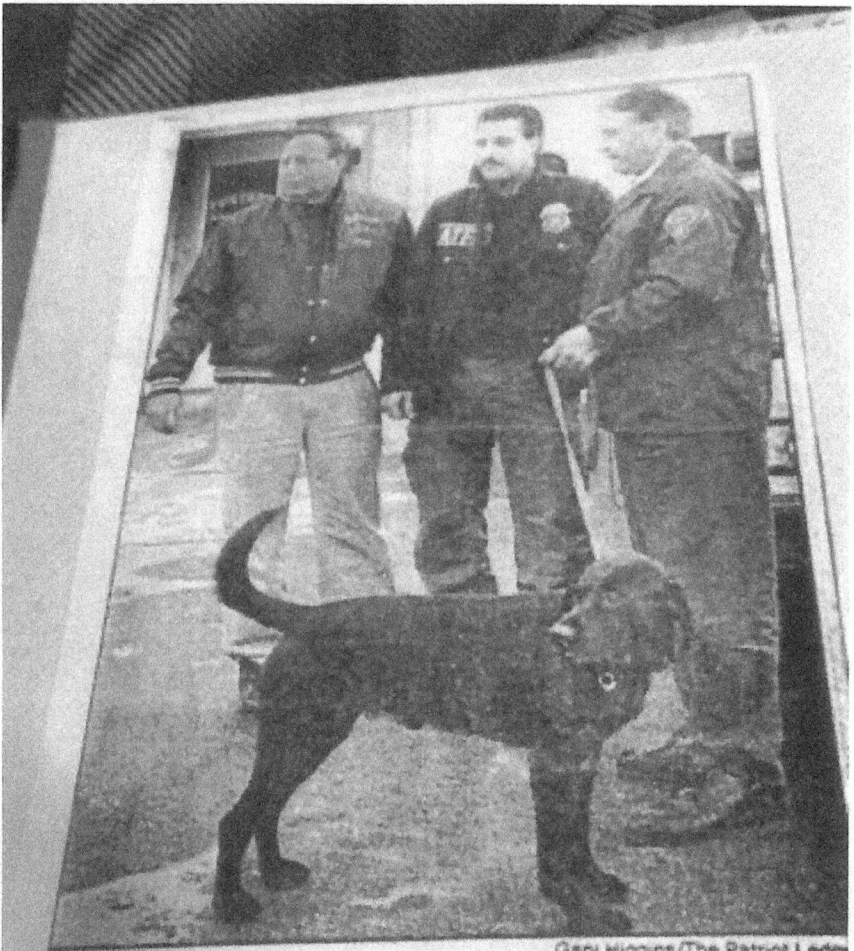

Gary Higgins/The Patriot Ledger

The team that has been investigating the "God and country" arsoni *includes, from left, Holbrook Fire Chief William Marble, Special Age* *Wayne Miller of the Bureau of Alcohol, Tobacco and Firearms and M* *chael Cherven of the fire marshal's office. They were aided by S* *Hulk, foreground, who is trained to detect flammable liquids.*

News article during arson case with Chief William Marble,
me, Trooper Cherven and Sgt. Hulk
(Patriot Ledger photo by Gary Higgins.)

The late Trooper Michael Cherven, one of the pioneers of the MSP's Ignitable-Liquid Detection K-9 Program, and Hulk work at the scene of a massive fire in Lawrence in the 1990s.

James Dix is at least 73-years-old now. His whereabouts are unknown.

Mike Cherven's career as a "road" trooper took him across Central Massachusetts and back home to the Foxboro barracks.

After 10 years of patrol, Trooper Cherven was assigned to the State Fire Marshal's office as an investigator. An opportunity came his way for an accelerant detection K-9, which was to be the first in Massachusetts State Police history. Corporal Bob Corry and Trooper Cherven were trained as dual handlers for Sergeant Hulk, the state's first arson accelerant detection canine.

Eventually, Bob would be promoted to Detective Lieutenant, and Mike was the sole handler of Sergeant Hulk. Trooper Cherven and Sergeant Hulk worked numerous high-profile arson cases throughout the entire state and throughout New England. As a testimony to the success of Sergeant Hulk, the State Fire Marshal's office now deploys five arson canines and five explosive canines in Massachusetts.

In 1994, Trooper Cherven was promoted to the rank of Sergeant and transferred to Troop C, Holden, as the evening shift patrol supervisor. On July 13, 1995, Sergeant Cherven went for a run, as he did many times each week, and collapsed from a heart attack. His wife Robyn and sons survive Sergeant Cherven. His sons, Trooper Mike Cherven, Jr. who is assigned to the State Police Barracks in South Boston and Trooper Derek Cherven who is assigned to the State Police Barracks in Belchertown.

Bibliography

United States of America v. James A. Dix, Mag. Judge's No. 93-0835-RC, 03/12, 19, 29/93.

Arson worries are somewhat outdated, The Patriot Ledger, Patrick Ronan, 11/30/12

Former Holbrook Fire Chief reflects on chasing suspected arsonist James Dix, The Patriot Ledger, Brian Benson, 10/09/10

Prosecutor: Plymouth arsonist wanted to go back to jail, The Enterprise, Patriot Ledger Staff, 10/06/10

Suspected 'God and country' arsonist faces new federal charge, Wicked Local.com-Holbrook, Lane Lambert, 11/24/10

Onetime serial arson suspect accused of setting office on fire, boston. com, The Boston Globe, Christine Legere, Stephanie Spyropoulos, 10/06/10

CHAPTER 13

Another Disaster Averted

In mid to late July 1990, the ATF Arson Task Force received some scary information from the Massachusetts State Police. They had an ongoing long-term undercover narcotics investigation with a confidential informant in the middle of making a serious dent in heroin trafficking in the greater Lawrence area.

Lawrence, an old textile mill city of over 70,000 people, had its struggles in the 1980s and early 1990s. With an overabundance of vacant mill buildings and multi-family structures, arsonists set scores of these buildings ablaze for various reasons. The Lawrence Police and Fire Departments joined with the State Fire Marshal's Office and ATF to establish an Arson Strike Force, working together to resolve the arson problem.

On this occasion, the State Police related their informant had learned the owner of a laundromat hired a heroin dealer to burn his business. However, the method to burn the building was extremely serious and potentially catastrophic.

The torch, known to us as Cookie, was planning to open a gas line in the basement and use an ignition source to blow the building up. This news presented several problems that had to be resolved. The first issue was a legal one. The State Police weren't ready to expose their informant to discovery being in the midst of that large-scale drug investigation.

After much discussion, we decided not to wire the informant. He was to be the driver for Cookie, so we would know exactly when Cookie planned to do his deed. ATF was the lead agency, but the other three agencies played major roles in the investigative effort. We also put the local gas company on notice to standby for any potential emergency, although we did not tell them the exact location.

I was the assigned case agent. This carried tremendous responsibility. Several members of each agency met at the Lawrence Fire Department. We discussed assignments with extensive planning, trying to avoid a disaster.

On the day of the event, around 7 p.m., surveillance teams took up positions. Initially, everyone located loosely around the laundromat, except for my mobile team. I was driving a nicely painted conversion van carrying three other team members, including Lawrence Fire Lt. Kevin Ord.

With temperatures hovering in the upper 80s, combined with the typical sticky New England summer humidity, the evening was extremely hot. The building sat within a triangular intersection. The narrow point of the structure bisected two fairly busy roads which ran alongside the building, with a dozen or more vehicles passing by every minute. An adjacent structure connected to the third side.

This was a densely populated Hispanic neighborhood with multi-family residences surrounding the target. None of the agents or the surveillance teams was of Hispanic heritage. We were all lily-white. Our teams had to be careful not to expose ourselves, cause suspicion and give our positions away. One surveillance team alerted us, "Subject vehicle approaching the target." From my position seated on the floor of the van, I looked over my left shoulder out the driver's side window.

Just then, the car driven by the informant pulled into the same parking lot where we parked. It came to a stop three feet from my driver's side door. The freaking torch was getting out of the car right next to me!

I not only was dripping sweat from the hot weather. The situation raised my sweat to an all-new level. All four of us were virtually shitting our pants. And holding our breaths.

Cookie stood right outside my door, where he nonchalantly took a piss right there. I could have held his dick for him; he was that close!

Once he completed his task, he made his way across the street to a side door that led to the basement of the building. The laundromat filled an entire triangular-shaped block. On the side of the building facing us, one and a half stories were visible as the structure was on a hillside. The opposite side was where the laundromat main door opened to grade.

I watched as Cookie unlocked the basement door, entered, and closed the door behind him. I noted the time, 7:25 p.m. Moments later, 37 seconds to be exact, Cookie exited from the doorway. Thirty-seven freaking seconds!

What the heck was that all about? The car next to us backed out and picked Cookie up in the street. My mind started racing. He couldn't have done whatever he was going to do in the building. I was thinking and speaking out loud to the other investigators there was no way he completed setting up the building to burn in that short time.

Inside, I was turning into a hot mess, mulling over the possibilities. If he completed the fire setup, while we just sat there, we would be screwed. At least I would be because I was in charge of the operation. If I don't react and act correctly, this entire block might blow up with who knows what for other collateral damages, including possible injuries or death.

We ATF Agents always joked about being sent to Detroit when we screwed up on the job because back in those days, being sent to Detroit was less than desirable. Now, I faced something more serious than exile to Detroit. I radioed to all the mobile surveillance units surrounding the area to hold their original positions.

After wrangling with my thoughts for another few minutes, and no explosion had occurred, the car containing Cookie pulled up, stopping in the middle of the street next to the basement doorway. He jumped out of the vehicle, which drove away, as he re-entered the laundromat. Super heavy sigh on my part! But now I revved up for what was to come next.

I advised all units to tighten up around the building. And I instructed Lawrence Fire Investigator Kevin Ord, who was sitting in the van with me, to photograph Cookie as he exited the building silhouetted by the door frame covered by one of those little gabled roofs. Kevin was the designated photographer for this occasion.

Two ATF Agents left our van, walked across the street and positioned themselves, one on each side of the door. A team of State Troopers and Lawrence Police, who positioned against the far side of the laundromat reported hearing multiple banging noises as metal on metal. Then, using a more urgent tone, the team said there was a strong odor of gas coming from the building.

Kevin and I moved from the van to the street directly across from the doorway. Moments later, the door opened, Cookie exited, Kevin snapped a picture with his 35mm camera.

After a couple steps into the street, as Cookie spotted Kevin and me, the other two ATF Agents tackled Cookie from behind, knocking him face down on the street. They immediately cuffed him. I walked up to him, grabbed him by the cuffs and roughly assisted him to his feet. Not a simple task with the 200 plus pound, out-of-shape perpetrator.

"What were you doing in the building?" I asked Cookie even before I read him his Miranda rights. Time was of the essence at this point.

"The owner gave me a key so I could sleep in the basement," he responded.

"Okay, let's go see your sleeping area." I held him by the cuffs with one hand. My other hand guided him by the shoulder. I pushed the door wide open. On the top of the first step was a lit candle. There were only four steps down into the basement. In rapid order, I told Kevin to grab a photo of the candle before I stepped forward to blow it out.

From that position, I smelled the powerful, pungent stench related to natural gas. That was scary enough, but I also heard the constant swooshing sound of a large open gas line under high pressure.

Rather stupidly, I took Cookie down those stairs into the basement. With my flashlight aimed directly across the 24-foot span of the basement, I observed, much to my chagrin, a two-inch main, wide open with an end cap removed.

There was no need to calculate how much gas was spewing into the basement; it was far more than enough to kill all of us if it ignited. I got us out of there as fast as my prisoner and I could move. Back outside, I ordered one of the other team members to call in the waiting gas company and the fire department crews to remedy the dangerous state of affairs. I don't think my nervousness showed. It couldn't have been a more tense situation. All the team members moved as far away from the building as possible, plus we blocked off the streets with our vehicles. It was only a short time before the cavalry arrived.

In the meantime, I read Cookie his rights. He wasn't willing to talk except to say he would only speak with recently retired ATF Special Agent Henry "Hank" Foderaro because, once upon a time, Cookie had been an informant for him. I questioned Cookie about the owner wanting to blow his building up, using him to do his dirty work. I explained we would speak with the prosecutor if he would cooperate with us. We needed him to call the owner of the laundromat as soon as possible. Our plan was for him to tell the owner he should hear about the building burning or blowing up any minute, hoping the owner made some incriminating statements.

But Cookie wasn't biting without speaking to Hank first. He had been a street criminal for many years. That and his drug addiction made him very wary of law enforcement and any potential promises of leniency.

By the time we contacted Hank, and he spoke to Cookie, there was too much of a delay, so we never made the call to the owner. Within days, I spoke to the owner, but he admitted nothing. We never made a case against him. Except for Cookie's word and the key in his hand, we had no evidence to arrest the proprietor.

Here's a little kicker—Kevin Ord had forgotten to put film in his camera. So, the shots he took of Cookie coming out the door and of the lit candle on the basement stairs were nonexistent. In the days before digital cameras, this isn't the first time this ever happened. I don't mean this brief note to make fun of or demean Kevin. Besides being a good man, during this period, he was a dedicated civil servant who was straight out as the only Lawrence Fire Department investigator in this busy city.

Cookie ended up pleading guilty and went to prison. This was so typical. The little guy who gets caught with his hand in the "cookie" jar goes to jail; the bigger fish gets away. Fortunately for me, ATF kept me in Boston until I retired. Oh, yeah. The reason Cookie exited the laundromat after only 37 seconds was because he forgot a flashlight.

A few short years later, our friend Kevin died of brain cancer. God rest his soul. And in early 2020, as I was writing this manuscript, another good man, friend to all, Hank "The Footer" Foderaro passed away after a long period of declining health. Gentlemen, rest in peace.

Thanks for assistance to Retired Lawrence Fire Captain (retired) William "Bill" Lannon.

CHAPTER 14

Richie, the Most Interesting Criminal I Ever Met

What do you do when a guy confesses to an arson-for-profit 10 years after the fire, long after the statute of limitations had expired? That's just what Richie did. His life story is one of the most interesting I have ever come across.

Richie has always been a business owner of one type or another. Sometimes his work involved a criminal aspect. Richie lived on that Massachusetts flexed arm peninsula of Cape Cod, that playground and fishing Mecca in the most southeastern section of the state. Among his other pursuits, he turned his love of fishing into a fish business, selling both wholesale and retail. As part of his business, he had fishing boats.

However, he also wanted to get rich quickly, so he got heavily involved in marijuana smuggling. One hazard associated with that business is getting caught. DEA seized one of his fishing boats with multi-tons (I heard the amount was over 20 tons) of the herb. After his arrest and conviction, Richie went to prison for a few years.

Once back out in the streets and on the seas, a large-scale federal indictment for conspiracy to import and sell marijuana, charged Richie as a co-conspirator. This conspiracy included the largest marijuana smuggler in the northeast. Richie pleaded guilty. The Federal judge decided Richie had now learned his lesson, so he sentenced Richie to no jail time, only probation.

Then, a few years later, Canadian authorities arrested one of Richie's fishing boat captains for attempting to smuggle swordfish from Canada to the United States. Both countries have strict laws regarding smuggling swordfish and the authorities seriously pursue smugglers. Canada banned catching swordfish because of mercury content above .5 parts per million, while the US allows 1 part per million in swordfish. So, some Canadian fishermen catch the fish and sell it to US boaters, who then sail back to the US where they make a tidy sum on their load.

Richie's next brush with the law resulted from his captain's arrest. After legal proceedings, Canada flew the captain to Boston's Logan Airport. The story I heard was Richie met his captain there. In the parking lot, somehow Richie discharged his .357 handgun, killing the man. Richie had only purchased the gun a couple days prior to the shooting.

Police arrested Richie, charging him with homicide. During the subsequent trial, Richie's attorney argued Richie accidentally shot his friend. Even the victim's mother testified on behalf of Richie, saying there was no way Richie intentionally killed her son. The jury acquitted Richie of any homicide charges.

A few years later, as his retail and wholesale fish business chugged along, his building caught fire. The firefighters had to force entry into the building. They readily extinguished the fairly small blaze.

Enter ATF to assist the local fire and police investigate the loss. This was March 1991. I had been an ATF Certified Fire Investigator by then. But I brought in reinforcements to help with the origin and cause investigation. I had a friendly and professional relationship with a New York investigator, Robert Doran. Bob had been around quite a few more fires than I had. Fire investigators all over the country, including me, had great respect for him.

The fire building had a sizable retail area and an even larger wholesale area. Customers could walk into the store for fresh seafood—lobster, scallops, clams, cod, and more. The wholesale business had gone well for some time. Besides having many restaurants as customers, Richie had large international companies, including Campbell's Soup and Mrs. Paul's, as customers.

The corrugated metal structure had no direct fire damage. There was a limited amount of heat damage showing on the upper section of the painted metal. There was only smoke and water damage on the main level of the business with no fire damage. We easily eliminated everything on the ground level as being related to the fire cause.

Technically, there was no second floor. There was only a loft area with the heating system and storage, mainly flat-folded wax-coated boxes used for shipping seafood. These boxes supplied most of the fuel for the fire. The burn patterns appeared to have originated from the vicinity of the oil-fired boiler. Standing on the wood loft platform, we could nearly touch the metal-clad roofing. Thus, the fire easily caused heat patterns on the metal, but not nearly enough to buckle the roof.

The exterior metal jacket of the boiler closest to the charred boxes was heat damaged, but as soon as we opened the boiler, we found the interior components virtually undamaged. The evidence eliminated the boiler as being related to the fire cause.

We also eliminated two fluorescent light fixtures suspended by chains from the roof assembly. The lights had been "off" at the time of the fire. Interview information revealed nobody smoked in the building, and nobody allegedly had been in the building for at least eight hours prior to the fire.

With no other potential ignition sources in the area, we concluded someone intentionally set the fire within the readily combustible boxes next to the boiler to make the fire appear accidental. The actual ignition source was unidentified but was likely a simple time-delayed device or open flame.

With the building found secured upon arrival of the firefighters, we had limited choices as to who set the fire. We only had to account for a few keys. Besides Richie, three or four other employees had keys. A few interviews helped to eliminate two of those, leaving three people with keys—his handyman who had moved to Massachusetts from Texas only two years earlier, his manager, and the business owner, Richie.

I still remember Richie's response when I asked him to explain his activities on the night of the fire. He was great at pointing out the obvious to the point where his explanations were so obvious they became not obvious at all if that makes any sense. He replied, "If I was going to set a fire, I'd make sure I had a solid alibi. After 7 o'clock I was home all night." And he was alone the entire time.

For the rest of this investigation, Special Agent Terry Barry and I teamed up with a local detective, Mike, who knew just about everything about Richie, his associates, and almost everything else that moved in his town. The three of us made an excellent team. Over the next 12 months, we spent a few hundred hours together putting this case together.

We interviewed about 100 people during the investigation. Our goals were to identify the actual arsonist, if possible, and to determine the motive or reasons for the fire. The interviews ranged from competitors of Richie's fish business, other fishing crews, restaurant owners, vendors and suppliers, plus friends and associates of Richie.

Some other fish dealers filled our ears with their dealings with Richie. They didn't have any facts that would double as evidence, but they implied he was less than scrupulous. They pointed us toward local restaurants, telling us they might have useful information for us.

Several restaurant owners told us within the months leading up to the fire, they stopped buying seafood from Richie because his products were no longer reliably good. At least one owner said the fresh scallops weren't so fresh. They had to return the scallops a few times before they cut ties with Richie. Some restaurants learned Richie even washed the returned scallops, possibly with a bleach solution, then rinsed them with lemon juice. Sounds yummy!

Campbell's Soups and Mrs. Paul's, who had large national contracts for Richie's seafood, canceled the contracts because the fish products received from Richie were no longer up to their standards.

Another financial catastrophe hit the business within several weeks before the fire. For the holiday season, Richie had hundreds of lobsters, which he stored in lobster traps in the harbor. His lobsters started dying. It is my understanding when several lobsters are stored in such close quarters, and a lobster dies, it decomposes quickly, causing the others to die. The result was the loss of several thousand dollars' worth of product.

One of the most interesting interviews was of a man I will only identify as John. He told us he became friendly with Richie because of their love of fishing. He was on the Board of Directors for a major bank in the Boston area. And his bank lent Richie $1.2 M.

Maybe that seems like no big deal. But here's the kicker; the bank loaned the money with no paperwork! When was the last time you received a bank loan with no paperwork? John said he does this occasionally. He said he did it for his friend. That explanation made no sense. We couldn't prove it, but their transaction had all the earmarks of a money-laundering scheme. Something wasn't right about John and his money.

We never resolved this mystery. However, the FBI found enough wrongdoing with that bank to shut it down completely about three years later.

The financial motive kept piling up. We uncovered more evidence supporting his motive than any other case I ever worked on. Over the next 12 months, our little team of Agent Barry, Detective Mike, and I developed 70 Government witnesses.

The case was coming together. We had already confirmed the arson determination. The firefighters found the building secure upon their arrival, and we narrowed the opportunity to those who had access to the building, Richie and his handyman. Plus, neither person had a confirmable alibi. The handyman had no motive for setting the fire for himself. Only Richie had a motive.

Back at our ATF office, Agent Barry and I put a criminal case report together. We laid the events out in chronological order, and we enclosed each witness statement and every item of evidence included in a neat, organized package.

The day came to carry the blue jacket (the case report always had a blue cover on it) to the United States Attorney's Office. We already had an Assistant United States Attorney assigned to ATF arson cases. He will remain nameless in this story since I have nothing good to say about him.

One agent each from the IRS, the DEA, and Customs accompanied me to the US Attorney's Office because the assigned AUSA had already shown reluctance to take this case. These agents all had an interest in Richie because he previously violated laws that involved each agency. They all had suspicions he was still committing crimes, but they had insufficient evidence to support any prosecution. They came with me to back me up, support me with my spiel to the AUSA.

Crowded into the AUSA's office on the 11th floor at the granite block Federal Courthouse at Post Office Square, I laid out the specifics of the case. When I finished, the short curly-haired AUSA began a song and dance. He said the evidence was purely circumstantial. He explained the case only had a 50-50 chance at success and with the 70 witnesses just for the prosecution, the trial probably would take four or more weeks.

I got a little hot under my dress shirt collar. I implored the AUSA to reconsider, to at least seek an indictment. Further, I explained this was exactly the complex arson-for-profit case that was ripe for prosecution. That's what the system was for. The other agents all spoke up, explaining what they felt was at stake. They said Richie was a career criminal and ATF had a case worthy of prosecution.

All our efforts were to no avail. The AUSA declined to prosecute the case. My feelings were so raw. I thought of him as a wimp with no balls. I just wanted to hang him by his ankles from his 11th-floor office window, threatening to let go of him until he acquiesced. I was so pissed off. My anger was palpable.

After I cooled some, I have to admit I shopped this case around to the State Attorney General's Office and the Barnstable County District Attorney's Office. They both passed on the case, knowing the US Attorney's Office refused to prosecute.

I could not believe I spent most of a year investigating this case just to have it filed in a cabinet. That was one of the most frustrating moments in my career, even more than losing a trial, because, at least, the case got tried and the jurors spoke.

Now comes the kicker, or twist to this case. About 10 years later, US Customs caught Richie again, charging him with several counts of smuggling swordfish from Canada. These violations were serious felonies, worthy of a Federal prison sentence.

The Customs' office was right across the hall from ATF in the Tip O'Neill Federal Building. For some reason, when Customs was processing Richie, he asked the agent handling his case whether he could speak to me.

The agent checked if I was in the office. Luckily, or maybe not, I was. The agent marched Richie over to one of our interview rooms. To say I was shocked would be an understatement. Richie nonchalantly confessed the entire arson scheme, including naming his handyman as the torch who burned the fish business at his behest. He knew the statute of limitations had passed. Richie could not be held responsible legally for the fire. His confession was just Richie being Richie. It was his way of laughing in my face.

I had been right all along. His confession brought up some of those angry emotions I had 10 years earlier. I even checked the mail fraud portion of the arson, when mailings occurred because an owner intentionally burned their property, which was beyond the statute of limitations. It was. I moved on. There were more fires awaiting investigation.

✳   ✳   ✳

As I began writing this chapter, I contacted Richie so I could get his input for this story. It was an unusual move on my part. We had not spoken since that day in my office. I didn't know how he would react. During the phone call, when I identified myself and refreshed his memory I had investigated the fire at his business, he told me to fornicate with myself, that I was an A-hole, and I had a lot of nerve. Click! I didn't even get a chance to explain my thoughts to him, so I wrote him the following letter. I figured I had nothing to lose.

Richard,

I am sorry my reaching out to you upset you so much. I did take a chance by contacting you, but I wanted to run something by you, not cause you grief. Please take a moment to read this, and then at least you will see where I was coming from.

I retired from ATF in 2001. Last year I published a book, Burn Boston Burn. It was one arson case with nine guys involved, including three cops and three firefighters who burned 264 buildings in and around Boston from 1982 to 1984. One of the arsonists has helped me with a lot of the inner details after 10 years in prison.

I am now writing a second book, short stories, all real cases, some on firearms, a couple of bombing cases and some arson cases. I plan to write about your fire as it was very fascinating because of you.

I honestly consider you one of the most interesting men I have ever met. Your past is extraordinary. I recently spoke to a couple of ------ -- authorities who had nothing but good things to say about your past 20+ years. I really would like your input for the story so I could get it right, not just from my investigative side. I can even write it without mentioning you by name or using the business name. I didn't demean, slander or wreck the guys involved in my first book. I don't plan to do that to you now. We could put in what you want to. Do you remember when Customs got you for swordfish smuggling and you came into my office and told me the story of the fire?

With your gracious help, this chapter could be the best one in the book. I know you have a least 1 adult child, a business and a new life. Maybe you just want to keep it all in the past. Of course, I don't know what your son knows about your past. If you assisted me in this project, I will keep your identity completely out of it. In a strange way, having your story in a book will forever keep you alive, a legacy of your wild past.

You may not care, but I would respect your decision, whatever it is. If you don't want any part of this and want me to go to hell, so be it. As an agent back then, I was doing my job and I don't think I ever disrespected you. If you would like to talk or tell me your decision, please feel free to call me, ----------. Take care, stay safe, regards,

✻   ✻   ✻

I thought I presented a persuasive argument. Richie never responded. I had so many questions for him. I just wanted him to tell me whatever he felt comfortable with, whether or not he was truthful. The story would have had Richie's flair. Since we never arrested him for this fire, although he later confessed to me, I wrote this story in this fashion without using his full name, the name of the business, or even the town where the fire occurred. Only those who have direct knowledge of the fire or the man will know this story.

Thanks to the town police and fire departments and one retired police Lieutenant for their assistance. I hope you understand why I chose not to identify you.

CHAPTER 15

Just Something I Wanted to Share...

It had to be the early 1990s when a large multi-family (20 units) apartment building was the subject of a fire. Due to the efficient work by the Malden Fire Department, firefighters had confined the physical fire damage to only a couple of apartments. However, the damage to the structure made it temporarily uninhabitable.

During the origin and cause scene investigation, I checked each separate room within the building, including all the apartments. Following my usual protocol, there were two reasons to examine every area, even those spaces with no fire damage.

One, I take a couple photographs in each apartment to document them, showing the lack of damage. These photos could show any interested person I eliminated those areas as being the fire origin. Second, I examine these units to check for any incendiary device or fire set that did not ignite and to record the contents or the lack thereof.

The main door to each unit was open, allowing free access. About midway through my inspection, for some strange and unknown reason, a framed newspaper article hanging on a wall above a bureau caught my attention. The article referred to the life and car accident death of Robert Kimball, which had occurred a couple years prior. Why did this story pique my interest?

Robert Kimball "Kim" had been a Vietnam veteran who had suffered severe head trauma while deployed in Southeast Asia. Kim survived his injury after doctors replaced part of his skull with a large metal plate. However, he spent years in pain, so he devoured pills for relief. The pills also caused him to get in trouble with law enforcement. That's how I met Kim, who became one of my early confidential informants in the late 1970s.

He had introduced me to several people in an effort to locate sources for illegal guns, ones usually stolen from a legal firearms owner. One guy Kim had been friendly with was a bookie/loan shark. Nearly four years later, I interviewed that gentleman after his "office" burned as a result of an arson fire. But, arsonists, who were the subjects of my first book, *Burn Boston Burn*, had set that fire.

Kim was a very likable character. We had a good connection. But we didn't make any cases. Because of this lack of success, over time, we lost contact.

Kim lived in Norwood, Massachusetts, a suburb to the southwest of Boston, 30 miles from the north shore town of Malden. The apartment in Malden had been his sister's place. This is one of life's weird coincidences. Why I noticed that article was one of those mysteries of kismet. I was sorry to learn Kim had met a tragic ending.

CHAPTER 16

Troubles with Arson-for-Profit Prosecutions

It is often said arson is one of the toughest cases to prove. Well, it isn't so much as the arson fire itself; it is finding the person(s) responsible for the fire that haunts investigators. And it is even tougher to arrest and convict someone in arson-for-profit cases. Statistics support arsons have a very low solvability rate with arrests and convictions among the lowest success percentages of all felonies.

Some investigations presented below, in which I worked with state and local investigators, show the difficulties encountered while trying to perfect a criminal case. People think, often correctly, you have to catch the arsonist with the match in hand. In far too many situations, I found this to be true.

When a person or multiple people decide to burn their property, in effect selling it to the insurance company, this choice is often a business decision. For some unknown reason, they become desperate for money, so they try to steal it from the insurance company by committing arson and then following up the fire with insurance and mail fraud. Their money problems could be because of drugs, gambling, divorce, a poor economy, just plain money mismanagement, or some other plight from a countless list of issues.

Most of these people have never been arrested for any crime during their lifetime. They hardly consider their act a crime. This type of arsonist considers their act a victimless crime, as long as nobody physically gets hurt. The insurance companies have lots of money so their fire wouldn't hurt them. And the reason it's a firefighters' job to fight fires, so if they get hurt, it is just part of their job.

These rookie arsonists often make lots of mistakes. Many suppose they are much smarter than lowly investigators, assuming their local investigator won't have a clue. They aren't familiar with the teams of well-trained investigators who work these fires. Setting a fire intentionally often leaves behind telltale evidence that doesn't disappear during the fire. Investigators can trace their associated criminal activities before and after the fire.

Then why do so many of these arson-for-profit criminals get away with their crime? In my personal experience, there may be something related to white or professional privilege in play here. I remember reflecting after these cases that juries made up entirely of white jurors found it troublesome, believing that white professional defendants sitting before them could have committed the crime of arson. It's also possible that the juror's felt for the individual over the large impersonal insurance company, even though arson fraud fires tend to increase everyone's premium. This held true even when there was overwhelming evidence to support a conviction.

✳   ✳   ✳

The address in question was 1330 High Street in Westwood, Massachusetts, an upscale suburb immediately to the southwest side of Boston. The target was a two-story, two-family apartment building situated only feet from the main drag, also known as Route 109. To the right side of the house was Pond Street, which ran past an elementary school, Buckmaster Pond, and a large, residential neighborhood.

The wood-frame building was over 100 years old. It looked well-maintained on the exterior with its solid white exterior clapboard siding. The interior was another story. It needed serious attention and upgrading. If you walked with your eyes closed, you'd be lucky not to trip on the uneven, "hilly" floors. The ancient boiler was unsafe, a heat source with the potential to cause a dangerous fire.

On a routine rolling patrol, Westwood Police Officer Paul McCarthy edged his cruiser off High Street into the parking lot of the Sheehan Elementary School. He was checking the area for any nefarious activities at the school, which was less than 100 yards from the 1330 High Street dwelling. The Officer continued behind the school, turning right around one back corner heading toward the exit onto Pond Street. As it was after 9:30 p.m., the summer sun had already set. Darkness had deeply settled in on the clear night.

As Officer McCarthy's vehicle crawled to the front corner of the school, a man with sandy hair wearing blue jeans and a blue shirt walked directly in front of the cruiser. Both parties were lucky the Officer had been inching his way along. The man, white, approaching middle age, never hesitated. He continued with the same steady gait past the front of the cruiser, past a parked Volkswagen Jetta, through a stand of trees and into the athletic fields.

Approaching the exit, the officer noticed a woman seated in the driver's seat of that parked silver Jetta. He turned onto Pond Street. At the stop sign with the 1330 High Street property to his right, Officer McCarthy noticed the odor of wood burning but discounted it as someone with a campfire or something similar. Thinking about the man at the school, McCarthy turned around to check on his whereabouts.

As he drove back to the school parking lot, he saw the Jetta woman pulling out. Now, it was plenty dark enough to warrant the use of car headlights. But the woman initially didn't turn on her lights until she was driving up Pond Street.

After a quick, but unsuccessful search for the guy, Officer McCarthy drove back toward High Street until a frantic female waved him down. She advised him the house at 1330 High was on fire. Moments later, he saw fire coming from the basement at the rear of the house.

Officer McCarthy's cruiser (blue). Mrs. M's Jetta (red).
(Google Maps 2021)

Front view of 1330 High Street, Westwood
(Google Maps 2021)

Immediately, Officer McCarthy radioed his station, asking for fire department response and requesting additional patrol cars to assist in looking for the strange couple he observed just before the fire's discovery. Upon the arrival of Westwood firefighters, he began his own search for the suspicious duo.

Only moments later, he saw the VW Jetta turn into a neighborhood off of Pond Street. Now, Officer McCarty flipped on his blue overhead lights pulling over the female driver who was still alone in the vehicle. Sidling up to her driver-side door, he inquired what she was doing as he requested to see her license.

Mrs. M said she was the owner of the house at 1330 High Street. Upon hearing that, Officer McCarthy advised her of her Miranda rights. She stated she understood her rights, and she agreed to answer his questions. Mrs. M stated she was waiting for her husband.

"You mean the guy with sandy hair wearing jeans and a blue shirt?" he asked. When she answered in the affirmative, he added, "He just walked past your car and kept going right into the field. What's going on?"

Mrs. M responded with a story of three young men who had occupied one of their apartments within the house down the street. The tenants were being evicted because she and her husband planned repairs for the building. Her husband told her to remain at the school because the tenants might get violent. He was going to retrieve the apartment keys from them.

The Officer deliberated aloud, "Well, he just walked by my cruiser and then past your vehicle into the field. He wasn't running from anyone." When he asked why he walked right past her, she told him she didn't see him as she was looking at the cruiser. Mrs. M gave no response why she drove away without her husband and why she didn't turn on her headlights.

She asked if she could walk over to the house, which he allowed. McCarthy accompanied her.

Black smoke was visible, forcefully pushing out of the structure, masking the nearby clear night sky. The Officer detained the woman and called in the situation to the Westwood dispatcher.

Coincidentally, at nearly the same moment Officer McCarthy saw the fire, Westwood Fire Lieutenant William "Billy" Scoble was heading eastbound on High Street in front of the building in question when he, too, detected wood burning and saw visible smoke spewing from the old wood house. Not knowing what was going on a few hundred feet up the road behind the house, Lt. Scoble also called dispatch to notify them of the apparent structure fire. He forced entry into the house in case occupants had become trapped. However, an intolerable black, acrid smoke from tires burning in the basement forced the Lieutenant to wait for assistance.

Westwood FD rolled, arriving on the scene within three minutes. A firefighter on the first nozzle in the front door tumbled down the missing burned-out stairs to the basement. This close call could have been disastrous, but lucky for him, he only wrenched his knee.

Firefighter Rich Cerullo, who later became Deputy Chief, drove the ladder truck to the scene. He maneuvered the stick to the roof where firefighters vented the roof and second-floor windows. Although the fire was burning in the center stairwell from the cellar to the second floor, the firefighters did a great knockdown, minimizing the overall damage.

In the meantime, Officer McCarthy, now a Massachusetts State Trooper, shadowed Mrs. M, monitoring her every move. He noticed she kept scanning the crowd, paying little attention to the blaze at her property.

Her husband was still missing. A short time later, the Westwood Police started receiving phone calls from several residents in the Buckmaster Pond neighborhood reporting a man running through their pitch-black backyards.

Westwood firefighter "Rocky" signaling from a second-floor window.

After Officer McCarthy's information and description of the missing Mr. M, the dispatcher put out a BOLO (be on the lookout) for Mr. M.

Cops flooded the area, including Officer Abdou, knowing who they were looking for. When he heard McCarthy's radio transmissions, he responded to the Pond Street area. He checked the streets in the high-density residential neighborhood. One local resident approached the Officer, telling him a man ran up the street a few minutes earlier. Abdou stayed near the Jetta left by Mrs. M, hoping Mr. M would either return to the car or head to the fire.

It didn't take too long for Mr. M to approach his car. At 10:22 p.m., Officer Abdou spotted him. He made contact, asking him to identify himself and what was he doing in the area. Mr. M stated it was his house on fire and his tenants had summoned him earlier to meet them there. He added two tenants were chasing him, so he was running from them. When Officer Abdou noted fresh blood leaking from a cut on Mr. M's forehead, he asked what had happened. "I told you, I was just running," was Mr. M's curt response. Police Officer Abdou radioed he had the previously missing person at the car.

Upon arriving at that location with Mrs. M, Officer McCarthy instantly recognized Mr. M as the man who had walked past his cruiser a short time before. McCarthy advised him of his Miranda rights, to which he replied he wished to speak with his attorney.

As he read the rights, the Officer made several observations of Mr. M, including an odor of alcohol and slurred speech, plus there were fresh cuts on his forehead and one of his hands, and there was grass and woodchips on the back of his blue shirt. Officer McCarthy hadn't seen the cuts or the debris on Mr. M when he first saw him 30 minutes before.

When he mentioned the cut on his hand to Mr. M, he said he had hurt it while working on his automobile that afternoon. The two police officers gave each other a look of disbelief as the wounds on both his forehead and hand showed fresh, uncoagulated blood with loose skin tissue.

As the officers discussed the incident, they overheard Mr. M. mutter to his wife, "Oh, I did it." The cops couldn't believe what they thought they heard. A few minutes later, Mr. M again quietly made a remark to his wife with a disappointed tone, "Oh, I did it."

Mrs. M replied, "Oh, well." The couple began walking back toward the fire. The officers followed and pulled their Sergeant aside to update him as to their observations.

Another Westwood Police Officer, Patrolman Paul Sicard, who was off duty, came across the activities at the fire scene, so he stayed to help. While the others briefed Sergeant Cunningham, Officer Sicard watched the suspects. He was acquainted with Mrs. M. When she recognized him, they exchanged greetings.

Moments later, Mr. M started speaking either to himself or to the officer. He said he was having problems with the tenants and he knew they did this. Mr. M further stated he traveled to the house to meet them when the "whole place went up." He added they previously made death threats against him and he thought they were trying to kill him so he just ran away.

Mr. M also informed the police he had come to the house to retrieve keys from three young men who they had evicted from the apartment. He evicted them because he planned to renovate the building. He was afraid there might be violence, so he told his wife to wait at the school.

At the house, the tenants started chasing him, so he fled and they must have set the fire. But his story didn't explain why he casually walked in front of the police cruiser, not running, not panicky and without notifying the police officer. Nor does his story account for why he walked right past his wife in the car and ran throughout the neighborhood.

After a quick trip back to the fire scene, Sergeant Cunningham advised his officers that firefighters recovered a gasoline can from the scene. Fire Lieutenant Billy Scoble had already begun his investigation of the fire. He knew from the distinct fire patterns only in the stairwells from the basement to the second-floor that someone had intentionally set this fire. He relayed his findings to his counterparts.

With this extra information plus the odd behavior of the owners of the burning house, Officer McCarthy asked Mr. M if he could sniff his hands. Mr. M gave his permission. The Officer noted the distinct odor of a petroleum product on Mr. M's right hand and forearm, but he repeated he had been working on his car that afternoon.

They awaited the arrival of Detective John Nash, a long-time investigator before they made any arrests. Just before 10:30 p.m., he arrived. After receiving updates on the investigation, he walked over to the rear cellar door of the building. There he met with Fire Lt. Scoble who had a 2 ½ gallon metal can on the ground. There was a yellow spout in the can, but the top screw cap was missing. He saw an oily film on top of the can and he smelled a strong petroleum odor, fuel oil, he guessed.

Nash knew he had enough evidence to merit arrests. Based upon the initial fire scene information, plus lies from the husband and wife team, combined with the on-scene presence of Mr. M at the time of the fire, otherwise known as an opportunity, Westwood Officers placed them under arrest for arson of a dwelling.

Officer Abdou and Nash transported Mrs. M to the station for booking. After being read her Miranda rights, she requested an attorney. The officers swabbed Mr. M's hands with his consent and placed the swab in an airtight package for later analysis. They had the suspects' vehicle towed with the plan to get a search warrant so they could search it.

Detective Nash returned to the scene after leaving Mrs. M for booking. Lt. Scoble exited the basement bulkhead with a charred and distorted, partially melted plastic "Jerry Jug." Nash took possession of the container and kept a small amount of a light-colored liquid that smelled similar to lacquer thinner for later analysis.

*   *   *

So what do you think of the evidence thus far? Do you believe it warranted the arrests at that time? Do you sense they could have developed more evidence before the arrests? Were the suspects a further threat to anyone since they may only have burned their own property? It is unlikely they would have burned anything else. Do you think they were flight risks? Do you suppose they planned, conspired to set the fire and then did it? What do you make of Mr. M's story of being chased and his wounds?

What about the young tenants who allegedly chased Mr. M? Wasn't 9:30 p.m. an unusual time to meet with your evicted tenants to retrieve their keys? Could they or anybody else in the world set this fire? Or maybe Martians set it?

By the way, Mr. and Mrs. M were both schoolteachers in a neighboring town and they had at least one child and a house in an adjacent town.

❋ ❋ ❋

One former tenant contacted the Westwood Police that night after a friend notified him the house was on fire. He told the police he had never met Mr. M and never threatened him or his wife, plus he had no plans to meet his landlords at the apartment since they already evicted his roommates and him for nonpayment of rent. They withheld payment because the house was in a dangerous state of disrepair.

The two other tenants of the second floor also had strong, confirmed alibis. One tenant had been in a Providence, Rhode Island club much of the evening. He knew the bouncer, and they conversed that night. Plus, when interviewed the day following the fire, he still had the red stamp on the back of his right hand with the name of the club on it.

As a normal course of processing a prisoner by the Westwood Police, they took the sneakers and clothing of Mr. and Mrs. M into custody. An olfactory check of Mr. M's clothing and sneakers detected no odor of petroleum products. The police packaged his clothing and sent them to the State laboratory for testing.

Routinely during fire investigations, samples are taken from fire scenes for analysis, checking for ignitable liquid residue. When a suspected arsonist gets caught in a timely manner wearing the same clothing as when the fire was set, authorities should have the footwear and clothing tested.

Westwood Police Officer McGilly booked Mrs. M, again advised her of her rights, and stayed with her until being bailed out 4 hours later. But at 12:30 a.m., Mr. M asked to speak with his wife. During the conversation, Officer McGilly stood nearby, but outside the cellblock. She heard Mr. M say, "We knew this would happen. They said they'd get us and they did."

A few minutes later, Officer McGilly allowed Mrs. M to call her mother. During the call, while standing about 10 feet away, the officer heard Mrs. M explain to her mother they planned to meet their tenants at the house, but the house burned, and the police arrested her and her husband for burning the house.

After returning Mrs. M to her cell, she spoke freely with the officer who kept her company for the next two hours. Mrs. M said her mother already learned of the fire before she called her because the insurance company had notified her, but Mrs. M was puzzled how the insurance company knew about the fire and why they called her mother.

Additionally, she related her husband previously was married and his children live with his ex-wife. His former wife remarried, so he didn't pay alimony anymore, but he still paid child support. Visitation rights disputes had been contentious and the two women had an altercation. She added she and her husband spent $10,000 for legal fees.

Mrs. M detailed problems at the house, including the boiler that had cracked and needed repairs, but first an asbestos abatement was necessary. She said the first floor was vacant, and they recently evicted the second-floor tenants. Mrs. M's parents bailed her out at 3:15 a.m.

In the morning, Detective Nash wrote two affidavits by hand to seek search warrants at Dedham District Court. The court issued two warrants, one for the vehicle and the other for closer examination of the fire scene. Both warrants allowed searches for any evidence relating to arson of the dwelling.

Later that day, after issuance of the warrants, MA State Trooper Mike Cherven and I assisted Lt. Scoble and Detective Nash with the scene inspection. I first worked with Bill Scoble a few years earlier when a young man burned a car before he broke into the basement of a Jewish temple, also setting fire there. It was a simple case to solve because after setting the fires, the police followed a set of sneaker prints in the fresh inch of snow that covered the ground overnight.

The origin and cause analysis, in this case, was also fairly easy. Besides moderate heat and smoke throughout much of the house, the bulk of the direct fire damage and resultant char patterns were confined to the stairways from the cellar to the second floor.

With limited fire damage in a structure, it is unusual for a fire to burn out or heavily char stairs. Even if a fire originated on the stairs, the normal fire progression is for the heat and buoyant fire gases to extend toward the upper walls and ceiling, following the natural flow of the chimney effect to the upper floors. The resulting heat and char patterns under these conditions are always to the upper walls and ceilings in a stairwell unless there is a readily ignitable fuel, such as gasoline, or another fuel stored on each stair. Often, the upper railings and balusters burn away and have the heaviest charring. Unusual fire damage on the stair treads, risers and lower railing requires further investigation. Heavily charred stairs and burned-away stairs are what we observed at 1330 High Street.

Trooper Cherven, along with Massachusetts State Police Lieutenant Robert Corry, were the first in our state, and one of the first in the country, to become handlers for an Accelerant Detection Canine (ADCs). ATF began training ADCs in 1986. These highly trained specialty canines detect a variety of ignitable liquids often used to start a fire. They can perceive the smallest amounts of residue remaining after a fire from areas where liquids had touched.

Mike put his dog, Sergeant Hulk, to work at the scene. Hulk alerted to several locations. Mike then took samples from the specific sites to send to the State lab for analysis. It is a necessity to have the canine alerts verified by the laboratory. It is unknown exactly what the ADC alerted to, but the lab ran their tests to identify the components.

At the Massachusetts Department of Public Safety Crime Laboratory, chemists analyzed the 15 samples taken from the burned house by gas chromatography-mass spectrometry. The analysis provides certain peaks on a graph that chemists compare to known compounds.

Here, the testing confirmed lacquer thinner residue on Mr. M's sneakers, but not on his jeans or shirt. In addition, the lab identified the liquid in the partially melted red plastic container as lacquer thinner. It is difficult to explain away the existence of thinner on your sneakers when you were at the building, but allegedly not inside, when a fire starts, plus your story is full of holes. Investigators don't believe in coincidences such as this.

The lab also found gasoline residue on two samples from the stairs and the first-floor wood door trim, plus gasoline was in a recovered 5-gallon container. Gasoline comprises over 200 components, but as with other compounds, the GCMS analysis readily identifies and confirms the presence of the substance. A third combustible liquid, fuel oil, was in the metal container taken from the basement. We concluded Mr. M intentionally set the fire using an open flame on the stairs from the basement to the second floor with the aid of poured combustible liquids to spread the fire rapidly.

The case against Mr. and Mrs. M proceeded. The evidence appeared to be substantial. Our investigation proved the stories provided by Mr. and Mrs. M to be false. The three men they allegedly were to meet were nowhere near the Westwood house when the fire occurred. All three had confirmed alibis; two were in nearby towns, one was out of state. Mr. M was at the house when the fire originated.

According to Mr. M, the reason for the evictions was because of the planned renovations. In fact, it appeared Mr. and Mrs. M intended for the insurance company to pay for the renovations. Our information fulfilled the trifecta of evidence—the motive, means and opportunity. We all felt we had a strong arson-for-profit case.

This case was tried in Norfolk County Superior Court. From the outset of the trial, things weren't going well. The state court system in Massachusetts is agonizing. Cases often take 18 to 36 months to come to trial.

Here, the defense got the trial date pushed back several times. As we filled the courtroom to seat a jury, the defendants were a sight to behold. Mrs. M was seven months pregnant. She cried and sniffled throughout the proceedings. How do you think this played with the jury?

We know how it played with the judge who happened to be female. (Now before any female readers curse me out, please understand I have worked regularly side by side with many, many female investigators, attorneys and judges with no problems or issues. Anybody who knows me knows I worked with anybody and never complained if they did their job.)

During the trial, the judge exhibited extreme bias, making every ruling in favor of the defendants—stuff that seemed like she was bending over backward far beyond protecting the rights of the accused. She handcuffed the prosecution team. Just before reading the verdict, the judge said with giddy excitement, "Well, let's not keep everybody in suspense!"

I was nervous and not optimistic. The announcement came, "Not guilty," on all counts. The judge, with a broad smile on her not-so-judicial face, showed her elation. She congratulated the former defendants.

This is what happens in a trial with two white professional suburbanite defendants with no prior arrest records in their 35 years of life. The spouses were both schoolteachers in a nearby town. How would you feel about them teaching your children?

Remember a "not guilty" verdict does not mean the defendant is innocent. It only means the prosecution did not prove the case beyond a reasonable doubt. Either way, however you judge these schoolteachers, they were tried and walked away free. I do not know whether they collected the insurance money after the fire. I don't recall ever having contact with any insurance people relating to this case.

How many times have you heard arson is a tough crime to prove, practically needing to trap the arsonist with the match in his hands? That match had barely left Mr. M's hand when the police officer first spotted him with the building burning about a hundred yards away.

We found combustible liquids on his footwear and at the scene. The defense did not contest the fire cause determination. The activities by both the husband and wife at the scene were very suspicious. We used the lies they told when they were first questioned against them. We established a strong financial motive for them to set the fire. What else could we have done to perfect this case?

I'm not sure where we fell short to convince the jurors. Maybe we should have checked gas stations to see if Mr. M had purchased a container of gasoline. They only lived six miles from the fire scene. There might be 50 gas stations in the area. That's where old-fashion legwork comes in.

One thing that often bothered me in cases prosecuted in state courts was the prosecutors chose to not have me testify during the trial. This happened at three trials in Connecticut, two in Massachusetts and one in New Hampshire. The defendant in each case walked free.

I'm not suggesting I was any better than the local investigators who testified in those cases. However, I usually had more experience and training than the local investigator. I feel that using a Federal Agent in these situations could have added a fresh perspective, a higher authority so to speak, someone who is an outsider, not so connected to the town where the crime occurred. I sense that was especially true back when these cases occurred. The Federal badge garnered more respect in those days.

Today, with this same case, I would suggest holding off on an arrest until uncovering more evidence. We had sufficient evidence to get search warrants, but we possibly could have developed additional evidence.

Investigators could examine any computers the teachers had access to in order to look for any searches relating to the crimes of arson and insurance fraud. Today, with the abundance of security cameras in use, Mr. M may have been digitally captured as he entered the house, perhaps with a gas can in hand. With today's technology, investigators could strengthen their case by using forensic GPS and cell phone information to eliminate the three young tenants who Mr. and Mrs. M tried to implicate for setting the fire. Investigators could secure evidence, such as the containers, possibly finding the DNA of any suspects.

Feel free to contact me with additional thoughts about this case or any other via my email: authorwaynemiller@gmail.com. I would be happy to discuss cases or assist in any way possible with your case.

This is not the only arson-for-profit case that went to trial and ended up frustrating me to the point I didn't want to work on these types of cases any longer. But I did anyway. Maybe I'm a slow learner.

Thank you to the Westwood Fire and Police Departments, retired Westwood Fire Chief William Scoble, Deputy Chief Richard Cerullo, and Norfolk Superior Court Clerk Colleen McCarthy for all their assistance with this story.

CHAPTER 17

Doctor, Doctor Give Me the News

The recession of 1987 affected many people in so many ways. It especially hit the top-end real estate market. During the first 2 weeks of October, the stock market lost 15% of its value, then on October 19, the Dow Jones stocks fell 508 points, a whopping 22% plummet on what Wall Street termed "Black Monday."

Arson investigators fully expected a sharp uptick with intentionally set fires all over the state over the following months. The rash of arsons never materialized. I remember looking at several vacant motels on Cape Cod, thinking they were prime targets for business owners who were suffering through financial losses. But they never burned. As a law enforcement officer who often viewed the integrity of people with skepticism, this lack of fires gave me hope for humanity.

Then, my friend, Trooper Mike Cherven, and I came face to face with an interesting investigation. Dr. Barry Lehman, DDS (I am not an anti-dentite as prescribed in a famous Seinfeld episode) lived in a McMansion overlooking the rocky ocean shoreline in the wealthiest section on the neck of Marblehead, 16 miles northeast of Boston. On June 19, 1989, late in the afternoon, he went to check on one of his investment properties, a beautiful 150-year-old house with 25 acres in Dover, Massachusetts. Shortly thereafter, the house burned.

This is another story that illustrates how difficult it was, and is, to prosecute an arson-for-profit case successfully. These cases are even more challenging when a defendant is a professional person with no previous felony arrests. Jurors, especially prior to the internet and plethora of TV crime shows, had a hard time finding white-collar criminals guilty.

This particular case gave further credence to the belief held by so many that you practically had to catch an arsonist with the match in hand to prove an arson case. Today, over 30 years since this case, with advancements in fire investigation and technology, arsons, like many other crimes, have become a little easier to prove.

However, after you read what follows, maybe you'll agree there was nothing much from the investigation standpoint that could have changed the outcome of this investigation. I plan to present much of the facts and information brought out in a subsequent trial.

Dr. Lehman had been a practicing dentist for several years when he got involved in high-end real estate. The Doctor had done well financially. People saw him speeding around Marblehead in his expensive sports car. He also drove a large Jeep Wagoneer. That oceanfront home he built was worth a couple of million dollars in 1987.

He teamed up with a few other real estate investors on three major projects. On the island of Nantucket, nearly 30 miles off the Massachusetts coast, the investors were working on a large hotel conversion, making it into more of a resort property. At another resort tourist location, in Newport, Rhode Island, the same group was deep into a mid-size condominium venture on a wharf in the downtown section.

The third property was in Dover, an affluent country town 20 miles west of Boston. This exclusive town showcased its idyllic woods, rolling fields, and horse pastures.

Dr. Lehman and his partners had purchased 25 acres on the narrow, winding, former cow path, Farm Street. There was a large white, two-story, wood-frame multi-room 1800s house at one corner of the land.

A small strip of grass and a New England-style stone wall erected during that era separated the building from the street. During the past 400 years, property owners built these stone walls, like thousands of others in the northeast, not only to divide properties but also to clear the fields full of rocks, making farming the fields less difficult. The current real estate venture divided the property into five five-acre lots, with one having the old "mansion" as part of the package.

As I recall, the lots were selling for $600,000 each, except for the lot with the mansion that was listed for $1.1 million. After several months, none of the lots sold. All the investments soaked up tens of thousands of dollars from the investors. Neither Newport nor Nantucket was close to producing money. They were still in construction. It was imperative some Dover lots were sold to help the bottom line.

BRICK END FEDERAL COLONIAL
Dover, Massachusetts

Sales pamphlet for the Dover mansion
(Courtesy of Jay Hughes, Dover Country Properties)

Barry Lehman cried poor-mouth to his partners, turning his pants pockets inside out, telling them he had nothing left to put in their investment pot. As proof of this, on that June day, Dr. Lehman traveled 90 miles through Boston area traffic from his Marblehead home to Falmouth on Cape Cod. The purpose of this trip was to complete the sale of his boat. This sale brought in $187,000, a nice little boost for his bank account, but it came with the loss of one of his biggest toys.

*   *   *

A young couple had just settled into their canoe to do some fishing on the pond about 100 yards behind that big old white house at 21 Farm Street. They saw smoke at the house but thought there was a runaway barbeque at the rear of the building. Minutes later, hearing sirens approaching, they looked toward the road. Now, they saw heavy smoke emanating from the roof of the old mansion.

Since Dover was a small country town, the fire department was a fully volunteer call department, except for Chief Peter Sherman and Inspector Dave Tiberi. Lt. Jay Hughes was the first firefighter to arrive on the scene. As a kid growing up in a couple of New England towns, Jay started chasing fires, pedaling his bicycle to the scenes. Now, he not only had been working several years for Dover FD, but he was also a real estate agent in the family business in town. He was quite familiar with this Farm Street property. His agency had the listing.

Lt. Hughes opened the trunk to his personal car, grabbing his gear, fire boots, a helmet and a rubber coat. Smoke was pushing out of the second floor and roof as he sized up the structure. Fearing the live-in caretaker, a real old-timer, might be inside the burning structure, the Lieutenant made immediate entry into the house via an unlocked rear door.

He instantly reacted to the distinct odor of gasoline. Jay noticed the lack of burning on the first floor, only scorching of the floor and wall surfaces. But yet, he saw the heat had wafted downward from the ceiling with upper wall paint sagging from the heat of the fast-burning gasoline. Checking the second floor, the raging fire halted his advance. There was no sign of the caretaker, whose bedroom was a rear first-floor room.

First arriving Dover fire engines pulled up the driveway to the rear of the house. The fishing couple abandoned their angling efforts to get a closer look at the burning building.

Dover Firefighters, with mutual aid help from nearby towns, saved much of the structure after wetting down the first floor, battling a bigger fire on the second floor, and conducting an exterior attack of the major fire that took down a portion of the massive hip roof. After nightfall, once the fire was completely out, Dover called the State Fire Marshal's Office for help with the fire origin and cause investigation.

Trooper Mike Cherven, assigned to the South Team, regularly worked in Norfolk County where Dover is located. He caught this investigation. Mike called me to join him in Dover the following morning. It didn't take long for evidence to pile up.

We located the fishing couple. Theirs was the first interesting story of many in this fascinating investigation. They related that about 3 p.m. they turned onto the property via a break in the stone wall about 100 feet past the old house. There was a path through the field of tall grass that ran from the street to the pond. After only traveling a few yards, they saw a Jeep Wagoneer coming toward them through the grass from the direction of the rear of the house. They turned to approach the vehicle and came abreast with the oncoming driver.

A white male driver, between 40 and 50 years old, asked them what they were doing. They told him the previous owner had permitted them to fish on the pond. Lehman, who did not identify himself to the couple, simply said okay, and drove off. They said he appeared to be acting normally when he drove off at a normal speed. They added it was only five minutes later when they noticed smoke from what they thought was a runaway grill.

A local man who heard about the fire offered additional information. He reported shortly after 3 p.m. the previous afternoon, he was driving along Farm Street. As he passed the break in the stone wall by the old house, some guy, driving a Wagoneer, recklessly sped out through the opening onto Farm Street, nearly crashing into him. He added the guy never hesitated or paused but kept going.

The fire scene spoke volumes, not in words, but in fire patterns and other evidence. We viewed and photographed all four sides of the house. After not observing any exterior fire damage except the partial collapse of the roof, Trooper Cherven, the Dover Chief, and I inspected the interior. When the fire occurred, the dwelling was unoccupied. There was active electrical service to the structure. Otherwise, no other potential accidental ignition sources were present, including cooking, smoking, candle use or any other inherent heat source. The scene had yet to tell the complete story of the fire.

First-floor damage was very minor, but that damage was telltale. From the kitchen and down a center hallway, light scorching was visible on the wood plank flooring and on the lower plaster walls of the hall. The odor of gasoline was prevalent. There was no charring at all.

The burning of gasoline vapors from gas poured on the floor created these minimal patterns. The vapors initially burned rapidly, causing that sagging of the wall paint observed by Lt. Hughes. But the flames burned out before imparting sufficient energy to ignite any nearby materials.

This was an early indication of what occurred. Someone intentionally set this fire. We had an arson fire, but there was much more site work to do.

Throughout the second-floor center hallway, there was heavy fire damage with substantial charring and smoky soot deposits, but no fire in any bedrooms. This fire damage was a separate and distinct fire from the first-floor hallway fire. Aside from the fact firefighters extinguished the fire in the second-floor hallway before it spread any further laterally, the other primary reason for the damage being confined to the hallway was the lack of readily available combustibles.

We found the pull-down stairway to the attic extended down into the hallway. Patterns showed it was open during the fire. Because of the weakened state of the stairs, we used a ladder to gain access to the attic.

Most of the attic floor assembly was still intact, with the second-floor ceiling attached to wood joists. Recently installed fiberglass insulation between the joists helped protect the joists from fire. We could see the sky where the fire had burned through the roof, causing it to collapse. This burning fall down material caused additional burning to the lower portions of the attic.

The fiberglass insulation throughout the attic was a great material to save as evidence. It soaked up gasoline used as an accelerant to assist with the initiation and spread of the fire. We took several samples. Back on the second floor, we also took samples from the charred wood baseboard lining the hallway. Laboratory analysis of these samples tested positive for residue of gasoline.

Now that we concluded someone intentionally set this fire, we had to identify that someone. A logical place to start is with the property owner, especially one who was at the property minutes before the discovery of the fire.

The fire science analysis, coupled with the scene evidence and initial interview information, supported that someone set this fire shortly before the couple on the pond first observed smoke. That timeline put Dr. Barry Lehman on the property when the fire started. We needed to speak with him to assist our investigation. But any interview with Dr. Barry Lehman was going to be delayed. He had already flown to Europe for the next 10 to 12 days with his girlfriend (mistress), leaving behind his wife and child.

In the meantime, we caught up to his wife and several of his business partners. The following is some information we learned while he was away.

On the afternoon of the fire, after concluding the sale of his boat, Lehman traveled from Falmouth, driving another 75 miles to the Dover property. His "purpose" was to check if landscapers had cut the grass around the house. By this time in mid-June, uncut grass could be about 12 inches tall, rather unsightly when trying to sell the property. For some reason, he chose not to call the landscapers to determine if they had cut it. Instead, he traveled one to two hours out of his way before heading toward home to do some last-minute errands related to his trip.

We learned from several of his business partners Lehman told them he was broke with no money left to contribute to the real estate ventures. However, we discovered he paid for the entire European romp to the tune of some $12,000. So much for not having any money.

I found Lehman's Wagoneer parked outside a Jeep dealership north of Boston. Allegedly, one of his windows was not working properly. At the lot, I walked around the Jeep. It was in great shape. In particular, after peering through the windows, I noted the interior was spotless. Aside from the interior furnishings, I saw nothing, absolutely nothing. It was the cleanest vehicle I had ever seen. And I obsess over keeping my personal vehicle clean.

Even though we inquired, Trooper Cherven and I could not persuade the Norfolk County District's Attorney's Office to seek a search warrant. We wanted to get inside the vehicle with an accelerant detection canine to sniff the interior.

This arson violated state law. There was no Federal violation for burning this house as it did not affect interstate commerce, a requirement for a fire to fall within Federal guidelines. That's why we took this case to the DA's Office.

Most often, if someone transported a gasoline container within a vehicle and the container was used to pour gas, the liquid or vapors should leave some residue on the interior surfaces it came in contact with. In and of itself, this wouldn't mean Lehman was guilty of setting the fire. There could be other explanations for having gasoline inside the vehicle, but when combined with a litany of additional information, the discovery of gasoline residue could be a valuable puzzle piece.

Further, with the ongoing poor economy, there had been no bites on the Dover properties. Since the other properties needed an influx of cash to complete construction, it appeared the financial motives for Barry Lehman to burn the Dover property were mounting.

We dubbed the old white mansion as the "White Elephant" because it was an expensive property, costly to the project. It was somewhat useless as it added little to the value of the parcel. Perhaps the house was an annoyance, a nearly worthless burden to Lehman unless he sold it to the insurance company. There was an adage that stated if the roof burns off a building, the insurance company considers the building a total loss. That means a nice payday for the owners of the policy, without having to go through the stalled high-end real estate market.

Over the nearly two weeks between the fire and return of Dr. Lehman, Mike and I, along with the local investigators and a Norfolk County Assistant District Attorney, built a case against the Doctor for arson. After all, we had a clearly defined incendiary fire, a timeline for the fire placing him at the scene, and we had substantial evidence of financial stress.

That all adds up to motive, means, and opportunity. To our way of thinking, all the evidence supported only one person could have set this fire, Barry Lehman. A judge rewarded our efforts when he issued an arrest warrant for Barry Lehman.

On the day Lehman was due back from his European trip, we had a team meet him on the Boston side of US Customs. As he filed into United States territory, agents placed him under arrest for a State arson violation. During his transport to Norfolk County, where we planned to process him, Lehman requested to speak with his attorney.

While this activity was taking place, another team targeted his Wagoneer. We found the Jeep in motion, driving along a Marblehead thoroughfare. With the search warrant in hand, we flipped on the blue lights and chirped the siren, directing the vehicle to the curb. We were a little surprised to find Barry's father in the driver's seat. After questioning him, we moved the Wagoneer into a safer spot in a parking lot.

First, we visually searched the vehicle. What we found was not what we expected. The floor carpets and the rear storage compartment were uniformly wet, not soaking, but more than damp. After sweeping my hand across the surface in the cargo area, I smelled my moist fingers. The odor of soap was prevalent.

When questioned, Mr. Lehman replied he had just come from the car wash where he had the vehicle washed inside and out as requested by his son. To me, this seemed unusual since the interior of the Wagoneer was spotless when I looked through the windows days earlier. It was also a red flag since it appeared they did the shampoo job to hide any residue of gasoline.

We then led the State Fire Marshal's Accelerant Detection Canine, Hulk, into the vehicle's interior. With the olfactory senses of these specially trained canines being so keen to detect combustible liquids at the rate of parts per million, we wondered if Hulk would alert to anything.

We all understood if gasoline spilled or dripped directly onto the material, washing the carpet with soap most likely would not remove the volatile liquid sufficiently so that Hulk could still detect it. However, if gasoline dripped or had run down the side of the container, then dried before contacting the carpet, a good washing could mask the liquid from detection. It is also possible Lehman placed a container on top of something else that someone removed from the vehicle.

A day or two later, we learned the fire investigator from Dover, who was part of our investigative team, innocently mentioned to a friend and associate that we planned to use the dog to sniff the vehicle for gasoline. This person was not only a real estate developer but also one of Lehman's partners. Research on this guy revealed two of his properties had also burned. When we questioned him, he said he spoke to Lehman while he was away, mentioning our proposed investigative plan to him.

Our thought was once Barry heard about our plan, he duped the elder Lehman to shampoo the vehicle before he returned from vacation. The clean-up worked. Hulk didn't alert at all within the vehicle. This was disappointing, as it would have bolstered the case. But we made do with the cards dealt us. Barry's father had nothing to tell us that hurt or helped the investigation.

✳   ✳   ✳

During the ensuing weeks after Lehman's arrest, one of our ATF Auditors examined his finances line by line. Lehman's financial records revealed his net worth decreased from approximately four million dollars to one million in a year's time. That is a stressful situation for most people. For us, it established a financial motive to burn the property.

Now, we felt we established Lehman's reason for setting the fire. His opportunity seemed clear since he was at the building at the time we concluded the fire started. Only the means, the tools or method used to commit the arson was weak. We knew the arsonist used gasoline, and the evidence supported it was lit with an open flame. Nothing suggested anyone placed a time-delayed device to ignite the fire. But it would have been nice to have positive physical evidence that tied Lehman directly to the fire.

Who else could have set the fire? Pouring gasoline on three different levels of the building and lighting the fire took some time, at least several minutes. Barry Lehman was allegedly only driving on the property to check if landscapers cut the grass. His presence at the property coincided with the same time someone set the fire.

Who else had the motive, means and opportunity? No other vehicles or people were on the property, except for the couple on the pond. But the timeline established the fire was already underway, and they were never near the building. We found no evidence anyone else had any motive to burn the property.

Lehman tried blaming the caretaker for setting the fire, but he had been out all day with family members for a doctor's appointment. Plus, he had no identified reason to set the fire.

❉   ❉   ❉

A Norfolk County Grand Jury indicted Barry A. Lehman for the Burning of a Dwelling in January 1992. The wheels of justice move painfully slowly in the Massachusetts court system. Lehman hired the highly capable attorney, John McBride. He would be one of my first choices for a criminal attorney if I ever needed one. Throughout 1992 and most of 1993, McBride filed motion after motion and sought delay after delay. He twice sought dismissal of the case, but Judge Charles Spurlock denied the motions.

Finally, in mid-November 1993, the trial began. Over the years, I took part in many November trials that always ended around Thanksgiving. This case was one of those.

Assistant District Attorney James F. Lang prosecuted the case. Lang became an Assistant United States Attorney a month after this trial, eventually becoming a Massachusetts judge. He put previously mentioned people on the stand as witnesses. He laid the case against Lehman before the jury.

On the fourth day of trial, I testified as an expert origin and cause witness. I described the elements that proved this was an arson fire. My testimony also established Lehman as the only person who could have set this fire. The timeline of the fire with him on the property was powerful evidence. Defense Attorney McBride motioned to strike this portion of my testimony because it hurt his witness. Judge Spurlock denied the motion.

Other witnesses established the motive. Our ATF Auditor laid out Lehman's losses over the year prior to the fire. Our case-in-chief seemed to go well. The judge also denied McBride's obligatory motion for a finding of not guilty when the prosecution rested.

The defense only called a couple witnesses. Lehman did not testify. But his mother did. She sat on the Board of Directors of a local bank. Mama Lehman testified Barry wasn't broke or even financially stressed. She could get him any money he ever needed. Defense rested.

On Monday, November 22, 1993, the case went to the jury. Two days later, the day before Thanksgiving, the jury acquitted Barry A. Lehman on all counts. It is difficult to convince a jury a man with $1,000,000 is destitute when the average juror made about $40,000 a year. And who would believe a dentist burned his property? After all, the jurors didn't want to be classified as "anti-dentites"!

✳   ✳   ✳

Eventually, a new owner restored the beautiful old mansion several years later. All the properties involving Lehman were subsequently completed. All made handsome profits. The partners and their banking associates ended up in the courts over disputes.

Thanks to Retired Dover Fire Chief Jay Hughes, Norfolk County Superior Clerk Colleen McCarthy. Without their help, this story could not be written.

CHAPTER 18

Reverse Sting in Vermont

Several Vermont Northeast Kingdom farmers reasoned if the Federal Government paid them hundreds of thousands of dollars not to produce milk at their dairy farms for five years to help bolster the milk prices, their empty barns would probably go to hell. During the latter half of the 1980s, the Federal Government designed the dairy termination program, also known as the Whole Herd Buyout Program, to reduce milk production to stabilize the market prices. The Government paid farmers to slaughter their herds and not produce dairy products for five years.

So when someone suggested to some farmers a means for their vacant barns to produce income, they decided to sell those barns to the insurance companies. A feed supplier from Canada asked farmers if they wanted to return to milk production. The farmers in this area had all joined the federal program around the same time, and the five-year limit was expiring. Essentially, the feed supplier asked, "Do you want to go back into business in the old dumpy barn or a new one?"

Local black sheep, Timothy Roberts, was there to help the dairymen with a solution. Over a six-week period, Timmy burned four dairy barns. From the top of the rolling hills, these nighttime fires were spectacular blazes, one after another in the otherwise sleepy pastoral town of North Troy, Vermont in the shadow of the Canadian border.

By the time the rural volunteer fire departments poured water on any of these infernos, the barns had collapsed, leaving little but some timbers and lots of ashes. The farmers allegedly hired Roberts to set three of those fires. The fourth one was an accidental arson. Timmy mistakenly hit the wrong property on that night.

For someone of Roberts's inabilities, this error was easy with so many barns close to one another. He later admitted that he wasn't even familiar with the area. You get what you pay for, but in this case, of burning the wrong property, nobody paid him.

Timmy was a rather busy criminal during this period of 1987. Not only was he an arsonist, he was also an occasional drug user, and a small-time marijuana and firearms dealer. His ex-girlfriend introduced Timmy to a new buyer. Too bad for Timmy, this client was an undercover Vermont State Trooper.

Roberts had other faults, too. He talked and bragged too much about his felonious exploits. At one meeting Timmy asked the undercover Trooper, "Do you know anybody that needs a building burned?"

The Trooper jumped on this new opening. He asked Timmy what he was talking about, figuring Roberts would open up. He did. Timmy couldn't help himself. After hearing this story, the Trooper advised Roberts he knew a guy who needed to get rid of a building. He would get back to him.

The Trooper went to his superiors, who notified our ATF office about the situation. This was exactly the type of case ATF designed their arson program to investigate.

Special Agent Thomas Perret became the case agent. Tom was one of those agents who came on the job in Boston during June 1976, the same as me and a couple dozen others. Tom was always a hard-charging, very straight agent. Fastidious in his appearance, tall and slim, Tom was always fit looking in his suit and tie, always well-groomed. His interviewing and investigative efforts were top-notch.

Tom would spend the next ten months full time, putting thousands of miles on his government vehicle driving all over Vermont.

Our supervisor assigned me to work with Tom. We traveled to the Green Mountain State, one of the most beautiful gems in this country. With State Police assistance, we came up with a proactive game plan. We planned a reverse sting operation.

✳   ✳   ✳

Law enforcement has legitimately used reverse stings for years in drug and gun cases. These sting operations are controversial because when not performed correctly, the question of entrapment arises. Offering a lot of money to someone to commit a crime or creating the thought of committing a crime to entice someone who hasn't committed that crime is entrapment.

When done properly, undercover (uc) officers with something to offer, such as drugs, guns, prostitution, or stolen goods, can open new doors to those people already involved in similar illegal activities. Let's say an undercover agent has been working on an illegal narcotics case. To get the interest of some upper-echelon players, he presents a large shipment of drugs for sale. The agent has only offered the drugs; he has forced nobody to make or arrange the deal.

You may have heard of reverse stings used in terrorist investigations. An agent who has infiltrated a group intent on committing terrorist acts might introduce explosives or weapons that can be used to complete their plans. Terrorists looking for such weapons now have the choice of whether to purchase them. The people involved are already predisposed to commit the crime. This tactic allows the investigators to control the action rather than the buyers seeking weapons from some unknown seller.

There is one other purpose for considering using a reverse sting as an investigative strategy. We liked to use some of these arsonists as a stepping stone. If property owners previously hired the torch to burn their buildings, like the farmers hired Timmy Roberts, and we successfully arrest the torch, we want to flip the arsonist. Their cooperation is critical toward perfecting an arson-for-profit criminal case against the property owners.

The Boston Arson Task Force had been in operation for several years, since 1982. With our principal focus on arson-for-profit fires, we became proactive in our approach to catching, not only the "professional" arsonist but those who hired the torch. We succeeded at least eight times where informants introduced our uc agent to a self-proclaimed arsonist and presented him with an opportunity to ply his illegal skill.

I took part in every one of those cases. In one case, I was the undercover agent who hired a torch to burn a building. Several times I was on the surveillance team keeping an eye on the arsonist or on the building.

On one Halloween night, Tom and I spent several hours standing against the enormous trunk of a thick fir tree on the side of a busy residential Brockton, Massachusetts street. Dozens of trick-or-treaters, some with parents, traipsed past us, almost close enough that we could snatch their candy.

Nobody discovered us in our hiding spot, not even the two hired torches, who walked by us, then returned by us again as they checked out the target building. Once more they tramped by us as they made their last approach to their target.

Each time they passed us, Tom and I relayed a message via walkie-talkie to the other surveillance teams, keeping them apprised of the arsonist's movements. Although we worried that any squawk on the radio would alert the bad guys, the plan went off without a hitch. Other agents arrested one man as he entered the house to burn it. The remaining guy ran in our direction. Tom jumped out from our hiding place and tackled him, preventing his escape.

On another occasion, the hired arsonist took our down payment money but never showed up. We had to protect the target building until the torch was located. Once we did, we warned him if anything happened to the building, we would arrest him. We couldn't even get our money back. Since we had given the money to him, we couldn't charge him with anything (except maybe Breach of Contract.) He didn't steal the money.

Another time, in the northern Massachusetts city of Lawrence, an arson epidemic was ongoing. ATF was part of an Arson Task Force with the MA State Police, the Lawrence Police and the Fire Department. Within 18 months the Task Force had made 129 arrests, knocking out the entire problem.

One night, after we hired an alleged torch to burn a house in the city, our surveillance teams saturated the area. Additional agents hid inside the house, but nobody had an eyeball on the torch. The suspect failed to show at the property, well after the midnight deadline. Again, we had to protect the building until he was located.

Supervisor Jack Dowd, who headed up this operation, relieved everybody but asked me to stay with the property until daytime when he would relieve me. I backed deep into the darkened driveway and settled in, but I was a little uncomfortable as I could only see two sides of the building.

Thirty minutes later, about 4 a.m., a man who fit the description of our intended arsonist came walking from the block to my right. He crossed the street and strolled past the front of the target house, out of my sight.

I got on my radio calling for anybody in the area. Special Agent Dennis Leahy (a great friend and agent who left this life too soon) just left the Lawrence Police Department. He said that he'd meet me within five minutes. As he said it, the subject walked back into my view. Dennis arrived shortly thereafter. The torch-to-be walked back toward the house. We jumped out of our cars and stopped him across the street from the house. He had a bottle of gasoline in a bag he was carrying. He confessed back at the station, but for me, it was a close call.

*　　*　　*

In the case involving Timmy Roberts, wherein he had already burned several barns, Roberts asked the uc Trooper if he knew someone who needed a building burned. Predisposed to set buildings on fire for money, Timmy was looking for more "work."

If the uc had not been working on this investigation, Timmy would have looked elsewhere. He would not have stopped burning buildings until someone caught him. As in some other serious cases, it was imperative that we jump on this investigation immediately, before someone got killed in one of his fires.

It was time for the planning. We required a target for Roberts to burn. It had to meet several suitable criteria. One, it was best if it was a commercial building that affected interstate commerce so that the case could fit under the Federal statute, 18 U.S.C., 844 (i):

> *Whoever maliciously damages or destroys, or attempts to damage or destroy, by means of fire or an explosive, any building, vehicle, or other real or personal property used in interstate or foreign commerce or in any activity affecting interstate or foreign commerce shall be imprisoned for not less than 5 years and not more than 20 years, fined under this title, or both; and if personal injury results to any person, including any public safety officer performing duties as a direct or proximate result of conduct prohibited by this subsection, shall be imprisoned for not less than 7 years and not more than 40 years, fined under this title, or both; and if death results to any person, including any public safety officer performing duties as a direct or proximate result of conduct prohibited by this subsection, shall also be subject to imprisonment for any term of years, or to the death penalty or to life imprisonment.*

We needed to find someone or some entity willing to lend us their building to use as bait. That building had to look like something an owner might want to burn. It also had to be a structure we could protect and one that wasn't too close to others in case something went wrong. The building also had to be close enough to Timmy Roberts' operating area, but at the same time, a location outside his comfort zone.

Tom found the property that fit our complicated conditions through a local contact in the little town of Hartford, Vermont, at the confluence of the White and Connecticut Rivers, bordering New Hampshire. The building was a two-story beat-up wood-frame carpet warehouse owned by a man from Boston. The place was so rickety; we felt anxious that it could burn anytime with no one's help, or that the owner would take advantage of our plot.

Next, we needed to select our undercover agent who would pretend to be the owner of the carpet warehouse. Senior Special Agent James Karolides was perfect to play the leading role. A card-carrying thespian, Jimmy acted in local plays. For his real-life role in eliciting a confession from a Boston cop in the major arson ring that was the subject of my first book, *Burn Boston Burn*, Jimmy won an acting award.

We also required a meeting place where the Vermont uc Trooper could introduce Karolides to Roberts. It had to be a place where we could control the situation to protect our agent. In nearby White River Junction, there was a hotel belonging to one of the major chains close to our target building. It suited our needs.

Here's how the meeting unfolded. The State uc cop told Timmy he had a guy from Boston who owned an old warehouse in Hartford who wanted to sell it to the insurance company. He needed it burned, and he wanted it done quickly.

The Trooper met Timmy in the hotel parking lot. If anybody paid any attention to the two scruffy-looking men talking by a pickup truck, one might think they were up to no good. Roberts was a 30-something wiry, short guy with an unkempt appearance. His mop of dark brown hair was already receding, and he kept a full beard covering his lower face. The duo headed inside.

Our Boston ATF Tech, Special Agent Dave Watts, arranged the hotel room with a minute pin-hole camera and a transmitter.

Both were secreted, aimed directly at a small table with two chairs between the large room window and bed.

I checked on Karolides to see if he had everything he needed. To get Timmy sitting in the chair facing the hidden camera, Jim poured a drink into one of the hotel glasses (actual glass, not plastic). He placed the glass on the table next to the chair closest to the camera so that his back would be to the camera.

The three of us, Dave, Tom Perret and I moved into the adjacent hotel room ready to watch, listen, and record everything going on next door. We conducted a video and sound check, while also monitoring the video feed and test conversation. Everything looked and sounded perfect. So on with the show.

Agent Karolides was all set, waiting for the curtain to rise. Except for a little less of his slicked-back gray hair and a few more years of normal wear and tear, Jimmy looked like he did on that December 1982 night when he played his role so brilliantly while interviewing Boston Police Officer (turned arsonist) Robert Groblewski about his part in setting 264 buildings on fire. Now, as he did on that night, he had on a dark pin-stripe suit over his round countenance with dark-rimmed glasses. He appeared to be the perfect aging business owner.

Back in the viewing room, we heard a knock at the bedroom door. Jimmy walked out of view, opened the door and greeted his guests. After the undercover Trooper introduced Roberts to Karolides, Jimmy booted the uc out to reduce the number of witnesses and be able to discuss business more freely. As the pair came into view on camera, Jimmy offered Timmy a drink, motioning him toward the best seat in the house as Jimmy sat by his own drink.

Jimmy didn't beat around the bush. "So, I understand that you might have a service that I could use." This is a good line to open with to avoid the entrapment issue.

With immediate brash cockiness, Timmy responded, "I've never seen a building I couldn't burn!" It appeared Timmy was inclined to burn a building with no offer dangling before him.

Agent Karolides explained he had this old building nearby that he hoped to burn. He further said the insurance coverage on the building was expiring soon, so the property had to be torched before that time. Jimmy asked Roberts if he could get the job done on time. He also asked Timmy what he charged for something like this. Roberts simply said that he could do the job whenever needed and he could do it for $3000. Jimmy quibbled at the amount. They settled for a lower fee and arranged for the fire to happen the following week.

Out of the clear blue, Timmy stated, "You know, this works on other things."

Having no clue what Timmy was talking about, Karolides quizzically replied, "What do you mean?"

"Arc welders do a good job on horses." Roberts told how you wet the grass under a horse and use an arc welder to electrocute the animal. It would look like the horse got hit by lightning. He bragged about being paid to kill a horse in this manner so the owner could collect the insurance proceeds.

In the adjacent room, we each had incredulous looks on our faces. We couldn't believe what we had just heard. In a rural area like Vermont, people would hang Timmy if they ever heard this recording.

During the intervening week, Agent Perret was extremely busy, arranging meetings for the State Police and other ATF Agents. He set up the surveillance teams, working with two dozen team members, ensuring they were familiar with their assignments.

Tom also conferred with the police and fire chiefs to alert them to the plan. With their help, Perret secured the second floor of the Hartford Water Department, directly across the street from the carpet business. ATF Tech Watts planned to use this area to watch the street, parking area and front door of the target building. From that observation post (op), he could video Timmy Roberts' arrival and radio the rest of us as he approached. Tom had the streetlights turned off for better operation of a video camera with a night scope attached.

When the day for the fire came, October 13, 1987, Jimmy met Roberts again in the hotel to finalize the plans. Timmy had his girlfriend with him waiting in his pickup truck while he was inside.

To solidify Robert's propensity to commit arson, Karolides inquired of Timmy, "Listen, what I don't want is for firefighters to find your body in the building. How do I know you really can do this?"

In response, Timmy said, "Not a problem, I set several dairy barns on fire about 70 miles north of here." He rattled off his qualifications citing he had burned those barns in North Troy within view of the Canadian border. Roberts explained how he set four fires, but farmers hired him for only three fires. Laughing, he clarified he set the wrong barn on fire one night. Timmy quipped that the farms all looked alike at night.

Around 4 p.m., the two planners headed out in Jimmy's ATF undercover car. The sun was sinking low in the western sky on this exceptionally chilly fall day.

With Jimmy still wired for sound, we could hear every word of their conversation as they drove to the carpet warehouse in the downtown village of Hartford. Plus, we had a dozen moving surveillance State Police and ATF vehicles following Karolides in the event a problem arose. With so many vehicles covering the area, we joked that had there been a car accident in town that night, it would have been between two government vehicles.

The plan was for Karolides to show Timmy the target. After perusing the building from its front parking lot, Jimmy K asked Roberts if he still wanted to go through with the job. This question further allowed the person with criminal intent to back out of the scheme if he wished. It again showed that the Government wasn't twisting his arm to do the deed. Timmy reassured his new employer that he would take care of the place tonight.

Karolides then handed Timmy the key to the front door. Jimmy also gave Roberts half of the agreed-upon payment, planning to pay him in full the next morning after the building burned.

As they made their way back to Timmy's truck, the rest of our team geared up for the next phase. From that moment on, we, representatives of the Federal Government, had to protect the bait, the target building we borrowed from a cooperating US citizen.

A Federal Agent had just identified the intended target to the arsonist and gave him access to the interior via the front door! It would have been more than embarrassing if we allowed the property to be torched. Imagine the liability!

As soon as the pair left the hotel, we also abandoned our station in the adjacent room. And when Jimmy and Timmy drove away from the warehouse, I joined with three other Special Agents to take our place inside the building to await Timmy's arrival.

The interior of the structure had two contiguous, but completely separate areas. There was no access between the two sections, which were divided by a wall, separating the front from the back. Two agents were to protect the rear half of the building.

It was unlikely Timmy would try making an entry in the rear since Karolides had shown him the front and he had the key for the front door. But better safe than sorry. The only benefit for him breaking into the rear of the building would be it didn't face the main street. With its small parking lot, the front door was only about 30 feet from the road, but this area is eerily quiet after 8 p.m.

Special Agent Jerry Gallo and I were positioned inside the front section of the warehouse. Jerry came on the job two months after me in the summer of 1976. He was a dark-haired, dark-complected Italian kid from the Boston area. He was one of the fittest guys I have ever seen, staying in great shape throughout his career. It was always nice having Jerry as your back-up or having him in front to kick in a door. On this night Jerry carried a pump-action shotgun while I had my 9mm Sig Sauer pistol.

This ancient building had a large open room immediately inside the front door. There were numerous carpet rolls in small stacks lined against the back and right side of this room. To the left of the room were a couple old-style enclosed offices with solid lower half walls and fully glass-encased upper walls.

Very little light infiltrated through the translucent upper half of the front door. Tom Perret worked with the town and utility company who shut off all the streetlights on the street. Since the business was supposedly closed for the night, we kept the interior pitch black. The darkness helped secrete our presence.

I advised Jerry of our plan, "As soon as Timmy gets in the front door and closes the door behind him, count to yourself, 1001, 1002, 1003. I'll shine my flashlight in his face and announce our presence with 'Freeze, police!' I'll have him covered with my pistol. At the same instant, you pump a round into your shotgun. Timmy will immediately recognize that sound."

Now, we prepared ourselves to wait. Since it was shortly after 5:30 p.m., we could be in hiding for over six hours if Timmy showed up late, but before the midnight deadline. It was damn cold in that unheated warehouse with the outside temps now in the 30s.

Our surveillance teams followed Timmy and his girlfriend in his pickup truck from the hotel across the state line into West Lebanon, New Hampshire. His first stop was at a store in a shopping plaza where he purchased a flashlight, batteries, and a red plastic gasoline container.

One agent from the surveillance team followed Timmy into the store. As soon as Timmy left the store, the agent pulled the clerk aside. After identifying himself, he requested a copy of the receipt for Roberts' purchases and asked them to hold the security camera footage to be subpoenaed within the next few days.

The surveillance teams watched as Roberts gassed up the pickup and put fuel into a container in the bed of his truck at a self-serve gas station. Back in White River Junction, a small village within the town of Hartford, Timmy pulled into a convenience store down the street from the hotel where he bought two of those wide-neck bottles of juice.

Finally, Roberts drove toward the target building. The surveillance teams kept us informed of his movements. Meanwhile, we waited in that cold dark room sitting on rolls of carpeting. As each minute passed, and Roberts got closer to our location, my anticipation level rose with a controlled nervousness.

After all, a guy who uses and sells drugs was to come through that front door shortly. Since he also sold guns, he may be carrying one, increasing the possibility of a dangerous encounter.

Plus, we didn't know how he was going to set the fire. What if he had an incendiary device and ignited it as we were arresting him?

My portable walkie-talkie chirped with an update that Roberts parked his pickup about two blocks from our location. They added he was outside his vehicle doing something near the rear of the truck bed. The agents couldn't see what he was doing. But the surveilling agents were close enough to Roberts to see him tuck something into his jacket pockets.

We later learned Roberts started using diesel fuel when one of his barn fires set with gasoline flashed on him. The farmers built many barns in North Troy into hillsides.

One night when setting a barn on fire, Roberts drove his pickup right into the upper level, the loft level. Once there, he poured a lot of gas directly out of a container. At least once, he went down to the lower level after pouring the fuel upstairs. He saw the liquid dripping from above and running down the interior walls. When he lit the fire, the ensuing blast blew him out the door. It's a wonder he didn't kill himself!

Next, agents passed word Roberts was walking toward us. My pulse quickened. Another surveillance team cloistered in darkness now had visual contact with Roberts. He was only a block away. Across the street from us on the second floor of the town water department building, Special Agent Dave Watts, our tech man, spotted Timmy walking down the street. He advised us he was now in the front parking lot of the warehouse.

Inside our blackened hideout, Jerry Gallo was positioned in a front corner about 30 feet to the right as one enters the front door. I was directly in front of the door, about 20 feet in, behind an opened office door that had wood on the lower half, the upper half being glass.

As Watts alerted us that Timmy was at the front door, I could barely see his silhouetted shadow through the translucent glass of the upper half of the front door. My heart thumped loudly in my chest, my telltale heart.

I was no longer cold. Heart racing faster. This was about to happen. I could hear the key trying to find the lock as Timmy struggled to turn the key in the lock. My breath caught in my throat. The door opened. I'm ready for action, whatever that may be. Timmy stepped inside, closing the door behind him. "One thousand one, one thousand two, one thousand three," I whispered inside my head.

"FREEZE, POLICE!" I yelled with authority. As planned, I illuminated Timmy with my flashlight and aimed my gun at him. On cue, Jerry cranked a shell into the chamber of his shotgun.

Timmy absolutely froze. I ordered him to put his hands in the air. He didn't move. "Turn around and put your hands against the wall," I barked as I started closing the distance between us with my pistol aimed at the center of mass, his chest. He still didn't move.

Petrified, Timmy remained locked in place. I swear he must have gone to the bathroom before he got to this moment in time because he was so shocked and scared he would have pissed or shit his pants had he not gone recently.

I grabbed him, then spun him around and raised his limp arms and hands, placing them against the wall above his head. Jerry covered Roberts as I frisked him. Timmy ended up not having a gun on him, but in his jacket pockets, on his left and right sides, he had two 12 ounce juice bottles filled with fuel. That's what he was doing at the bed of his truck about 10 minutes earlier.

He also had a cigarette lighter on him, but he didn't smoke. I snugged my handcuffs around his wrists. We radioed our covering team that all was safe and we were coming out with Roberts.

Immediately upon hearing we had Roberts in custody, Tom Perret ordered a surveillance team to take Timmy's girlfriend, who was still sitting in his pickup two blocks away. When they got her out of the truck, they searched her purse where they found the down payment cash that Agent Karolides paid her boyfriend a few hours earlier. The agents arrested her for conspiracy, which carried the potential for a five-year prison sentence.

In an ironic twist, her father was a retired Fire Chief of a local fire department. In court the next morning, her father cried as he watched his daughter's initial appearance. The arrest ended her romantic relationship with Roberts. Dad made sure of that.

Tom Perret and I had a lot of work to do to put this case together on those who had hired Timmy Roberts to burn those dairy barns. Several times we crisscrossed the state from Newport to Burlington, where the United States Attorney's Office was located. There were no highways that ran between the capital city nestled on Lake Champlain along the western edge of the state and the Northeast Kingdom.

On some of these 80 plus mile drives, I had to get my fill of Ben & Jerry's Ice Cream which was sold in every small convenience store since Vermont is the home of the company. One afternoon, after we left Burlington, I had just expressed to Tom that I needed my B & J fix. Less than a minute later, around the next bend in the road, lo-and-behold, the Ben and Jerry's manufacturing plant was directly in front of us. Hallelujah!

We had to stop. I ended up with my favorite ice cream pint, Cherry Garcia, named after the Grateful Dead's Jerry Garcia by the two hippies that formed the company. What a delicious way to pass the time!

To further this investigation toward prosecution of the farmers who allegedly hired Timmy Roberts to burn their barns, we asked one farmer to take a polygraph test. I recall a weathered dairyman about 55-years-old came to a hotel where our Polygraph Examiner, Special Agent Gerry O'Reilly had a room all set up for administering an exam.

Gerry O. was a friendly grandfatherly type who was great at his job of talking with a test subject, explaining and trying to ease their nervous minds.

The farmer, in a plaid flannel shirt and jeans, took a seat at the small table where the "lie-detector" recorder was ready for use. O'Reilly sat across the table. I took a seat off to the side behind the subject, affording me a unique ringside seat for this session.

S.A. O'Reilly told the farmer he would ask him a series of questions pertaining to the fire at his barn. Each question required only a yes or no answer. But first, before asking those pertinent questions, he was going to run a sample test. Gerry told the man to write seven women's first names on a sheet of paper, including his wife's name. He added he was not to list his wife's name first or last. Gerry said that he would ask, "Is your wife's name...?" He instructed the subject to answer "no" for each question. Then Gerry would show him the test results, including when he lied (or was not truthful as polygraphers like to say) about his wife's name.

After the farmer completed his task, O'Reilly wired the guy up for the test with monitors wrapped around his chest and on his finger. The exam commenced. "Is your wife's name, Susan? Is your wife's name, Mary?" He continued with seven questions. The farmer responded with a "no" to each query.

When Gerry correctly told the man his wife's name, the farmer hunched over the table in front of him. His breathing became labored, heaving heavily. Sweat broke out on his forehead. As I was thinking he was having a heart attack, the farmer ripped the monitors off his finger and from his chest. He pushed himself up from his chair, gasping, "I can't do this," and he walked out of the room. Test over.

My duties related to this case also ended here. Tom teamed up with State Police Detective Sergeant Rick Hall from the St. Johnsbury barracks. Rick loved life and loved being a good trooper and investigator. When I say they teamed up, the two became brothers. Tom worked hundreds of hours with Rick, also spending time with Rick's wife and family, frequently enjoying dinners together after a long day.

Their work on this case was often demanding. Assistant United States Attorney Tom Anderson prosecuted this case with the help of Tom Perret and Rick Hall. Initially, Roberts, with advice from his defense attorney, resisted confessing and cooperating with the government. This delay didn't help the case. We would have liked his immediate help. With Roberts as a cooperating witness, ATF could wire him while he met with the farmers trying to elicit incriminating conversation.

In an early court hearing, Roberts told a story trying to diminish his culpability in the attempted arson. He testified about when he was trying to find the keyhole in the dark, he decided what he was about to do was wrong and turned to walk away. Just then the door opened. A big arm reached out, grabbed him and dragged him into the building.

How could Roberts and his attorney make such a big mistake? Luckily for the government's response to this ludicrous allegation, our tech man, Dave Watts, had filmed everything from Timmy's approach to the building to his entry into the front door under his own control.

In early December, Perret convinced defendant Timmy Roberts to cooperate. During the debriefing process, Roberts confessed to burning the four dairy barns, including the one he burned by mistake. Timmy described how the plans unfolded and how he set the fires.

He related that a feed supplier from Canada, who serviced the dairy farms in the North Troy area, was quite familiar with the United States program to shutter the dairy barns for five years. Roberts said it was this man who came up with the idea to burn the barns.

He and Roberts had known each other for a while. Being familiar with Timmy's propensity for the illegal side of life, this feed supplier brokered Timmy to the farmers as an arsonist.

When Roberts spelled out the details of each barn fire, the investigators' eyes popped wide open a few times. In one story, Timmy explained he got into and out of the barn through the "shit chute", the moniker given to the chute that carried manure to a holding area, typically a pit dug to store manure during the winter when snow prevented access to the fields.

In a meeting with the AUSA, Agent Perret, Roberts and his counsel, Roberts made a surprising admission. He revealed he burned the barn of his friend, Reginald Riendeau on June 23, 1984, long before being hired to torch the other barns in North Troy. Riendeau hired Roberts to burn his property so he could collect on his insurance.

With that additional information, the Government told Roberts that he could help himself with a recommendation for a reduced prison sentence if he wore a wire, met with Riendeau and tried getting him to make admissions relative to his barn fire. Timmy, knowing he was facing a lengthy prison sentence for the arson charges, agreed.

Perret and Rick Hall devised a script for Roberts to follow the best he could while speaking with Riendeau. During their first meeting, Roberts was incapable of even conversing with Riendeau, he was so nervous. The investigators then prepared a fake letter on the defense attorney's stationery. The letter laid out Roberts' cooperation and mentioned Riendeau hiring Roberts to set his property on fire.

The day came for the undercover contact. Perret had to secret the recorder and transmitter on Timmy's body. Normally, we taped the devices and associated wires directly to the undercover person's body using surgical tape, which adheres well without tearing the skin or body hair. But Tom didn't have the tape with him. Roberts saved the day by coming up with some tape. It wasn't quite the same tape we used. It was duct tape! And Timmy was hairy front and back, with black gorilla hair. But the tape held well.

When the meeting occurred between the two Vermonters, Hall and Perret listened to the conversation. It stunned them to hear how badly Roberts handled himself. Perret described Roberts as being so stupid, he couldn't follow the script or think on his feet. The fake letter helped slightly. Reggie wasn't much brighter than his friend.

After he read the letter with the sentence that mentioned his property, Reggie inquired, "You're not going to tell them about burning my barn, are you?" Except for that one statement, Roberts elicited no other conversation to make a strong case against Riendeau. At least, Tom Perret, with tears of laughter, relished in the howls of pain as he ripped the duct tape off the hairy Roberts.

Shortly after this meeting, Riendeau was indicted, then arrested for the arson of his barn and for mail fraud associated with trying to collect the insurance for the loss of his barn. He was released on bail, pending his trial.

On February 9, 1988, Roberts pled guilty to three counts of arson. The following week he was to turn himself in to begin his prison sentence. However, another development created more work and new headaches for the investigators all the way to the Federal Appeals Court.

The day before Roberts was to surrender to the U.S. Marshals, he contacted Rick Hall with an urgent situation. Timmy explained he discovered two bullet holes in his pickup truck. He said he was in fear for his life and that of his family.

Perret was already in St. Johnsbury for Roberts' surrender. He and Rick Hall inspected the truck. They saw the two dents where the bullets hit the vehicle, plus they found one spent round on the ground. To them, Riendeau most likely sent a message to Roberts in retaliation for getting him arrested. Roberts was taken into custody to begin his prison sentence. He was due to start it anyway, but this was partially for his safekeeping.

Immediately, the government moved to revoke Riendeau's bail, but the motion was unsuccessful. Roberts remained incarcerated the next day, as planned. Timmy's mouth once again was to get him in trouble.

Two weeks later, Detective Hall received a telephone call from someone who had just spent a weekend in jail with Roberts. Relaying how Roberts told him he shot up his own truck, the new informer detailed where Roberts hid the gun.

With that information, Perret and Hall received consent from the owner of the property to search his barn. Roberts was living at this house prior to being locked up.

The informer's information was spot on. They found a .22 caliber pistol hidden in a wall cavity in the barn. Tom Perret still has the photos taken when he reached in the hole between the inner and outer barn walls.

While still at the property, the owner of the barn told investigators Roberts asked him to shoot the truck and even shoot Roberts in the arm, but he declined. The investigators felt good finding the gun. But they were very unhappy their star witness against Riendeau was now a major problem.

This is where the investigation becomes the crux of an appeal subsequently filed by Roberts. Tom and Rick interviewed Roberts while he was in custody. There was no attorney present representing Roberts. The focus of their interview was an additional matter unrelated to the fires, so Tom and Rick figured Roberts didn't need representation unless he asked for it.

Still, they handed Roberts a Miranda statement of rights form. He wondered aloud why they were giving him his rights. Perret replied they hadn't recently advised him and they wanted to question him on some old issues and some recent issues. Roberts signed the form without asking for an attorney.

The questioning began. Perret and Hall asked him if he had shot his own truck. Roberts denied doing it. Tom was so pissed. He pulled out the recovered Roberts' gun. Slamming the gun so hard on the table in front of Timmy, other troopers in the barracks where they were questioning him thought Roberts was getting a beating.

Just when Tom and Rick got up to leave, Roberts told them the truth. He confessed he shot his truck, hoping to improve his odds for placement in the federal witness protection program.

His actions had the opposite effect. The US Attorney's Office pulled their agreement with Roberts. Instead of two counts of arson, the government now charged Roberts with four counts of arson, one attempted arson, and one count of possession of a firearm while under indictment. However, the case against Riendeau was still going forward.

ATF had their auditor, Alan Graham, do an exhaustive audit on Riendeau. Graham, one of the best forensic accountants in the country, found a strong financial motive for Riendeau to burn his barn.

Based on Riendeau's own utterance while Roberts wore a wire, plus using arsonist Roberts as a witness, and with proof of motive, the government felt their case was still strong enough to proceed.

The trial against Riendeau did not go well. Many hours of trial preparation with Roberts failed to make him a solid witness. Predicated on Roberts' previous lackluster undercover performance, the prosecution knew that using him was an uphill battle. Roberts ended up making a terrible witness. His credibility was so damaged that the AUSA could do nothing to rehabilitate him in the eyes and ears of the jury.

The defense put the final nail in Roberts' testimony when they used Timmy's fake shooting against him. Besides the Roberts fiasco, Riendeau's father testified on behalf of his son. He perjured himself by claiming the farm finances were in good shape and by suggesting the electrical system condition was so poor, it was the likely source of the fire. The jury must have believed him more than Roberts. In short order, the jury found Riendeau not guilty of arson.

Because they lost that case, the US Attorney's Office declined to go any further with cases against the other dairy farmers who had their barns torched. Tom has shown the undercover audio and visual recordings taken during this case many times when teaching proactive investigation techniques at the ATF Academy.

In July 1988, the judge sentenced Roberts for his crimes. Special Agent Tom Perret and Vermont State Police Detective Sergeant Rick Hall stood in the courtroom behind Roberts as the judge read Roberts' sentence. On Count 1, the gun charge, the judge gave Roberts one year. For the burning of Riendeau's barn, Count 2, the sentence was 10 years consecutively with Count 1, totaling 11 years. On Count 3, the attempted arson, the judge sentenced Roberts to 10 years to run concurrently with the previous sentence.

Perret tapped Hall, telling him to watch Roberts. Tom could see Timmy adding up the years in his head, looking extremely nervous. Then, on Counts 4, 5, and 6, for each count, the judge read 10 years to run concurrently. Tom saw Timmy swaying. His unsteadiness increased as he continued to calculate his prison sentence. Timmy summed it up to 51 years in prison because he didn't know what concurrent meant. When he was about to go down for the count, his attorney supported Timmy explaining to him he only received 11 years in total. Although relieved, Timmy needed aid as he was shaking when led from the courtroom.

The case wasn't quite over yet. Roberts moved to suppress statements he made to Perret and Hall when questioning him about his shooting. The Federal District Court ruled in his favor saying he had an attorney for the arson case so this still entitled him to representation. However, the Federal Appeals Court

Timmy Roberts, 60-years-old in 2018, no longer with his black hair. (Courtesy of Vermont Fish and Wildlife)

overturned that decision because Roberts signed the Miranda form, never asking for counsel.

✳ ✳ ✳

Timmy Roberts got his 11-year prison sentence in July 1988. Rick Hall got far worse. Rick noticed a persistent pain deep in his throat. In September, doctors diagnosed Rick with esophageal cancer.

Tom Perret and Rick had become like brothers. They enjoyed each other's company since the day they met. Each had the other's back.

Within days, Rick underwent surgery. Tom traveled to northern Vermont to see Rick. At the hospital, Tom asked, "What room is Rick Hall in?" The response was he was seeing no visitors today. Tom, not about to take that reply without his own rejoinder, "I drove all the way up here from Boston."

The nurse asked, "Are you Tom?" He shook his head. "You're the only visitor he wants to see."

It was a solemn meeting. Rick told Tom, "They didn't get it all. I can feel it." For those of you who have been through this, you know what it feels like seeing your family member like this. Others can only imagine the ache in your gut and your heart.

When Rick developed an infection, they transferred him to a top-notch medical center near Dartmouth College. Around Christmas, Tom visited Rick, who was at home being cared for by his wife and a visiting nurse. As he walked into his room, Tom saw the end was near for Rick. He was out of it with his eyes wide open, vacantly staring into space. Suddenly, Rick became lucid, "Did you bring Ashley?"

Tom's daughter was only four years old. Rick had heard so much about her but never met her. They had discussed their families as friends do. "Not this time, Rick. Next time." It felt like a knife stabbed deep into Tom's chest.

On January 1, 1989, Rick Hall's wife called Tom notifying him of Rick's passing. Rick had gotten the ultimate sentence. Way too soon.

Tom attended the service for Rick, but they couldn't bury him because of the deep freeze in Vermont. So Tom returned to Vermont in the spring. His "brother," Rick, wanted him as one of his pallbearers. To this day, Tom chokes up when he thinks about the loss of his good friend and fellow Navy veteran.

Many thanks to ATF Special Agent (retired) Thomas F. Perret. His recollection of this story not only made it factual, but he put the human touch to it.

CHAPTER 19

This Story Bugs Me

Since I have very little psychology training, I don't intend to discuss the basis for the extreme hoarding habits of some people. During my last 20 years of fire investigation, I have seen many houses turned into storage units. The occupants lived within the confines of piles of 'stuff,' often in filthy conditions. My first such encounter with a hoarder is one I will never forget.

Twice during the mid-1990s, I had the fortunate experience of being assigned to work with the Washington, DC Fire Department (DCFD) for six weeks at a time. This unique cross-training provided ATF Agents the opportunity to see all types of fires, with many extinguished while still in the incipient stage. This gave us invaluable insight into fire patterns created early in a fire's development.

Since the fires ATF Agents often investigated were large events, understanding a fire's early growth and resultant physical remnants is crucial to becoming proficient at analyzing a fire's history. The patterns created during a fire change every minute from the moment of ignition to the time of full extinguishment.

The DCFD investigators learned from our extensive training. By that time, we Certified Fire Investigators had about 1000 hours of training and maybe 500 fires under each of our belts. Relative to the

ATF Arson program, the Bureau did the right thing to assure that we became some of the best explosion and fire investigators in the country.

Effectively applying one's training to fire scene investigations can only truly be accomplished after seeing a great number of fires, both accidental fires and intentionally set fires. The DC investigators went to every single fire within the city. This gave them a broad investigative background that they could share with us.

One of these DC fires provided me with working my first hoarder fire. The ATF Agents were guests of the DCFD Fire Investigation Unit. We slept in the same rooms as the DC investigators did at the firehouse, waiting for the call to overnight fires. Around 10 p.m. on a chilly early April weeknight, we rolled into the beautiful Georgetown section of the city.

The large apartment building had four or five floors with six units on each floor. It was a rather nice-looking place in a pleasant neighborhood. The firefighters knocked the fire down, containing the fire damage to a second-floor front apartment. Nobody had been home at the time of the fire.

My gear was simple in those days. Over my jeans, I wore a pair of navy blue BDU (from Battle Dress Uniform) pants with 6 pockets. I had a lightweight nylon jacket over my ATF t-shirt. I routinely wore protective boots with steel toes and shank, and I always carried good work gloves and wore a helmet when conditions dictated.

The DC guys and I made our way up a wide center stairway to a large second-floor lobby. This lobby looked neat and clean. The powerful odor of smoke was prevalent, but there was no evidence of soot. Several geared-up DC firefighters who had extinguished the fire were awaiting our arrival. I walked into the apartment with one of the firefighters.

As soon as I took my first step into the unit, I was no longer walking on the floor. I was actually about 6 to 12 inches above the floor. I asked my escort if his guys were responsible for these conditions, to which he replied that this was the way they found it.

This was a large studio unit, one open room with a bed against the front wall, a living area near the door, and a kitchen area also along the front wall. A bathroom was the only separate room in the corner off the kitchen. Soot blackened the room, but there was very little visible fire damage. This smoky fire caused the activation of a smoke detector within the apartment before the fire propagated to any great extent.

There was no floor space to walk on, none. The entire place was full of contents. This was puzzling. It was about this time the occupant of the apartment returned home from a night out on the town. The young man, in his 30s, spoke with a thick Middle Eastern accent, making understanding him somewhat difficult. Being patient with me, he related he lived in the apartment for a couple years. As we walked into the space, I asked him what all this stuff was. He replied he was constantly buying from QVC and the Home Shopping Network, so all the items spread throughout his apartment were new, mostly never used.

After I asked him about the three refrigerators in this little apartment, he explained the full-size refrigerator that came with the apartment stopped working after a few months. So, he bought one of the smaller dorm room size models. That one also stopped working after a short time. Pointing toward the newest, under-counter size refrigerator, he stated he had that unit for about six months.

Just looking over the fire scene indicated what may have occurred. The fire had only been at and near floor level. Nothing above the level of the pile on the floor had any heat or char damage. There was no fire or heat damage around the full-size refrigerator, but the tenant had stacked packages completely around the base of the appliance. The conditions were identical around the "faulty" mini-fridge, no fire damage, but "junk" piled around the unit.

However, the situation around the newest mini-fridge was dramatically different. I found many boxed items still encased in plastic wrap on the floor around the fridge, fused together from the heat with charring of the box surfaces. This warranted further investigation.

I took a short-handled shovel and hit the fused debris, trying to move it while seeking the ignition source.

What happened next obliterated my focused attention on doing my job. With my first stroke into the debris, hundreds of reddish-brown cockroaches streamed up from below as if I opened the door, the proverbial Pandora's box, releasing crawling inmates from floor level. The flattened, oval-shaped creatures scrambled in every direction. I can do snakes and rats, but I don't do bugs, with cockroaches being my special bane. I nearly convulsed upon the invasion of the creepy-crawly creatures.

A quick conclusion to my investigation entailed flipping over the mini-fridge with the second battalion of bugs coming out of hiding to invade my space. It became obvious, based on the data, albeit limited, that the compressor motor overheated because of the junk piled around it, causing the combustibles in direct contact with the unit to pyrolyze. The process of pyrolysis is the breakdown of items due to the heating process, ultimately producing melting, charring and/or the smoke that activated the smoke detector. After I formed my opinion, I bailed out of the apartment to the main street below.

Immediately, I ripped off my jacket and T-shirt and banged them on the sidewalk, trying to beat any cockroaches off the fabric. I then pulled off my boots and peeled off my BDU's, also pounding them silly. I was tempted to pull off my jeans right then and there to repeat the cleansing process. That night in DC, after returning to quarters, I couldn't sleep with the constant itching created by my imagination. My behavior may be extreme and over-the-top, even irrational, but I'll bet a few readers are getting a little squeamish right about now!

That event reminded me of my first encounter with cockroaches. While going through the second half of New Agent Training at the Federal Law Enforcement Training Center in Brunswick, Georgia, I joined a bunch of young agents on a Friday evening at one of our favorite watering holes, Murphy's on St. Simon's Island. No sooner had I sidled up to the bar to order my first beer of the night, I felt something strange just above my ankle.

I instantly reached down, grabbing my lower leg. Too late. By then, whatever it was, had reached my thigh. I grabbed at the unwelcome invader to stop the upward assault. Simultaneously, I rapidly waltzed across the dance floor toward the men's room while undoing my pants belt. Once inside the door, *dropping-trou* as fast as possible, I trapped Mr. and Mrs. Palmetto bugs, those southern over-sized cockroaches, in my hand, only bug-sized steps from my groin. I tossed the pair into the toilet and smiled as I flushed. My feet never touched the floor the rest of the night!

In the ensuing 38 years of conducting over 2300 fire scene examinations, only one other time did I have a nasty encounter with bugs, but this time it was fleas. I ended up with about 300 flea bites covering both lower legs, both forearms and my lower back. The pattern at the top of my sock line looked similar to one of those barbed wire tattoos. An allergic reaction overtook my system from the sheer number of bites. The itch and welts lasted for weeks. It was freakin' gross!

In telling these buggy-hoarder stories years and decades later, my skin still crawls. I'm feeling itchy all over again. I still have the scars, both mentally and physically. It's a post-traumatic stress thing for me.

CHAPTER 20

Was It Arson —
Murder in the North Country?

This is a case that caused me a lot of heartaches. I am going to present you all with the best information that I had on this investigation and let you make your own call. I am also going to give you as many of the defense arguments as I can recall or gather from records.

Although I didn't know it in the 80s and early 90s, I always utilized the scientific method during my fire and explosion scene analyses. The data collected relative to the fire origin always included witness information, fire patterns, fire dynamic analysis and some form of arc mapping, plus a timeline of events. The fire cause analysis always included a review of all potential ignition sources within a defined origin area, plus I made inquiry as to the first fuel ignited, the competency of an ignition source and the actions or inactions that brought the fuel and heat source together, defined as the fire cause scenario.

I used this same methodology for an arson-murder investigation in Vermont.

✳   ✳   ✳

How many of you have experienced a fire in your residence? Now, how many of you have experienced two fires in your residence? Further, how many of you have lost a family member in each of those fires? One more question, how many of you have had two fires in your residence with a family member dying in each fire within just a few minutes of you walking out of your residence?

Ruth Lizotte of West Rutland, Vermont, was such an unfortunate person who suffered two tragic losses. But there is a lot more to this story. Of course, there is, or I wouldn't have written about this case.

Late in 1987 Ruth Gaudette Lizotte, her husband, Terry J. Lizotte, and their five-year-old son, Jay, welcomed home their newest family member, Micheal Joseph Lizotte, who was born on November 2, 1987. The home was a "garden-style" apartment in Rutland. Terry was an assembler in the plywood department at Carris Reels, a large local business that manufactures, among other items, those large reels or spools that often have wire cables wrapped around them. Ruth was a stay-at-home mom, at least sometimes.

For instance, on a cloudy, cool Thursday, April 21, 1988 morning, Ruth left her apartment to visit a nearby unit allegedly to make a phone call. She left behind five-year-old Jay with his five-month-old infant brother, Micheal. While visiting her friend to use the phone, Ruth extended her stay to have a cup of coffee that her friend offered to her.

Moments later, someone discovered a fire in Ruth's apartment. Then Ruth became aware of the fire. She ran over to her unit and pulled open the same door she had come out a few minutes earlier. Little Jay came running out the door. But because of the ferocity of the fire, Ruth couldn't make sufficient entry to get to her baby.

First arriving firefighters couldn't make the save either. Micheal perished, forever to be only five months old.

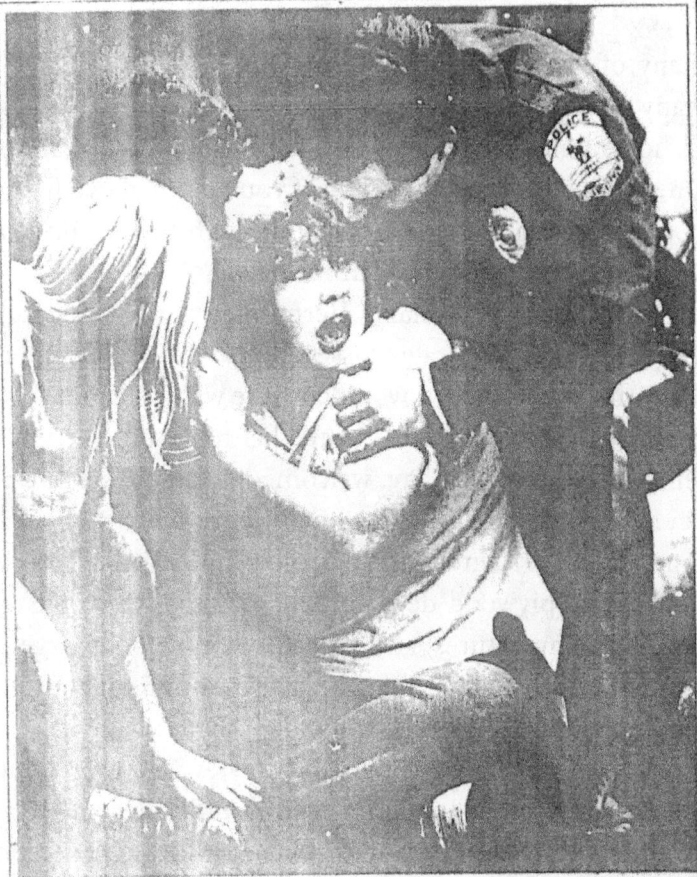

Two Rutland City Police officers comfort Ruth Lizotte, who collapsed after learning her 5-month-old baby died in a fire at the Forest Park Housing development in Rutland.

Forest Park Fire Kills Boy

By YVONNE DALEY

[...] child died [...] when a fire [...] reportedly set by accident by the infant's sibling, ravaged the family's two-story apartment at a low-income housing project in Rutland.

No one else was injured in the morning fire.

The fire occurred at 8:30 a.m. at the Forest Park Housing Project while the baby's mother, Ruth Lizotte, was at a neighbor's apartment two doors away making a phone call.

Officials said initial indications were that the fire was set accidently by Lizotte's 3-year-old son, who was apparently playing with a cigarette lighter. The fire, which caused about $35,000 in damage, is still under investigation.

Lizotte had left the infant son, Michael Joseph Lizotte, in a playpen in the living room with her 3-year-old son, Jay, while she made the phone call, according to Rutland Fire Chief Gerald Lloyd.

Lizotte was at the apartment of neighbors Evie and Rod Kenyon for only minutes, Rod Kenyon said, when the smoke alarm in the Kenyon apartment sounded.

The 75-unit Forest Park complex is composed of numerous blocks of apartments, each equipped with one or two smoke detectors that are connected electrically to alarms located in the other apartments in that block. In that way, if one alarm is activated, it triggers smoke alarms in the other apartments in that block, Theodore Cacioppi, manager of the housing project said.

When Lizotte heard the alarm, she ran out of the Kenyon apartment to her own apartment, neighbors said. Smoke was already pouring out of the apartment and, within seconds, flames had consumed the building, they said.

(See Page 16: Fire)

Ruth Lizotte after learning of her son's death.
(Rutland Daily Herald 4/22/88 by Vyto Starinskas)

The local fire and police departments, along with the District Attorney's Office and the Vermont State Fire Marshal's Office, who investigated this fire, determined the origin of the fire to be on or near the living room sofa. Ruth told the investigators Jay must have gotten a lighter and lit some newspapers on fire that were on the couch. The case was closed shortly thereafter.

Headstone of Micheal Lizotte (From www.findagrave.com Photo added by Jen Snoots)

I was not privy to the actual interview or the first-hand notes, but as a seasoned investigator, her information was very specific, so specific that one might believe that she had first-hand knowledge of the cause scenario for this fire. What would make someone suggest that newspapers were the first material ignited rather than just the sofa itself? How many mothers would readily blame their young child for setting a fire that killed an infant sibling? The questions could go on and on.

Three years went by for Ruth and Terry Lizotte. There were rumors of various problems with their marriage, including allegations that each had affairs and sexual encounters outside the marriage. There was also an addition to the family, as of this time, the infant was only a few months old. The family was now living in a two-story West Rutland apartment.

On January 11, 1991, at approximately 8 a.m., witnesses observed Ruth Lizotte on her front doorstep outside the apartment. The street in front of their unit was only a step away. Ruth's car was only a few more steps away, parked on the street.

Ruth had been awake since Terry arrived home in the wee hours of the morning, more than a little intoxicated. When he made too much noise while heading up to the bed, the baby awoke crying. Ruth got pissed. She threw a baby bottle at him, demanding he take care of the baby. At some point, Terry bedded down on the sofa in the first-floor living room, either banished from the couple's bedroom or hiding from Ruth's wrath.

Just a few short hours later, Ruth was up with Jay, getting him ready for school, an elementary school about a five-minute drive away from their residence. She also got the baby ready for the ride, having to bundle him up to face the cold Vermont January morning. It seems like a lot of work for a 10-minute trip when the baby easily could have stayed home in his crib while Dad slept. Just after Ruth got up, Terry went to bed in the upstairs bedroom.

Ruth put the kids in the car's backseat and started the car to warm it up. Two high school teens, brother and sister, who lived directly next door to the left side (as viewed from the front of the building, Side B in firefighter terms, with the front designated as Side A and moving clockwise around the structure) of the Lizotte's apartment, saw Ruth on that front doorstep, but they didn't observe her come out of the front door to the house. As the teens approached their car to head to school, they saw Ruth get into her car by walking around the rear of the vehicle and enter her driver's side door.

As they climbed into their car, the teenagers saw Ruth drive past the rear of their car, which was parked in their driveway. The teens later stated that from the moment that Ruth got into her car and drove off was only a few seconds. They had not seen her put the children into the car, but they saw the heads of the kids in the car.

The teenage boy put his car into reverse and looked to see if the road was clear for him to back out. As he did this, he saw an orange glow inside the first-floor living room bow window on Side B of the Lizotte residence. He instantly alerted his sister, who also saw the orange glow erupt into flames at the bottom of the window at the south end of the living room. They then observed the curtains to the side of the windows on fire.

After putting the car in park, the teen boy walked rapidly back toward his front door so he could call the fire department. His sister stayed in the car since she was on crutches because of a leg injury.

As he traversed the 37 feet to his front door (coincidentally the distance from his sidewalk to the living room window was also 37 feet as I had made the measurements), the bow window off to his right ruptured with red-orange flames immediately venting to the exterior of the building.

As a fire investigator, this is a sign that a fire in a room had now progressed to a room on fire, a transitional stage of fire growth known as flashover. As a quick, simplified fire science explanation, when a fire grows within a fuel in a room, in this case, we'll use a sofa, the flames, smoke, and hot gases extend toward the ceiling. When the fire by-products reach the ceiling, those components spread laterally, and if the fire continues to grow, the smoke and hot gas layer descends toward the floor, in a sense, an upside-down version of a bathtub filling with water. When the fire reaches a critical stage in terms of temperature and heat energy, virtually all other combustible items within the room ignite simultaneously, often causing the room windows to fail with the flames extending outside.

According to the two eye-witnesses, the total time from when Ruth was first seen on the front stoop to when the flames blew out the living room window was less than two minutes.

Terry Lizotte apparently woke up in his second-floor bedroom, but he quickly collapsed. Firefighters found his lifeless body on the bedroom floor, dead from inhalation of smoke and toxic gases.

This is the short story of two fires in three years with two family members deceased with Ruth leaving the scene shortly before the discovery of each fire. Red flags for sure, but investigators needed to investigate before anyone drew conclusions. Investigators don't like or believe in coincidences.

Sergeants James Freese and Albert Rouse, plus Lieutenant D.J. Clark, of the Vermont State Police, conducted the initial investigation of this fire. Their scene examination revealed the fire originated on or immediately around the couch within the south end of the first-floor living room. The investigator s eliminated several potential ignition sources in the sofa's area, including the heating system, the structural electrical system, and electrical appliances as being related to the fire cause.

Since there were no other inherent ignition sources in the area, they concluded someone introduced the ignition source to the sofa or some other item on or around the sofa. However, the authorities could not determine the cause of the fire at that time, as they could not eliminate improper disposal of smoking materials or the intentional setting of the fire.

Interview information from the widow, Ruth, filled in the timeline of the events prior to the fire. In any fire investigation, interviews of first eye-witnesses and those familiar with the property, plus any person who has first-hand knowledge of the pre-fire conditions relating to the origin area, room of origin or building of origin are all enormously important to fire investigators.

Ruth said she took the baby with her when she was dropping Jay off at school because she didn't want to leave the baby with her husband, who had come home drunk only a few hours earlier. She stated that when she came down to the first floor before placing the kids in the car, she smelled a slight odor of smoke.

After putting the kids in the car, Ruth returned to the living room to check for the source of the odor. Thinking Terry may have smoked when he went to sleep on the couch during the night, she thought maybe a cigarette within the couch was burning. She said she saw no smoke and checked around the cushions and sides of the sofa, but found nothing, so she left.

This could prove significant. To reiterate, according to Ruth, she observed neither smoke nor fire in or around the sofa, the defined origin of the fire, within a few brief minutes before a fire erupted from that area.

Another witness, a neighbor who lived directly across the street from the Lizotte apartment, related what he observed. He heard Ruth drive away from her place that morning. About five minutes later, when he became aware there was a fire across the street, he looked out from his second-floor window and saw flames coming out from a first-floor window. He recalled the flames had already extended about halfway up the left side of the building toward the roof.

Vol. 135 No. 1?
Rutland, Vermont • Copyright

Saturday Morning, January 12, 1991

Ruth Lizotte sits wrapped in a blanket, watching firemen put out an apartment house fire that claimed the life of her husband, Terry Lizotte, 32, of West Rutland Friday morning. The couple lost an infant son in a fire at the Forest Park housing development three years ago.

Man Dies in West Rutland Fire

Firemen work to extinguish blaze that claimed the life of a West Rutland man Friday morning.

Ruth Lizotte watching her second fire in 3 years.
Rutland Daily Herald 01/12/91

Photo 1

This photograph was taken with the camera facing northwest
and shows a view of the east and south elevations.

Fire Science Technologies, Inc.
Fire & Explosion Analysis

Front and Side B of building.
(Courtesy of Dan Slowick)

Headstone of Terry Lizotte
(From www.findagrave.com Photo by Jen Snoots)

Ruth buried her husband, the father of her children, the second person in her immediate family to die by fire within three years. Terry Lizotte was forever 32 years old.

Four days after the fire, Dan Slowick, a private fire investigator who operated his own company, Fire Science Technologies, conducted a second scene examination with the origin and cause analysis on behalf of the insurance company that insured the structure. Based on his investigation, Slowick independently opined that the fire originated in the immediate area of the living room sofa. He also eliminated any building electrical or electronic components for causing the fire with the belief someone introduced an ignition source to the fuel, but he did not conclusively determine the cause scenario.

Like the State Fire Marshals before him, he initially could not conclude whether the fire started from improper handling of smoking material or from someone intentionally setting the fire. To Dan's credit, he didn't have all the interview information at the time of his investigation in order to support a more definitive cause determination.

*   *   *

The investigation of the cause of the fire languished. The Vermont State Police didn't forget about this case, but the hot case became a cold case. Some investigators within the VSP decided to have more eyes look at this incident.

In October 1993, over two-and-a-half years after Terry Lizotte died, Sergeant Bernard Chartier asked me to review this case. By this time I had been an ATF Certified Fire Investigator (CFI) for five years.

*   *   *

The ATF CFI Program was a Federal initiative that was one of the best projects ever undertaken by ATF or the Federal Government. The goal of ATF was to have a cadre of agents with expertise in determining where and how a fire started. In order to graduate as a CFI, agents had to fulfill the initial criteria to attend and assist with at least 100 fire scene origin and cause investigations, plus get a certain number of hours training, both within the Bureau and from outside sources. We accomplished this while also working on criminal cases in our home office.

Once certified, the CFIs had to continue their education and training, at least 80 hours yearly, plus investigate another 25 fires per year at a minimum. The training included setting training fires in buildings in various ways while recording the fire ignition and growth visually, plus collecting computerized measurements of temperatures and fuel gases within the room or compartment. We also examined numerous electrical appliances by taking them apart and comparing accidental versus intentionally set fires with those appliances. ATF teamed up with the highly respected University of Maryland Fire Science Program, where CFIs had the opportunity to take their fire science courses.

By 1993 I had analyzed over 250 fire and explosion incidents, plus I had about 500 hours of training under my belt. As of this writing, after 38 years of working fires and explosions, I have been fortunate to have amassed about 3000 hours of training, set over 100 training fires while witnessing even more, and I have analyzed approximately 2300 fire and explosion incidents.

A fire analysis conducted through review of reports, photos and any other collected data is a legitimate means of conducting a fire investigation, but the information and photos that are the basis for the review have to be fairly thorough. Generally, inspecting and analyzing the fire scene firsthand is the best practice, but depending on the conditions of the scene, sometimes a review conducted after the initial scene work can provide even better information.

Interview information obtained by investigators near to the time of the incident needs to be thorough. However, when additional questions arise later in an investigation, it is crucial to conduct further interviews to clarify any issues.

With today's digital photography, it is obligatory to document scenes with hundreds of photos, not like in the days of expensive film and processing where we only took a couple rolls worth of photos. I have often reviewed my own photos repeatedly before producing an expert report or before my appearance at a legal proceeding.

There have been many clues as to a fire's origin and cause observed in the photos missed because of poor lighting issues at the scene and other conditions that hindered observations. Today, there are even better ways to document scenes such as the use of a total station optical/ surveying instrument that automatically photographs and measures every inch of a room that is visible to the device.

*   *   *

My review of the second Lizotte fire led me to concur with the prior origin determinations of the fire as being at the couch in the first-floor living room. I determined this based upon the interview information, fire patterns and an analysis of the fire dynamics, which is the science behind the initiation and spread of the fire.

Except for inspection of an electrical outlet, a duplex receptacle mounted in the wall behind the sofa, nobody conducted any other electrical arc mapping. Looking for electrical arc faults caused during a fire is another tool that can assist with finding where a fire started.

I based the cause determination on the elimination of all inherent potential ignition sources (items that are permanent or normally in place) in the area combined with Ruth's statements that did not jibe with the timeline and fire dynamics relating to a sofa fire. Developing a timeline was an important aspect of this investigation when combined with the physical evidence and fire science. My conclusion was that someone intentionally set this fire using an open flame on or around the sofa.

Looking back on this determination over 25 years later, with that many more years of education, training and experience, those conclusions remain the same. I understand according to National Fire Protection Association (NFPA) guidelines, they recommended other criteria to be fulfilled before a definitive cause determination is made, but I feel that an analysis of the evidence supports my conclusions.

For instance, identification of the first fuel ignited is one important element of cause determination. In this analysis of the Lizotte fire, with the short time frame of only a few minutes from the time Ruth left the living room, where she saw no smoke or fire, to when witnesses discovered the fire and the windows failed, is there really a difference whether the sofa, some newspapers on the sofa or some lighter fluid on the sofa was the first fuel ignited with an open flame? Well, yes, there can be a difference!

Every type of initial fuel package, with its make-up and its configuration, and its proximity to secondary fuels, plus the location of the ignition source, all play a significant role in the ignition and incipient stage of the fire. For instance, the open flame of a lighter or match placed on top of the center of a couch cushion versus in the corner where the cushion meets the back and arm of a sofa which often results in an easier ignition and more rapid growth in the latter scenario.

Cotton versus a synthetic material for the covering and the inner cushion material play their role. Flat, unruffled newspaper is more difficult to support fire spread than crumpled or balled-up individual sheets of the paper. Ignition of lighter fluid squirted onto a couch will readily ignite, but, again, it is the location and the quantity of liquid used that determines subsequent fire growth.

This is where the development of a timeline is significant to assist with defining a fire cause scenario. The interview information helped establish the timeline in this analysis. Ruth Lizotte's statements that she thought she smelled smoke but saw neither smoke nor fire anyplace around the living room sofa, are crucial when taken in context with the first eye-witnesses to the fire.

Assistant States Attorney James Mongeon handled the prosecution of this case. I spent hundreds of hours with him, instructing him on the nuances of the fire science and the fire patterns that were necessary for him to understand in order to walk me through my testimony and to cross-examine the defense experts.

Woman Denies Setting Fire That Killed Husband

By LIZ ANDERSON

Ruth Lizotte "had to know" a fire had started in the home where her husband slept on a winter day in 1991, an investigator said in court documents filed Tuesday.

Another official said there was no other possible cause for the fire than an open flame that was used to intentionally spark a blaze near a sofa.

Lizotte, 26, pleaded innocent in Rutland District Court to the charges of arson causing death and involuntary manslaughter stemming from the fire that killed her husband Terry in the upstairs bedroom of their West Rutland apartment.

The arson-causing-death charge carries the same punishment as first degree murder.

District Judge Francis McCaffrey ordered Lizotte to post 10 percent of a $40,000 bail requirement to secure her release; her attorney said she would be unable to do so and would remain in jail.

Lizotte was tearful as she walked out of the court after the arraignment.

Police filed charges against her this week after receiving a report from a federal fire investigator at the Bureau of Al-

(See Page 12: Fire)

Staff Photo by Vyto Starinskas

Ruth Lizotte is arraigned Tuesday in District Court in Rutland.

Ruth Lizotte being arraigned.
(Rutland Daily Herald 12/22/93)

Finally, on December 20, 1993, the Vermont State Police arrested Ruth Lizotte for the arson, manslaughter and murder of her husband, Terry. Over the next four-plus years, there were stops and starts for this case. The changes of defense attorneys and court challenges brought by Lizotte's defense caused several postponements.

Some defense motions resulted in lengthy hearings. Vermont allows depositions in their criminal cases, which, in my experience of testifying in several states, is unusual. This gives the defense a preliminary bite of the apple. The defense hears the testimony of prosecution witnesses well ahead of the trial, providing them with ample opportunity to dissect the testimony and tailor the defense accordingly.

The defense also needed an extraordinary amount of time to find various qualified experts who would testify on behalf of a suspected murderer. Then, the defense attorney needed time to prep with his experts with the aid of the detailed notes from prosecution witness testimony.

Although all defendants deserve good representation, many fire experts will not testify for the defense in homicide cases. Some investigators won't take these cases because of their ethics, but I also had another reason for not taking on these cases. Since the public authorities, meaning the local and state police, made these criminal cases, and I had so many friends in those groups, I couldn't go against them and ruin my relationships. There were plenty of other investigators available to represent the defendants.

Many years later, I worked on behalf of individuals in two different cases wherein the insurance companies had wrongly denied coverage to their insureds following fires in their properties. However, the police never charged either person with arson.

After an incredibly long delay, the trial finally began in the early spring of 1998. Ruth Lizotte was about to face the jury for murder, manslaughter and arson. Attorney Mongeon argued to the jury that if they could not find that Ruth had set the fire that killed her husband, they should be able to find her guilty of having a reckless disregard for human life when she left the house after allegedly detecting smoke that caused her to look for the source, and then, leaving the house with her husband left inside sleeping while in an impaired condition. Attorney Mongeon put this argument forth to solidify a potential manslaughter conviction if the jurors couldn't agree on the murder charge.

Defense Attorney William Buckman was a remarkable attorney who presented a strong case. He fought tooth and nail to convince the jury that the fire was not arson and that Ruth Lizotte loved her husband with no motive for killing him.

One of Buckman's first victories was convincing the judge to have all witnesses sequestered. Neither I nor any other witness was allowed in the courtroom during testimony. In addition, the ruling forbade witnesses from speaking with one another until after each had testified. This situation was a little different for me because I had often assisted the prosecuting attorney to prep Government witnesses before their testimony, and during testimony, I would provide questions to the prosecutor to ask the witness.

This ruling got me in some boiling water. On the first Friday night of the trial, my wife and I went out to dinner at a really pleasant restaurant in Middlebury, Vermont, the town where the case was being tried. Fire and Ice was (and still is) a favorite among locals and tourists alike. As part of their dinners, their salad bar is a big draw.

As I sidled up to the salad bar filling my plate with all sorts of goodies to go along with my ordered steak and potato, I virtually bumped into the West Rutland Fire Chief. I had briefly met him prior to this. He testified for about an hour earlier in the day. Standing next to him, being the friendly guy that I am, I innocently greeted him and simply asked how he was doing. No further discussion, end of story. Right?

Wrong. Attorney Buckman's co-counsel was also in attendance as a guest diner at the restaurant. She happened to witness the encounter between two sequestered trial witnesses. Come Monday at the courthouse, I was confronted with quite the brouhaha. Attorney Buckman was clamoring for my head. He had Attorney Mongeon in the judge's chambers looking to get me disqualified as a testifying witness. After all, if Buckman succeeded, the State's case would be all but over. I was the State's primary expert witness.

The judge held a hearing with both the Chief and me being sworn in as witnesses. We were both grilled by the defense attorneys, but the judge subsequently ruled that there was no wrongdoing on my part. However, he admonished me to stay away from any other witnesses so that there were no future misunderstandings.

That command was fairly easy to follow as I was the next witness to take the stand. My direct testimony went well with Attorney Mongeon following a script we planned to walk me through my qualifications and then explain to the court and the jurors the fire science and evidence that led to my conclusion that Ruth Lizotte had intentionally set the fire that killed her husband.

Another more significant victory for the defense occurred prior to the start of any testimony when the judge ruled there was to be no mention of the fire that killed Ruth's son, Micheal. This seriously hampered our case.

Prosecutors often like to get into evidence testimony of similar acts, or prior bad acts of a defendant to show the present case was part of a criminal pattern. In this matter, the defense didn't want that testimony to prejudice their client unduly by unfairly poisoning the jurors' minds. Part of their argument was Ruth had never been charged with the first fire as she had blamed her five-year-old son, Jay, for setting the fire.

It would have been nice to strengthen our case if we could have shown that the origin and timing of both fires were nearly identical, with Ruth walking out of the house shortly before the discovery of the fires that both started on or around the living room sofa. But we tried our best with the cards dealt us.

The ruling by the judge was not unfair, as the evidence presented during any trial is often not the full story. There frequently is plenty of pertinent information kept from jurors. One party to the litigation would like certain items admitted into evidence, but for one legal reason or another may not be produced, much to the consternation of that party. There are rules to be followed and rulings made along the way that befuddle investigators and even lawyers sometimes.

Over the course of two days, I was on the stand for nine hours. Defense Attorney Buckman beat me around the head and ears. In order to be an expert witness, one must be somewhat masochistic because sometimes the whipping you take on the stand leaves you bloody and bruised. He was good at his job. After all, Ruth was looking at a lengthy stretch in prison if his client didn't prevail, so he pulled out all the stops.

The defense must have scrutinized every line from the reports of witness interviews. Earlier I wrote that the teen neighbors had seen Ruth Lizotte on the front step outside her front door only a few minutes before they observed her living room on fire. Well, the defense pounded home the fact that they didn't actually see Lizotte come out the door; they only saw her on the front stoop. The questioning to me went something like this, "For all you know, Ruth could have had a cigarette while standing outside the front door, right?"

My response was, "It's possible, but we have no information that suggests she did. Ruth never said that when interviewed by investigators."

Defense: Well, they never asked her that specific question, did they? She could have actually been out on that step for several minutes while she smoked a cigarette, right? If she was on the step for, say, five minutes, then what does that do to your timeline for the fire? You testified that the fire must have started when Ruth was in the house because the fire appeared to have gone from nothing to blowing out the windows in only two to three minutes, right? Would another five minutes change your opinion as to the speed of the fire growth? Could an accidental fire have grown to the flashover stage within that new timeline?

This was a tough line of questioning, except I pointed out all potential accidental ignition sources were either not present or were analyzed and eliminated. It sounded good to me.

I explained to the jury the expected fire dynamics scenario if Terry Lizotte had left a lit cigarette within the confines of the sofa before he went upstairs to bed. We investigators had even conducted several sofa test burns using a sofa similar in size and style with the best information that we had.

Cigarette ignitions within upholstered furniture are complex. Fire scientists and engineers have studied and tested the various scenarios for decades. Despite all that excellent work being shared with fire investigators, after a real-life fire incident involving heavy destruction, it is difficult to apply the laboratory findings that can reliably explain the cause of the fire.

There are certain characteristics of a sofa fire that are fairly consistent, but there are many variables to consider. With the short time frame from the time Ruth checked around the cushions and sides of the sofa as she claimed to when the fire was discovered, whether that time was two minutes or even stretching the time to seven minutes – if Ruth had a cigarette on the front step outside the house, the observed fire doesn't fit the fire science associated with a cigarette ignition of upholstered furniture.

If Terry Lizotte dropped a cigarette some two, three minutes, or at any time before he went upstairs to bed, and ignition occurred, it would have been smoldering combustion rather than an open flame burning. Sometimes the smoldering within upholstered furniture can last for hours without a very noticeable amount of smoke production.

A cigarette can burrow into the crevices and into the cushions as the inner material burns or melts away from the cigarette hot zone. However, in those last few minutes prior to transitioning from smoldering combustion to open flame, copious amounts of smoke are produced as the heat energy consumes more fuel. This smoke is highly visible, rising toward the ceiling in a room. It is also extremely toxic and choking. Close to the couch, there may also be a noticeable rise in temperature.

When this occurs, the inner fuels within a sofa often preheat to the point when the changeover from smoldering to open flame happens, the sofa can virtually erupt into flames. But that does not happen if there is no smoke at all when someone inspects the cushions and sides of a couch only minutes before the windows of a room blow out.

So after I described to the court how a cigarette ignition occurs, I then explained other potential theories that fit the timeline better. The explanation included that, if Ruth used an open flame to ignite the couch itself or newspapers on the couch, or even used lighter fluid to accelerate the initiation and spread of the fire, this is likely how this fire occurred because the fire growth would now be more rapid than the cigarette ignition scenario.

The smoke and heat within the room would develop quickly causing more fuels to volatilize, that is, heat up and break down releasing more volatile combustible gases. When the hot smoke and gas layer banks down from the ceiling to the lower sections of the room, the criteria for flashover conditions often occur. Windows start failing with fire venting to the building's exterior and to other rooms.

Why did I choose to mention newspapers or lighter fluid may have been the first material ignited rather than just leaving the couch as the first item ignited? That's because a single ignition point of the sofa alone may not develop quickly enough to satisfy the timeline.

Investigators found a can of lighter fluid for a cigarette lighter on the first floor of the apartment in a position where it could have been used as an accelerant. Plus, a few years earlier, Ruth had previously explained how her five-year-old son Jay must have set fire with newspapers on the couch when the first fire occurred that killed her infant son. Even if she didn't set that first fire herself, she apparently knew that the newspapers were a likely fuel that boosted that fire rapidly to lethal conditions. Both additional fuels on upholstered furniture could cause the fire scenario that witnesses observed within the established timeframe.

Attorney Buckman hammered away at me and other witnesses about the timeline in the sense what was the exact time she left the house and when the fire happened. He designed this line of questioning to confuse the witnesses and the jurors. It made no difference what the actual time was, whether it was 8:20 or 8:30 a.m. It was the relative time between events that counted, such as two, three, five, or seven minutes from when she walked out of the apartment to the discovery of the fire.

When the State rested their case, the defense took over with their witnesses. Attorney Buckman used testimony from Ruth's friends to express Ruth had no motive to kill her husband; she loved him. Well, how many times have you heard of stories that a spouse couldn't have killed their other half? Sure, they loved their spouse to death.

I know that I'm being sarcastic. Many domestic spouse murder cases involve spouses that loved one another in some form, but some murderers who are mentally on the edge don't need a lot to get pushed over that edge. An argument can spiral into a heinous act rather quickly. And they often are sorry their actions resulted in their spouses' death.

The defense put on an electrical engineer as an expert witness. He may have been very good at his job, but his testimony was purely speculative. He opined that a duplex receptacle in the wall behind the sofa must have had a pre-existing fault (problem) that catastrophically failed when Ruth slammed the front door closed as she was leaving the house. The result of the failure was that an electrical arc or sparking must have occurred, ejecting tiny red-hot material toward the fabric on the rear of the sofa, causing ignition of the sofa.

This theory relied on no physical evidence as the receptacle no longer existed and there were no detailed photos of it. It only relied upon a lot of assumptions, including:

- there was a pre-existing fault,
- that fault failed,
- Ruth slammed the exterior door,
- the slamming of the door shook the house,
- an arc or luminous spark, which is molten metal, ejected from the receptacle,
- that item had sufficient heat energy to ignite a fabric material, and
- the hot material penetrated the fabric, rather than bouncing off the vertical surface.

You all know what assuming can lead to, but the defense presented their case well. As I listened to their expert, I was mentally rolling my eyes at the crap that he was spewing. Let's tick off the arguments against each of these excuses for the fire.

- Speculation
- Speculation
- No information that Ruth slammed the door
- Speculation
- Speculation
- Pure speculation
- Assumption

It is *possible* for a luminous spark of molten metal to eject from those narrow slots of a receptacle. Furthermore, it is possible the spark has sufficient heat energy to ignite material if it doesn't bounce off the vertical rear of the sofa. However, all the prerequisite conditions have to be perfect, and other electrical conditions have to be met in order for this to occur, making this theory highly unlikely.

Here's another factor that makes this theory less than feasible. The front door, on the A (front) wall, was at least 15 feet from the B wall and at least another 15 feet from where the alleged faulty receptacle was located. I know what a slammed door sounds like since I live in a townhouse condominium where the front doors are less than 20 feet apart. When a neighbor slams their front door, I can hear the noise from anywhere in my place, but it doesn't even rattle the decorative glassware mounted in various places.

Remember the timeline. If she slammed the door causing a small single-point ignition at that moment, there is virtually no way, considering fire dynamic principles for this fire to attain flashover within the time that jibes with the witnesses' observations. That scenario also makes little sense when considering Ruth's statements about smelling smoke.

The defense did not test this theory in accordance with the scientific methodology. However, all Attorney Buckman was trying to do was throw spitballs against the wall to see what sticks with the aim of getting the jurors thinking maybe something else happened. All he needed was to create reasonable doubt in the mind of one juror to get an acquittal.

This may have been where both prosecutor James Mongeon and I erred. As the defense presented this theory after my testimony, I tried to explain this to Attorney Mongeon so he could cross-examine the electrical expert, but maybe we should have gotten our own electrical expert as a rebuttal witness. We did not do this.

When a case situation goes beyond the expertise of your origin-and-cause witness, attorneys should use a specialized expert. Whether it is a Fire Protection Engineer, a heating and cooling specialist, or an Electrical Engineer, these experts can strengthen your case. In the Lizotte case, an engineer could have explained the requisite conditions for an electrical failure to manifest itself.

Attorney Buckman also had a former employee of The California Bureau of Home Furnishings and Thermal Insulation testify about cigarette ignition of a sofa. Between his credentials and experience, his testimony was impressive. It only lacked an explanation of an intentionally set fire using other items, like newspapers, to boost the initial heat energy.

He testified similarly to what I mentioned earlier that a sofa can burst into flames if a cigarette burrows inside the material spreading smoldering heat to a large internal area. When, and if, this transitions to a flaming fire, it can rapidly progress. There is one caveat, though. There is a tremendous amount of smoke produced before the eruption of flames. Given the timeline, Ruth should have seen smoke before she exited the apartment.

Finally, Attorney Buckman had a Fire Protection Engineer from Worcester Polytechnic Institute, a renowned school of fire science. I knew their expert well. He explained to the jury how flashover can occur in a room in a short period of time. But Buckman raised the issue of how plastic toys in the living room could add substantial fuel to the fire, reducing the time to flashover. With no prior information, Buckman introduced a hypothetical of lots of toys, including one of those cars with a roof that a child rides in. Again, he attempted to explain the fire's rapid growth to minimize Ruth's possible involvement in setting the fire.

These toys could change the dynamics if close enough to first fuel. Otherwise, they make almost no difference to the fire growth until moments before flashover. NFPA has a great video of a couch fire with a lamp on top of the end table next to the sofa. The cloth lampshade didn't ignite despite a raging fire on the sofa less than two feet away. It finally ignited when the heat energy substantially banked down from the ceiling. Therefore, toys only two or three feet above floor level would not add to the fuel load until far into the fire development.

Buckman's use of expert testimony played well with the jury. They gave the jury enough information for them to consider an alternative for the fire cause.

After a month-long trial, on April 2, 1998, the case went to the jury. The charges included arson, murder, and manslaughter. Attorney Mongeon, in his closing argument, made the appeal that if she didn't set the fire, Ruth Lizotte was at least guilty of having a reckless disregard for human life when she left the house after smelling smoke and knowing that her husband was in an impaired condition since according to her he was drunk when he went to bed upstairs.

During the trial, Attorney Buckman said that the Lizotte apartment had many electrical code violations that made it a fire hazard. This is what I have to say about that. First, he just threw that out to the jury with no specifics to back the statement up.

If you scrutinized the electrical service in every building in the United States, you would probably find code violations in about 50% of those properties. So drawing any correlation from code violations to fires starting from some structural electrical fault due to a code violation, then potentially 50% of all the buildings would burn.

Code violations don't mean that a fire will happen. Also, when making that type of statement relative to a specific fire, then the party making that allegation must provide evidence that proves a correlation between a specific violation and the fire cause scenario. But again, Buckman was throwing out as much as he could to muddy the waters, to create that reasonable doubt.

Apparently, his tactics worked. And seemingly, we, of the prosecution team, failed to present a convincing argument that Ruth Lizotte had intentionally set the January 11, 1991 fire that killed her husband. After only three hours of deliberation, the jury returned a verdict that Ruth was not guilty. That is not the same as being found innocent (as reported in the news) of the charges she set the fire resulting in her husband's fire death. Not guilty does not mean she was innocent.

Without more conclusive evidence, in 1998 Vermont, a jury found it difficult to find a woman who had no criminal record, guilty of setting a fire to kill her husband. I wonder if the jurors ever heard about the fire that killed her son. I also wonder, in this day and age,

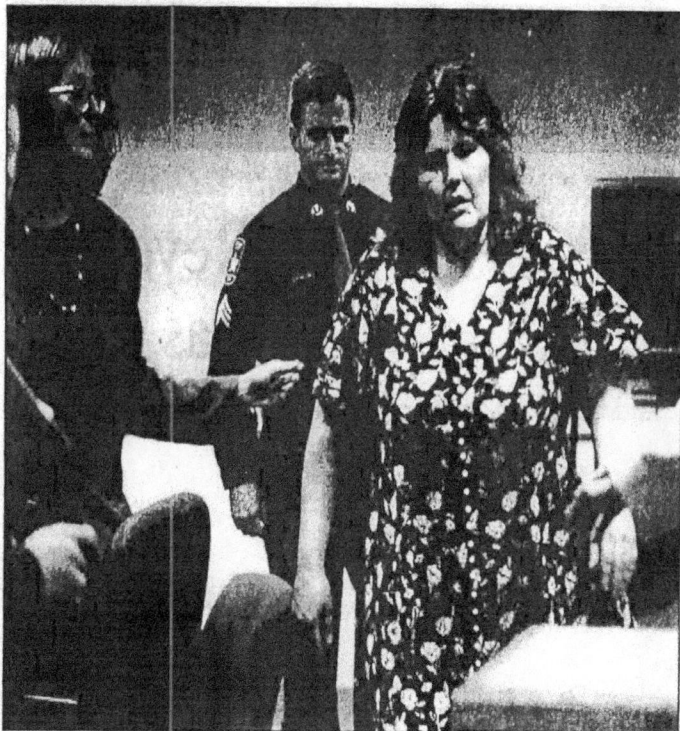

Innocent of Murder

ourthouse lobby
Buckman called
y unwarranted."
rsecution than a
d.
ney accused the
indreds of thou-
llars" on the case.
id County State's
Mongeon should
se long before it

e's evidence was

l: Lizotte)

ome
ge,
s Joy

IcKHANN
Staff
— Ruth Lizotte
hursday when a
of murder and
ges.
irs of sorrow shed
er late husband,
ther, three broth-
aid they were sad
e outcome of the

3: Family)

Staff Photos by Vyto Starinskas

Ruth Lizotte leaves Vermont District Court in Middlebury on Thursday after being found
innocent of killing her husband in a fire. At left is her attorney Anna Saxman.

Ruth Lizotte found not guilty.
(Rutland Daily Herald 4/3/1998)

with all the sensational cases in the news over the years of mothers and
wives who have been implicated in horrific murders of their family
members, whether a jury would have convicted Ruth.

In an interview with the local media after the trial, Terry Lizotte's
family expressed disappointment with the outcome of the trial. They
felt that State's Attorney James Mongeon did a poor job of presenting
the case during the trial.

It has been my experience that it is very difficult for a prosecutor who has never tried an arson case to learn enough about the details of fire science and fire investigation to excel during all aspects of the trial. It was my job to teach Attorney Mongeon and to assist him on the fly during the trial. So, as the fire expert that the state and the family relied on, I feel that I also bear some responsibility for the outcome of this case.

Maybe Jay Lizotte, that five-year-old boy blamed by his mother for setting the 1988 fire that killed his infant brother, has some recollection of that day that he would like to share with the world. He would be nearly 40-years-old now. He still lives in Vermont.

Thank you, Jessica Shurlow, Librarian, Rutland Free Library, who went above and beyond researching news articles from 1988 to 1998.

Thanks to Dan Slowick for his assistance and use of his report and photos.

State of Vermont v. Ruth Lizotte, Docket No. 1560-12-93 Rdcr, Motion hearing, Testimony of Wayne M. Miller, 06/01/95

State of Vermont v. Ruth Lizotte, Docket No. 1560-12-93 Rdcr, Deposition Testimony of Daniel Slowick, 06/03/96

Forest Park Fire Kills Boy, Rutland Daily Herald, Yvonne Daley, 04/22/88

Man Dies in West Rutland Fire, Rutland Daily Herald, Julie Hoogland, 01/12/91

Investigation of Fatal Fire in West Rutland Will Continue, Rutland Daily Herald, Julie Hoogland, 01/15/91

Woman is Charged with Arson Fatality, Rutland Daily Herald, Yvonne Daley, 12/21/93

Woman Denies Setting Fire That Killed Husband, Rutland Daily Herald, Liz Anderson, 12/22/93

Murder Trial Opens, Rutland Daily Herald, Mary McKhann, 03/10/98

Murder Trial: Lizotte Death is Described, Rutland Daily Herald, MaryMcKhann,03/18/98

Judge Denies Motion for Mistrial, Rutland Daily Herald, Mary McKhann, 03/21/98

Defense Witness: Evidence Lacking, Rutland Daily Herald, Mary McKhann, 03/31/98

Defense Finishes in Lizotte Case, Rutland Daily Herald, Mary McKhann, 04/01/98

Lizotte Found Innocent, Rutland Daily Herald, Mary McKhann, 04/03/98

CHAPTER 21

Honoring the Worcester 6

I would be remiss if I didn't cover one of the most horrific and tragic fires that occurred in New England during my career. Other stories have covered this heartbreaking inferno in detail, with the foremost book being *3000 Degrees – The True Story of a Deadly Fire and the Men Who Fought It* by Sean Flynn. With this short narrative, I would like to honor the memory of the 6 fallen firefighters by telling this story from my vantage point, through my eyes. Always remember these brave men, these firefighters, and their families in your thoughts and prayers. I will never forget.

Clockwise from top left: Firefighter Paul A. Brotherton, Firefighter Jeremiah M. Lucey, Lt. Timothy P. Jackson Sr., Lt. James F. Lyons III, Firefighter Joseph T. McGuirk, Lt. Thomas E. Spencer. I kept this photo at my desk for the next twenty years until I retired from fire investigation.

Early on Friday night, December 3, 1999, as I was watching TV, a news special cut into the show with the bulletin of a major fire at the Worcester Cold Storage and Warehouse with firefighters missing. Without hesitation or being told, I headed out to the scene after notifying my supervisor of the fire. Worcester, the second-largest city in New England, is about 20 miles from my house. I listened to the

Lost Firefighters. Never forgotten. Please ADD:
"From left to right, top line: Firefighter Paul A. Brotherton, Firefighter Jeremiah
M. Lucey, Lt. Timothy P. Jackson Sr. Bottom line: Lt. James F. Lyons III, Firefighter
Joseph T. McGuirk, Lt. Thomas E. Spencer

local AM radio news station as I mentally prepared myself for this horrific situation. That's when I learned six firefighters were missing. I thought, "My God, no!" I became sick to my stomach. I could hardly process what was swirling through my head.

Thirty minutes later, I stood in an empty parking lot across the street from the monstrous, block-long six-story brick warehouse. Little did I realize I would stand in that same lot for many hours over the next eight days during the interminable hunt for the 6 lost Worcester firefighters.

The blazing inferno continued on Saturday. With the collapse of the roof, along with the upper four floors crashing down onto the second-floor concrete deck, it was to be a long, arduous, painstaking search for the missing men. Firefighters from all over New England assisted at the location in one way or another. They raked, shoveled, and sifted for any trace of their fallen brothers.

Amazing and eerie photo of flames above the Worcester Cold Storage.
(Courtesy of Roger B. Conant)

The fire-breathing dragon.

Members of the Massachusetts State Police assigned to the Fire Marshal's Office were in charge of the investigation. They oversaw the delayering process. The first task at the building was to find the 6 men before investigators could conduct any in-depth scene work. But the Fire Marshals monitored everything removed from the building in order to maintain the chain of custody of evidence should a criminal case arise.

My job as an ATF Certified Fire Investigator was to assist the Fire Marshals, plus the Worcester Police and Fire Investigators. I was there to help with the scene origin and cause investigation, with interviews or with any fire investigation expertise necessary. Initially, I just waited, like so many others, for the firefighters to complete the recovery mission.

It took 40 hours after the first alarm to find the remains of Lt. Tim Jackson. Then, hours crawled by, leading to days before Jay Lyons was located. Another day and a half went by with no success. A massive memorial service at the Worcester Centrum was held on Thursday. Some 30,000 firefighters took part in the ceremony with the families and many other dignitaries, including President Bill Clinton. I attended the service inside the Centrum. Many times during the program, my eyes watered. It was a sad day within a miserable week, but the outpouring of support and the ceremony were uplifting.

Several days into the search for the last four firefighters, as I was standing in that parking lot across from the front of the killer building, an eerie, yet almost comforting sight caught my eye. It was one of those chilly December days when the sky was silvery gray with a pale, dim sun shining through the clouds. The rays of the sun suddenly glimmered down toward earth in separate straight-line waves. I likened those rays to those seemingly from Heaven I remembered from some old-time religious prints.

The fire-ravaged building had been partially demolished to make it safer for the continued recovery efforts. Delayering of many floors of collapsed debris had been underway since the day following the inferno. Just inside the B wall, there were remains of the metal stair railings. Dozens of firefighters had used this stairway during the fire to access the upper floors. The base of this stairway was also where District Chief Mike McNamee courageously stood his ground to prevent additional firefighters from searching for the lost 6 firefighters.

The railings and balusters at the third or fourth-floor level were still attached to the lower level, but the upper section was suspended in the open air. The faint rays extended from the sun, cutting through the black metal railing. My first thought upon seeing this caused me to pause and choke back tears. This was their stairway to heaven.

✳   ✳   ✳

Within the next couple days, I watched as the Worcester Fire Fighters carried out two more of their brothers, Joe McGuirk and Tom Spencer. Eight grueling days after the fire, the search unearthed the last two firefighters from the ashen debris. Every day as I worked at the site, looking at the dozens of melancholy, weary firefighters, I could only peripherally feel their anguish. They all worked hours on end trying to find any evidence of their fellow firefighters. They were beat, dead tired in body and soul, but they kept going.

My respect for these guys, and for all firefighters, increased exponentially during that terrible week. The circumstances made everything even worse because this all occurred within weeks before Christmas. It was heart-wrenching for me, and for all involved, including the people of Worcester and throughout Massachusetts.

During the solemn ceremonial removal of the fifth firefighter, Jeremiah Lucey, every firefighter lined up to salute as they removed his body. The search for Paul Brotherton began again with renewed energy. Only Worcester Firefighters handled the remains of their brothers from the time they recovered their bodies until they entrusted them to the Medical Examiner's Office.

Within hours, the firefighters announced the discovery of Brotherton's remains. As horrible as this was, simultaneously, a sense of relief filled the air.

The most mysterious event occurred within moments of that announcement. You might say it was divine intervention. High on the rear wall of the structure, about where the fifth floor once stood, flames appeared on the surface of the wall. The flames were like an eternal torch, only a foot or so wide with fingers of fire gently flickering less than two feet vertically.

Now, as an experienced fire analyst, this was difficult to explain. The flames were on an open-air section of the vertical brick wall. Decades ago, the cold storage business covered the wall's interior surface in cork impregnated with petroleum products to keep the inside cold. Styrofoam insulation even covered the wall to further insulate the rooms, although most of that burned away days earlier.

So after eight days, what was the ignition source for this ignition? There had been no apparent smoldering with absolutely no visible wisps of smoke during any time over that week-long span. I still have no way to explain this ignition scientifically.

The flames continued unabated while the firefighters gathered the bodily remains of Rescue Man Paul Brotherton. They then marched him between the rows of somber saluting fellow firefighters. Just as suddenly as the flames appeared, the fire self-extinguished as soon as the firefighters ritually carried him off the second-floor deck. This eerie incident still weighs heavily on my chest whenever I dwell on it.

✳   ✳   ✳

One longtime firefighter friend, retired Westwood Fire Chief William "Billy" Scoble, related some of his experiences with his two weeks involved with this incident. Billy had garnered high-level standing within the fire community, including at the State Fire Marshal's Office and the State Fire Academy. Worcester and Boston Fire Chiefs, who ran the deck recovery operations, asked Billy to act as the commanding officer overseeing recovery operations on the deck. He was well qualified for this. They needed his expertise because the long hours necessary to work the scene had overextended the other departments.

Once Billy responded to the site, he only occasionally left to grab a few hours' sleep. Day after day, just like all the other firefighters working the scene, he pressed onward until numbness settled in. He shifted into auto-pilot mode to keep his focus, using his years of training and experience to guide him.

At the end of the eighth day, after recovery of the last firefighters, Billy headed home to Westwood, roughly an hour's drive. When he arrived, his two teen daughters had a special request for their Dad. The girls, in a kind gesture that mimicked feelings of citizens throughout the Commonwealth, had flowers they wanted to place at the scene.

Billy, the dedicated firefighter and caring father, did the right thing. He got right back in his car and drove back to the city with his girls. At Worcester Engine 7, parked under the elevated highway, Route 290, the girls, Alison and Kristin, laid their flowers at the growing memorial. After a prayer and spending a few more moments with their solemn thoughts, the Scoble clan began the return journey home.

✳   ✳   ✳

Investigators couldn't examine the suspected area of fire origin until the searchers recovered the firefighters. It didn't mean that other investigative work hadn't occurred during that eight-day period. Investigators watched every pile of debris scooped by the heavy construction equipment. They oversaw the firefighters as they raked and sifted through each load. It was their duty to maintain custody of potential evidence located through the laborious sifting process.

On the night of the fire, firefighters had been in the abandoned warehouse conducting a search and rescue mission because they had received information two homeless people may have been in the building. Well, they had been when they caused the fire. But after the fugitive flames started growing, they fled from the structure. They hung out separately in the city. One callously stopped by a music shop, listening to tunes while the fire raged. Neither person reported the fire in the old warehouse.

Worcester detectives learned Tom Levesque and his former girlfriend, Julie Ann Barnes, had been using the building as their sleeping quarters. The detectives interviewed them to determine that they, in fact, used the place to flop. They admitted being there when the fire occurred. Next, the State Fire Marshals and Worcester Fire investigators questioned Barnes and Levesque to better understand how and where the fire started.

The stories from the pair were very similar, with only minor discrepancies. Keep this in mind as you read the following; this is their story, which I am not sure is the whole truth and nothing but the truth.

Both individuals had mental challenges. Levesque had a history of violence against women. Barnes was 19-years-old, pregnant with 37-year-old Levesque's baby. She had broken up with him the previous week, but she wanted to retrieve some belongings, including her puppy, which she left in their makeshift bedroom, formerly an office space.

Allegedly, Levesque wanted to have sex with her, but she wasn't willing to fool around. As they tussled, the single candle used by them, which they lit in the room, toppled over onto strewn clothing and fast-food wrappers, which immediately caught fire. Levesque may have tried to stamp out the fire, but it only spread further. Barnes tried to grab her dog and a kitten they shared, but she failed to reach them. They escaped from the warehouse, but neither attempted to notify anybody about the burning building.

By the following Tuesday, the Worcester County District Attorney's Office filed charges against Barnes and Levesque. They charged them with six counts of manslaughter, even before we conducted the scene examination or the search recovered most of the bodies. In Massachusetts, there is no law requiring someone to report a fire. There was none then, nor is there now. If nobody had died in this fire, the pair likely would not have been charged with anything.

Because of the DA's rush to make the arrests with the burden of the firefighter deaths weighing heavily on everyone, the investigators never re-interviewed Barnes or Levesque. Attorneys representing them would not let investigators further interview their clients, possibly implicating themselves with their words.

Additional questions often come up during the site examination. Investigators try to verify any new information by re-interviewing the eyewitnesses to the fire's beginning. Here, the investigators couldn't validate all the scene evidence because of the inability to re-interview the subjects. They could only compare the information to the initial eyewitness accounts.

✱   ✱   ✱

The day after the recovery of Firefighter Brotherton's remains, we concentrated on the fire origin and cause scene examination. Several of us, Worcester Fire, the State Fire Marshals and I worked on our hands and knees in that second-floor office where the fire allegedly began. Others continued decluttering the floor around the second-floor deck.

The reasons that the upper floors collapsed onto this deck, without further collapse, were two-fold. One, the lower floor, the ground level, didn't burn. The fire didn't originate there. Two, the floor assemblies of the upper levels were all wood components, whereas the second-floor deck was concrete.

We cleared the complete outline of the office as defined by the charred 2-inch by 4-inch wood base plates that had supported the partition walls. The room had a single 36-inch doorway where no base plate pattern existed.

Within the footprint of the office, we located the charred base of wood pallets where their mattress had been. We found empty tuna cans and cat food cans along with McDonald's wrappers. These items had all been preserved because the worst of the fire didn't occur within this room. Also, the collapse of the walls and ceiling protected items on the floor.

We raked and shoveled away the larger debris. In one corner, my shovel bounced off something on the floor. I got down on my knees to scrape away some charred debris. There I discovered the remains of the kitten and the puppy that appeared to have huddled together trying to hide from the approaching fire. After we took photographs, I placed the pet remnants into a large black plastic bag.

Upon cleaning the debris down to floor level, we found carpeting covering the floor. Carefully going over the carpet, we located re-solidified red candle wax that formed small globs. At least this confirmed a portion of the defendants' stories.

There were no other potential ignition sources within the room. We knew that there was no electricity, heating equipment, or cooking equipment. A person had to introduce the heat source to the fuel.

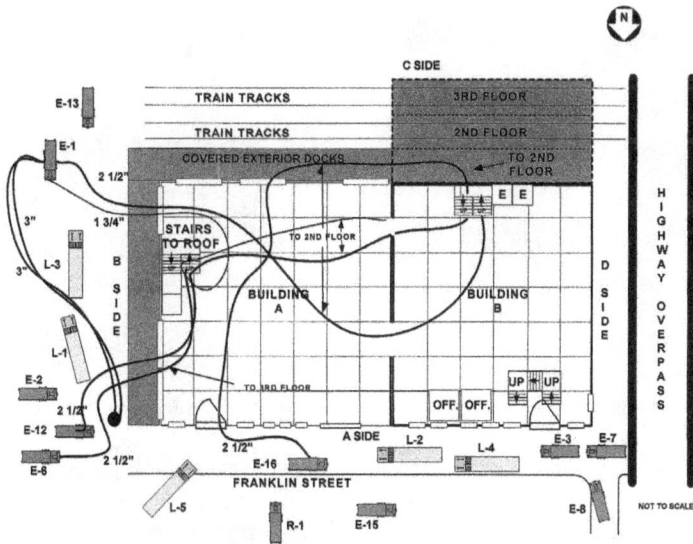

© 1999 Photograph by Telegram & Gazette Staff/Paul Kapteyn

Photo 6. *Firewall Between Building A and B, Cold-Storage and Warehouse Building*

```
                    KEY
          E  =  ELEVATOR SHAFT
         OFF. =  OFFICES                      C SIDE
                                    N

              TRAIN TRACKS                    3RD FLOOR

              TRAIN TRACKS
                                        STAIRWAY
                                         TO 3RD
              LOADING DOCKS              FLOOR
                                                    E   E
        B    L    STAIRWAY
             O    TO ROOF    BUILDING             BUILDING      D
        S    A               A                    B
        I    D                                                  S
        D    I                                                  I
        E    N    E                    OFF.              OFF.    D
             G                                                  E
             D    E                         OFF.
             O                      OFF.                OFF.
             C              APPROXIMATE ORIGIN
             K                  OF FIRE            OFF.
             S                                OFF.
                                                       OFF.
                                    OFF.
                                              OFF.
                                                    DN     DN
                                    OFF. OFF. OFF.

                                    A SIDE


                                    FRANKLIN ST.

                    FIRE WALL
```

NIOSH Sketch and Photos.

On the second day digging at the fire scene, the monster building almost claimed its seventh victim. Lt. Marty Fay, who was in charge of the State Fire Marshal's Fire Investigation Unit, was working along with a dozen of us. We were all extremely leery of the brick C wall of the building still looming almost four floors above our heads. It only takes a couple loose bricks or a sudden partial collapse to kill or maim anybody working within the shadow of that wall.

Mid-morning, with no warning whatsoever, as is usually the case, concrete blocks that had formed the elevator shaft came tumbling down from about 20 feet high. The blocks made a thunderous crash, shaking us on the deck. From my kneeling position in the room of origin, I heard a couple guys let out a loud yell.

I looked in the direction of the elevator shaft. A few State Troopers were leaping over debris toward the collapse. Only Lt. Fay's head and neck were visible under hundreds of pounds of blocks. He was fully conscious with blood running from a slight cut on his lip. We all started pitching those blocks away from him, hoping that he didn't have any crushing injuries from the load or broken bones from the force of the collapse.

Remarkably, as soon as the rescuers took the weight off Marty, his guys helped him to his feet. He was a little wobbly, but with a man on each arm for support, Marty walked under his own power. They rushed him to the hospital. After being checked out, Marty spent the night in his own home. And, although he was a few years older than any of us, the next morning he was back at the scene bright and early rearing to go. Marty Fay was a trooper in more ways than one.

✳   ✳   ✳

Later that week, a local news station played an audio and video clip taken at a Worcester convenience store sometime between the fire and arrest of Julie Barnes. The store manager was related to someone at the station. They thought the clip from the store would be newsworthy. The video showed Julie speaking with the clerk. When questioned about being at the fire, she told the clerk she wasn't actually in the room when it happened. She had already backed out of the room.

I had some concerns relative to the cause of the fire. If the candle was their only source of light in the room just before the fire, and they knocked it over, the room lighting situation would have instantly changed. Why couldn't they contain the incipient fire? How did the fire grow so quickly that they couldn't save the cat and dog? What did they use for light to escape the dark building?

There was unconfirmed information that Levesque had a flashlight. He also had a cell phone, but in 1999, the phone would have had no flashlight. Any screen light would not have provided sufficient light to see within that pitch-black warehouse with no windows.

Knowing Levesque's penchant for violence, plus he had two siblings already convicted of murder, could he have intentionally set this fire? Could he have been so angry with his lost lover as she walked out the bedroom door, leaving him sexually frustrated, that he intentionally knocked that candle over? Or did he use it to light a pile of readily combustible fuels? Did he yell to Julie, "Screw you and your little dog, too?" Is this why the fire took off unabated? The fire scene analysis could not provide the answer as to motivation or to the ultimate question. Was this fire the result of an accidental act, or was it intentionally set?

Over the next couple years, the District Attorney's Office dropped the initial case against Barnes and Levesque. Later, they re-instated new charges, but nothing ever became of the case. With no reporting law, they had no obligation to report that a fire was underway inside the Worcester Cold Storage and Warehouse Building, the building from hell.

*   *   *

Since retiring from ATF, I often present a large fire loss program. I discuss the fires and investigations of the New Year's Eve Dupont Plaza Hotel fire in Puerto Rico with 97 fatalities, the Philadelphia Meridian Bank Building with three firefighter fatalities, and this Worcester Cold Storage Building fire. For me personally, each fire left its mark on my mind and my soul.

But when I get to one slide in my presentation showing the memorial tributes to the Worcester 6, I always choke up. With a flutter in my chest and fighting back tears, I have to take a couple laps around the podium before I can continue. Well-wishers completely covered Worcester Engine 7 with flowers, but it is a sign on the passenger side jump-seat window that causes my reaction. The sign reads, "Firefighters saved my baby. I will always be grateful."

As I stated earlier, my admiration for all firefighters grew tremendously during those two weeks in Worcester. I had already met and worked with hundreds of firefighters and investigators by then, but this fire had the greatest impact on my psyche. These 6 men, as with firefighters all over the world, exhibited valor that was remarkably unquestioning. They were ready to give "the last full measure of devotion".

The dedication exhibited by all the firefighters throughout the fire and their efforts to locate their lost brothers was heroic. And District Chief McNamee displayed incredible courage when he had to make the heart-rending decision to hold back his firefighters from entering the warehouse with the 6 men already missing.

For me, reading Flynn's, book, *3000 Degrees* was highly emotional, renewing those feelings I felt at that Worcester fire scene over 20 years ago. Flynn covered each man in great detail, including specific interactions with their families and fellow firefighters. As I read the timeline of that fateful night, I was wishing it would have an alternative ending. Could the lost men find their way out or could rescuers find them before it was too late? But it was not to be. I'm sure that many who have some emotional connection to this fire have had a similar wish.

Very special thanks to Worcester Fire Captain (retired) William Metterville, Westwood Fire Chief (retired) Bill Scoble, and to Roger B. Conant for sharing their memories and photos of this fire.

Six Career Fire Fighters Killed in Cold-Storage and Warehouse Building Fire – Massachusetts, NIOSH Fire Fighter Fatality Investigation and Prevention Program, 09/27/2000

3000 Degrees: The True Story of a Deadly Fire and the Men Who Fought It, Sean Flynn, 03/29/02

Six Who Died in Worcester Remembered, The Boston Globe, Ellen Barry and Marcella Bombardieri, 12/06/99

Epilogue

As a student in high school and college, I had a keen interest in math, science, engineering and architecture. When I shifted gears to criminal justice, one professor said I was wasting my talents by not reaching higher to become an attorney. The way my career eventually unfolded, I realized I blended all of those earlier pursuits into my work. Isn't it strange how it all works out?

I totally enjoyed my work as a fire and explosion investigator and analyst. It was often a hard, difficult, and challenging job, but for me, it was rewarding to know I put in a good day's work to get the job done.

There were still many other complex fire cases that I didn't cover.

- The deadly DuPont Plaza Hotel arson with 97 fatalities in San Juan, Puerto Rico set by disgruntled employees who were arrested and convicted.

- The tragic 32-story Meridian Bank Building in downtown Philadelphia where three firefighters perished in a fire caused by the spontaneous combustion of linseed oil rags.

- A Lebanese bakery in Quincy, MA in which the two hired arsonists died when trapped in the basement while pouring gasoline. A deep dive into Lebanese organized crime resulted in no arrests.

- A bar/restaurant fire in South Boston that was originally called accidental disposal of smoking materials, until gasoline was found in the fire debris. No arrests in the case involving organized crime and political corruption.

- My first arson investigation of two brothers who had over 20 arson fires in their Boston properties. No arrests were ever made after two arsonists died using gasoline in one of their fires.

It is still difficult to perfect arson cases, particularly those arson-for-profit fires. It is now up to all of you to learn the trade to the best of your abilities and to apply your training, education and experience to stop these arsonists from having any future successes. Work hard. Stay honest. And come home safely. The best to you all.

If anybody would like to confer with me relative to any story in this book or about any fire case you are working on, please feel free to contact me through my email: authorWayneMiller@gmail.com

**Get your bonus chapter to *Bang Boom Burn*
by scanning this QR Code with your phone.
It will bring you to a link on my burnbostonburn.com
website! Enjoy!**

SCAN ME

Index

www.ingramcontent.com/pod-product-compliance
Lightning Source LLC
Chambersburg PA
CBHW030236030426
42336CB00009B/128